Alexander and the East

Alexander and the East

The Tragedy of Triumph

A. B. BOSWORTH

CLARENDON PRESS · OXFORD
1996

Oxford University Press, Great Clarendon Street, Oxford OX2 6DP
Oxford New York
Athens Auckland Bangkok Bogota Bombay
Buenos Aires Calcutta Cape Town Dar es Salaam
Delhi Florence Hong Kong Istanbul Karachi
Kuala Lumpur Madras Madrid Melbourne
Mexico City Nairobi Paris Singapore
Taipei Tokyo Toronto
and associated companies in
Berlin Ibadan

Oxford is a trade mark of Oxford University Press

Published in the United States
by Oxford University Press Inc., New York

British Library Cataloguing in Publication Data
Data available

Library of Congress Cataloging in Publication Data
Alexander and the East: the tradegy of triumph
A.B. Bosworth.
Includes bibliographical references and index.
1. Alexander, the Great, 356–323 B.C.—Military leadership.
2. Greece—History—Macedonian Expansion, 359–323 B.C.—Campaigns—Asia
3. Massacres—Asia—History. 4. Massacres—Mexico—History.
5. Mexico—History—Conquest, 1519–1540.   I. Title.
DF234.6.B67   1996   938'.07—dc20   96–21705
ISBN 0–19–814991–3

1 3 5 7 9 10 8 6 4 2

Typeset by Peter Kahrel, Lancaster
Printed in Great Britain on acid-free paper by
Bookcraft (Bath) Ltd., Midsomer Norton

DF
234
.6
.B67
1996

Preface

THE origins of this book are of some interest. In 1993 I was invited to give the Sixth Broadhead Lecture at the University of Canterbury, in Christchurch, New Zealand. For the occasion it seemed appropriate to give a general lecture on Alexander, developing many of the ideas I had only been able to adumbrate in my *Historical Commentary* on Arrian. It also gave me the opportunity to rebut some misapprehensions of my concept of Alexander's reign, which have become common currency. My work is not 'revisionist' (it goes back in fact to Niebuhr and Grote, before Droysen produced his classic encomiastic interpretation of the period), nor is it 'unromantic'. However, the romance is not the trivial picture of the wild-eyed, visionary Alexander. It is a much darker conception, its perspective that of the victims, the eggs in Alexander's ecumenical omelette. Before I came to the lecture, I had spent some years working through the text of Arrian. It was a depressing experience, cumulatively so, as the record of slaughter went on, apparently without an end. The slaughter was what Arrian primarily saw as the achievement of Alexander, and, for all his humanity, Arrian shares the Roman mentality which measured glory in terms of enemy casualties—with a lower limit of 5,000 enemy dead, the body count for a triumph. Alexander's most sympathetic chronicler in ancient times describes the reign as more or less continuous fighting, at times verging on massacre for its own sake, and his emphasis is certainly correct. Alexander spent much of his time killing and directing killing, and, arguably, killing was what he did best. That brute fact needed emphasis, and it was central to the Broadhead Lecture.

The Broadhead Trust stipulates publication of its lectures, and it seemed to me that 'The Shield of Achilles' would appear at best advantage as a thematic introduction to a set of studies exploring the background to Alexander's actions in the east of his empire, with particular emphasis on the period 329–325 BC, which I have come to consider of central importance for the entire Hellenistic Age. I already had an unpublished general lecture ('Alexander and the Desert'), which investigated Alexander's motives for conquest and the human cost of his passage through the Makran. The two pieces had a unity, and could be tied together by a series of detailed studies of the period. The result is the four central chapters of the book, in which I explore various overarching themes. I begin with the extant sources, with the problems of assessing variant traditions, and draw attention to the pervasive phenomenon of literary elaboration in the primary and secondary sources. The study of the sources leads naturally to investigation of their origins, the local informants exploited by Alexander and the accuracy of the information they imparted (Chapter 3, Information and Misinformation). In particular I was attracted by the remarkable complicity between questioner and informant which has bedevilled modern anthropological research. Alexander and his men had their prejudices and expectations about the lands they invaded. They expected to find Amazons when they believed themselves close to the Black Sea, and there were fabulous stories in circulation about the Indian lands, which they were eager to verify. Their informants duly obliged with a medley of material, both true and *ben trovato*, which was designed to satisfy the curiosity of their new masters. The most remarkable development, the evolution of the myths of Dionysus' and Heracles' conquests in India, is analysed in Chapter 4 (The Creation of Belief). Here I attempt to document how Alexander bolstered his conviction of divinity by evidence provided by his staff from their interrogation of the natives. At the same time I investigate the circumstances of the campaigning, when Alexander was isolated in the recesses of Sogdiana or Gandhara, engaged in vicious siege warfare, often with a mere handful of senior officers. The isolation encouraged the most extravagant concepts of his person and monarchy, and the absolutism of his last years is, to my mind, starkly foreshadowed as early as the Sogdian Revolt of 329. The circle is closed in Chapter 5 (The Justification of Terror), where I examine what conquest meant for its victims and how its atrocity could be justified in Alexander's eyes. His demands for sovereignty were absolute, and all peoples who had ever come under the sway of the Persians (or the mythical Dionysus) were automatically his subjects. Resistance was *ipso facto* rebellion, and it was treated as such, with indiscriminate massacre and enslavement.

In the course of these central chapters I make use of analogies from the Spanish conquest of Mexico, in particular the years 1519 to 1522, when Cortés moved inland from the coast of Yucatan to discover and ultimately destroy the Mexican capital of Tenochtitlan. I was attracted to the period because I felt that Alexander's mental development in the isolation of Sogdiana and India might have its counterpart among the Conquistadors in America. That proved a dead end. The analogies were relatively trivial, precisely because Cortés never experienced the intellectual isolation of Alexander. There was always a representative of the Church to remind the conquerors of their religious duties, and the enmity of Diego Velázquez (the governor of Cuba) meant that Cortés was always acutely conscious of the need to operate in the political contexts of Spain and the Indies. However, if the analogy did not work in macrocosm, it certainly did in microcosm. The interaction of the Conquistadors with their new subjects paralleled that of Alexander with the Indians in many ways. The use of interpreters was start-lingly similar, as was the interpreters' transformation of their subject-matter to accommodate the interests of their employers—and Doña Marina must have fulfilled for Cortés the role which men such as Calanus assumed for Alexander. Similarly the source tradition of the Mexican conquest, rich and abundant, is strongly reminiscent of the first generation of Alexander historians. It provides a working model with all the precise compositional dates and autobiographical detail which are lacking for the reign of Alexander.

One caveat must be lodged. I am not adducing the Mexican material as a general explanatory matrix. The differences between the two periods are profound, and the scale is quite disproportion-ate. Cortés took an army of a few hundred Spaniards (and several thousand Indian auxiliaries) to conquer the Valley of Mexico, a region densely populated but no more than 10,000 sq. km. in area, whereas Alexander headed the greatest expedition ever to leave Greek shores, and overran the eastern world as far as the border between modern Pakistan and India. The political settings, as we have seen, are totally different, as are the conceptual horizons. Alexander never entered a totally unknown world. At the Hyphasis he came closest to Cortés, the Cortés at Cempoala (August 1519), who had heard of the great inland empire of Montezuma and was eager to conquer it. That was Alexander's reaction to the reports of the Nanda kingdom of the Ganges, but his army notoriously failed to support his ambitions. Otherwise the two situations are distinct, and we cannot call upon Cortés to explain Alexander. However, the similarities of detail cannot be discounted, and, in my opinion, they may be considered parallel manifestations of universal phenomena, all the more impressive in that they are so separated in time and cultural context. Onesicritus' conversation with Calanus through his three interpreters does match Cortés' interviews with Montezuma via Doña Marina and Aguilar, and the distortions produced by the interpreting are remarkably similar. Even the justification of conquest is comparable. Alexander did not have or need a *Requerimiento*, but he conceived himself as justified as Cortés in the territorial claims he made, and saw his victims as insubordinate vassals. Similar modes of thought evoked similar responses. For all the differences of scale the Mexican conquest supplies a host of small-scale analogies which can illuminate the reign of Alexander.

As usual, there are many debts to acknowledge. To Kate Adshead and Charles Manning I owe the invitation to give the Broadhead Lecture, generous hospitality while I was a visitor at Christchurch, and, indeed, the primary inspiration for this book. Elizabeth Baynham discussed the subject-matter with me while she was in Perth on study leave, and read the entire work in draft, making a large number of very helpful comments and criticisms. At a late stage I had the advantage of the detailed observations of Simon Hornblower and Sir John Elliott, which materially improved my presentation of Chapter 2. I have also benefited from the acute eye of Norman Ashton, who has read and criticized much of the book. My department and university gave generous material support, in particular a Time Release Award for the first semester of 1995, which enabled me to do most of the writing in ideal conditions; and a subvention from the Australian Research Council's Large Grants Scheme gave me the opportunity to work on the Indian material at Oxford in 1994 and 1995. Finally, and most importantly, I should thank my wife, Jo, for her encouragement and understanding thoughout the gestation of this work.

This book is dedicated to the memory of my father, who was embroiled in a war he detested, witnessed some of the worst that man can do, and acquitted himself with dignity.

October 1995   A.B.B.

Contents

List of Figures   xi

Abbreviations   xii–xvi

1. The Shield of Achilles: Myth and Reality
   in the Reign of Alexander the Great   1

2. Windows on the Truth   31

3. Information and Misinformation   66

4. The Creation of Belief   98

5. The Justification of Terror   133

6. Alexander and the Desert   166

Appendix   Alexander and the Ganges:
   A Question of Probability   186

Bibliography   201

Index   211

List of Figures

1. The Porus decadrachm and a tetradrachm depicting an Indian archer and elephant (by permission of the Departement Oosterse en Slavische Studies, Katholieke Universiteit Leuven (Louvain)) 7
2. The modern topography around Jhelum 10
3. Alexander's crossing of the Hydaspes, according to Arrian 14
4. The cavalry engagement at the Hydaspes 17
5. Alexander's campaign in Bajaur 43
6. Operations at Mt. Aornus 48
7. The Strait of Hormuz 67
8. India East of the Hyphasis 75
9. An approximation of the configuration of the Punjab in antiquity (the river courses are wholly conjectural) 134
10. The Makran 168

Abbreviations

AFLM	*Annali della Facoltà di Lettere e Filosofia, Università di Macerata* (Padua)
Agrawala	V. S. Agrawala, *India as Known to Pāṇini* (Lucknow 1958)
AHB	*Ancient History Bulletin*
AJP	*American Journal of Philology*
AncSoc	*Ancient Society* (Louvain)
AncW	*The Ancient World* (Chicago)
*ASNP*³	*Annali della Scuola Normale Superiore di Pisa*, serie III
Atkinson	J. E. Atkinson, *A Commentary on Q. Curtius Rufus' Historiae Alexandri Magni* (Amsterdam and Uithoorn 1980–)
BABesch	*Bulletin Antieke Beschaving*
BASP	*Bulletin of the American Society of Papyrologists*
Bellinger, *Essays*	A. R. Bellinger, *Essays on the Coinage of Alexander the Great*, Numismatic Studies 11 (New York, 1963)
Berve	H. Berve, *Das Alexanderreich auf prosopographischer Grundlage* (2 vols.: Munich 1926)
Billows	R. A. Billows, *Antigonos the One-Eyed and the Creation of the Hellenistic State* (Berkeley and Los Angeles 1990)
BJ	*Bonner Jahrbücher*
Bosworth, *HCA*	A. B. Bosworth, *A Historical Commentary on Arrian's History of Alexander*, i– (Oxford 1980–)

Brunt, *Arrian*	P. A. Brunt, *Arrian* (2 vols.: Loeb Classical Library: Cambridge, Mass., 1976–83)
CAH	*Cambridge Ancient History*
CHIran	*Cambridge History of Iran*
CPh	*Classical Philology*
CQ	*Classical Quarterly*
CRAI	*Comptes-rendus de l'Académie des inscriptions et belles-lettres*
Droysen	J. G. Droysen, *Geschichte des Hellenismus* (2nd edn.: 3 vols.: Gotha 1877–8)
DS	C. Daremberg and E. Saglio, *Dictionnaire des antiquités grecques et romaines d' après les textes et les monuments* (Paris 1877–1919)
Edson Studies	*Ancient Macedonian Studies in Honor of Charles F. Edson*, ed. H. J. Dell (Thessaloniki 1981)
Engels	D. W. Engels, *Alexander the Great and the Logistics of the Macedonian Army* (Berkeley 1978)
Entretiens Hardt	*Entretiens sur l'antiquité classique* (Fondation Hardt: Vandœvres–Geneva)
FGrH	F. Jacoby, *Die Fragmente der griechischen Historiker* (Berlin and Leiden 1923–)
GJ	*Geographical Journal*
Goukowsky	*Essai sur les origines du mythe d'Alexandre* (2 vols.: Nancy 1978–81)
GRBS	*Greek, Roman and Byzantine Studies*
Greece & the E. Med.	*Greece and the Eastern Mediterranean in History and Prehistory*, ed. K. Kinzl (Berlin and New York 1977)
Green	P. Green, *Alexander of Macedon* (London 1974)

Hamilton, *Plut. Al.*	J. R. Hamilton, *Plutarch Alexander: A Commentary* (Oxford 1969)
Hammond, *KCS*[2]	N. G. L. Hammond, *Alexander the Great: King, Commander and Statesman* (2nd edn.: Bristol 1989).
Hammond, *Sources*	N. G. L. Hammond, *Sources for Alexander the Great: An Analysis of Plutarch's Life and Arrian's Anabasis Alexandrou* (Cambridge 1993)
Hammond, *Three Historians*	N. G. L. Hammond, *Three Historians of Alexander the Great: The So-Called Vulgate Authors, Diodorus, Justin and Curtius* (Cambridge 1983)
Heckel	W. Heckel, *The Marshals of Alexander's Empire* (London 1992)
Hoplites	*Hoplites. The Classical Greek Battle Experience*, ed. V. D. Hanson (London 1991)
Hornblower, *Hieronymus*	J. Hornblower, *Hieronymus of Cardia* (Oxford 1981)
IBK	*Innsbrucker Beiträge zur Kulturgeschichte*
IG	*Inscriptiones graecae* (1st edn.: Berlin 1873–)
JDAI	*Jahrbuch des Deutschen Archäologischen Instituts*
JHS	*Journal of Hellenic Studies*
JRAS	*Journal of the Royal Asiatic Society*
JS	*Journal des Savants*
Kornemann	E. Kornemann, *Die Alexandergeschichte des Königs Ptolemaios I von Aegypten* (Leipzig 1935)
MH	*Museum Helveticum*
Moretti, *ISE*	I. Moretti, *Iscrizioni storiche ellenistiche* (Florence 1967–)
Niese	B. Niese, *Geschichte der griechischen und makedonischen Staaten seit der Schlacht bei Chaeronea* (3 vols.: Gotha 1893–1903)

Orientalia Tucci	*Orientalia Iosephi Tucci memoriae dicata*, ed. G. Gnoli and L. Lanciotti (2 vols.: Rome 1985)
PACA	*Proceedings of the African Classical Association*
Pearson, *LHA*	L. Pearson, *The Lost Histories of Alexander the Great* (Philological Monographs 20: Am. Phil. Ass. 1960)
Pédech, *Historiens compagnons*	P. Pédech, *Historiens compagnons d'Alexandre* (Paris 1984)
POxy	*Oxyrhynchus Papyri*
Price, *Coinage*	M. J. Price, *The Coinage in the Name of Alexander the Great and Philip Arrhidaeus* (2 vols.: Zurich and London 1991)
PSI	*Papiri greci e latini* (Pubblicazioni della Società Italiana per la ricerca dei papiri greci e latini in Egitto)
RE	*Realencyclopädie der classischen Altertumswissenschaft*, ed. Pauly, Wissowa, Kroll (Stuttgart 1893–)
Robert, *OMS*	L. Robert, *Opera Minora Selecta*, vols. i– Paris 1969–)
Schachermeyr, *Al.*[2]	F. Schachermeyr, *Alexander der Große: das Problem seiner Persönlichkeit und seines Wirkens* (Sitzungsberichte der österreich. Akademie der Wißenschaften, phil.-hist. Kl., 285 (1973)
Siddiqi	M. I. Siddiqi, *The Fishermen's Settlements on the Coast of West Pakistan*, Schriften des geographischen Instituts der Universität Kiel XVI 2 (Kiel 1956)
SNR	*Schweizerische Numismatische Rundschau: Revue suisse de numismatique*
Stewart	A. Stewart, *Faces of Power: Alexander's Image and Hellenistic Politics* (Berkeley and Los Angeles 1993)

Strasburger, *Studien*	H. Strasburger, *Studien zur Alten Geschichte*, ed. W. Schmitthenner and R. Zoeppfel (3 vols.: Hildesheim 1982–90)
Studia Naster	*Studia Paulo Naster oblata*, ed. S. Scheers and J. Quaegebeur (Orientalia Lovaniensia Analecta 12–13: Louvain 1982)
SVF	*Stoicorum veterum fragmenta*, ed. H. von Arnim (4 vols.: Stuttgart 1903–24)
TAPA	*Transactions of the American Philological Association*
Tarn, *Al.*	W. W. Tarn, *Alexander the Great* (2 vols.: Cambridge 1948)
Tonnet	H. Tonnet, *Recherches sur Arrien. Sa personnalité et ses écrits* (2 vols.: Amsterdam 1988)
YCS	*Yale Classical Studies*
ZA	*Zeitschrift für Assyriologie und vorderasiatische Archäologie*
ZDMG	*Zeitschrift des Deutschen Morgenländischen Gesellschaft* (Wiesbaden)
ZPE	*Zeitschrift für Papyrologie und Epigraphik*
Zu Al. d. Gr.	*Zu Alexander dem Großen: Festschrift G. Wirth*, ed. W. Will (2 vols.: Amsterdam 1988)

I

The Shield of Achilles: Myth and Reality in the Reign of Alexander the Great

ONE of the most attractive—and admirable—qualities of Henry Broadhead's commentary on the *Persae* is his ability to see beyond Aeschylus' 'patriotic enthusiasm' for the Greek victory and appreciate the tragic pathos of the defeated Persian monarch. I hope that he would have sympathized with my own approach to the history of Alexander the Great and the negative emphasis upon the costs of conquest. We should perhaps begin with a paradox. Imperialism is no longer in fashion, nor is aggression for its own sake. Yet a positively rose-tinted aura surrounds Alexander, the leader of one of the most successful wars of imperial aggrandizement, pursued wholly for gain and glory under the specious pretext of revenge. He has become divorced from history and elevated into a symbol, the type of military invincibility and the culture hero with a mission to propagate Hellenic values world-wide.

The tendency to idealize began in antiquity. Within a generation of Alexander's demise the rumours and slanders of poisoning gave impetus to full-blown fiction. A body of romance gradually accrued which had reached the dimensions of a novel by the Roman period and continued to develop in practically every language and culture from Scotland to Mongolia until the advent of the printing press. The *Alexander Romance* is overtly fictitious. However, the supposedly historical tradition of Alexander's reign poses serious problems. It has been seriously distorted by the practitioners of rhetoric and popular philosophy. The primary historians of Alexander tended not to be widely read in antiquity. They provided examples which seeped into the popular consciousness through the medium of derivative literature. Alexander could be invoked in negative ways, to provide instances of irascibility, intemperance, and divine pre-

This chapter comprises the text of the Sixth Broadhead Lecture, delivered at the University of Canterbury in June 1993.

tensions.[1] There were also more positive examples, actions of generosity, magnanimity, and sexual restraint.[2] But the constant factor in this exemplary use of Alexander is that the details are taken out of context, geared to the author's own rhetorical or moralizing purposes.[3] The most famous and influential instance is Plutarch's ingenious treatise *On the Fortune or Virtue of Alexander*.[4] This followed the precedent of Alexander's contemporary, Onesicritus, who depicted the king in encomiastic vein and represented the Indian sage, Dandamis, acknowledging him as a philosopher in arms.[5] For Onesicritus this was simply a tribute to Alexander's intellectual curiosity, which remained unstifled by his military calling. Plutarch, however, developed the conceit and constructed a bravura portrait of Alexander, the philosopher under arms, with a mission to impose civilization—on the Greek model—on the lesser breeds without the law; 'he sowed all Asia with Greek magistracies and so overcame its uncivilized and brutish manner of living' (*Mor.* 328e). He was sent by the gods as a mediator and conciliator for the whole world, and using force where reason was ineffective, he united all mankind in a single mixing jar, producing a cosmopolitan unity, in which all

---

[1] The prime example is Seneca, whose view of Alexander seems uniformly hostile. Cf. *De ira* 2. 17. 1–2; 3. 23. 1; *De clem.* 1. 25. 1 (irascibility and cruelty); *De ben.* 1. 13. 1–2; 2. 16. 1 (*Ep. Mor.* 53. 10); 7. 2. 5–6; *Ep. Mor.* 94. 62–3 (grandiose ambition); 83. 19–23 (*ebrietas*). Not surprisingly, Seneca's judgements are echoed in a famous passage of his nephew Lucan's *Pharsalia* (10. 20–52), in which Alexander is stigmatized as the 'fortunate brigand' (*felix praedo*), important only as an ominous example of universal monarchy (27–8). Yet even Seneca (*De ira* 2. 23. 2–3) commends Alexander's trust in Philip the Acarnanian, which was all the more admirable given his general propensity to anger. See further A. Heuß, *Antike und Abendland* 4 (1954) 87–9.

[2] A crude but instructive sample is provided by Valerius Maximus' compilation of memorable sayings and deeds, published under Tiberius. Here Alexander is cited in a number of examples, evenly balanced between virtue and vice. On the credit side see 3. 8. ext. 6 (*constantia*); 4. 7. ext. 2 (*amicitia*); 5. 1. ext. 1 (*humanitas*); 6. 4. ext. 3 (*gravitas*). The negative examples are 8. 14. ext. 2 (desire for glory); 9. 3. ext. 1 (*iracundia*); 9. 5. ext. 1 (*superbia*).

[3] There are interesting instances where the same episode can serve differing and even contradictory purposes. The marriage to Rhoxane is sometimes excoriated as a morganatic union, contracted through passion, sometimes commended as an act of reconciliation between east and west, or even adduced as an example of self-control— Alexander abjured a conqueror's recourse to violence. Cf. Bosworth, *HCA* ii. 131–3.

[4] There is a convenient summary with pertinent discussion in Hamilton, *Plut. Al.* xxix-xxxiii. The most recent discussions are those by S. Schröder, *MH* 48 (1991) 151– 7 and M. R. Cammarota, in *Ricerche plutarchee*, ed. I. Gallo (Naples 1992) 105–24, both of which correctly define the work as a piece of epideictic rhetoric, playing upon paradox for its own sake.

[5] Strabo 15. 1. 64 (715) = *FGrH* 134 F 14a. Cf. Pédech, *Historiens compagnons* 108.

considered the world their nation, Alexander's camp their citadel, the good their kinsmen, and the bad aliens (*Mor.* 329b–c).

There is no denying the force of Plutarch's rhetoric, but it is rhetoric none the less, remarkably unsupported by corroborative detail. It is *assumed* that Alexander's foundations were intended to be centres of civilization,[6] and *assumed* that he had a policy of unification; but no instances are given. Plutarch's influences here are literary rather than historical. The underlying concept was, as we have seen, suggested by Onesicritus; and something is also owed to the great Alexandrian scholar, Eratosthenes of Cyrene, who commended Alexander for ignoring any sharp distinction between Greek and barbarian but promoting men of ability and virtue whatever their racial background.[7] Plutarch has broadened the picture. Eratosthenes' judicious selector of talent has become a visionary, supranational monarch, while Onesicritus' devotee of philosophy is transformed into a philosopher in action, achieving in reality what was only theory for Zeno and the Stoics. It cannot be stressed too strongly that this is a literary *jeu d'esprit*, a virtuoso juggling of standard themes to produce something strikingly novel and indeed paradoxical. Plutarch's Alexander is a creation of emotive rhetoric, its only contact with attested historical material a list of standard examples, not particularly apt to the theme.[8] None

[6] Plutarch simply lists Alexander's principal foundations (*Mor.* 328f), and states that they mitigated the primitive savagery (τὸ ἄγριον) of the natives. This does scant justice to the culture of the Achaemenids, and overstates the sophistication of Alexander's cities. From Plutarch's encomium one would never guess that the first reaction to the news of Alexander's death was a mass movement by the new colonists back to Greece 'out of longing for Greek upbringing and culture' (Diod. 18. 7. 1).

[7] Strabo 1. 4. 9 (66–7), towards the end of the Second Book of Eratosthenes' *Geography* (cf. 1. 4. 1; 2. 1. 1). The context was clearly the propriety of the geographical and moral division of the world between Greek and barbarian. Eratosthenes made much of the phenomenon of virtuous barbarian societies such as the Romans and Carthaginians (cf. Andreotti, *Historia* 5 (1956) 267), and observed that Alexander, despite the advice of Aristotle, recognized merit irrespective of race. He may have been thinking of Alexander's benefactions to such specific communities as the Abii or the Euergetae (see below, pp. 151–2), rather than a general *integration* of Greeks and barbarians. All that is obviously shared by Eratosthenes/Strabo and Plutarch is Alexander's disregard of Aristotle's advice to discriminate between the races (see Badian's analysis, *Historia* 7 (1958) 434–5). That *may* have inspired Plutarch to develop his imagery of Alexander the unifier, but the picture he draws of universal reconciliation and cultural harmony is unique. At least it has no obvious parallel in Eratosthenes.

[8] *Mor.* 332e–333f. Plutarch states that all Alexander's actions can be said to be those of a philosopher (φιλοσόφως), but he can only adduce the marriage to Rhoxane, the honour paid to Darius' corpse, and Alexander's trust in Hephaestion. These are

the less there *is* something supremely attractive in Plutarch's portrait, the universal conqueror who is simultaneously the civilizer and benefactor of mankind. It has been extraordinarily potent in shaping modern views of Alexander. The German concept of 'the policy of fusion' (*Verschmelzungspolitik*) is essentially a restatement of Plutarch, while the once influential theory of Sir William Tarn, that Alexander promoted the ideal of the brotherhood of man, is explicitly based on and inspired by Plutarch.[9] A recent writer even concludes that Alexander's principal claim to greatness lies in his creation of 'a supranational community capable of living internally at peace and of developing the concord and partnership which are so sadly lacking in the modern world'.[10]

This last statement is virtually a paraphrase of Plutarch. It takes the rhetoric at face value and makes it the basis for historical reconstruction. Even Plutarch's whimsical picture of the children of Persia, Susiana and Gedrosia, declaiming the tragedies of Euripides and Sophocles has been taken as an authentic echo of the educational curriculum which Alexander is said to have devised for the training of his youthful Iranian infantry (supervised by a battery of His Majesty's Inspectors).[11] Once the rhetoric is accepted, the

certainly standard exempla (see above, nn. 2–3), but they hardly attest a philosophical disposition.

[9] See particularly Tarn, *Al.* ii. 437–41, criticized in detail by Badian, *Historia* 7 (1958) 432–40. In an instructive footnote published some years before, Helmut Berve had insisted that Plutarch's picture of unification applied only to Macedonians and Persians, the Aryan *Herrenvölker* (*Klio* 31 (1938) 167 n. 1); Tarn and Walter Kolbe were therefore wrong to adduce a policy of universal brotherhood. Naturally so. In the Nazi ideology the worst of evils was cosmopolitanism, in which racial characteristics were obliterated and national individuality weakened. Berve was in effect attempting to salvage Alexander's reputation from the indictment that he had betrayed his 'Volk'. A reader with a good library and a strong stomach might care to look out Fritz Schachermeyr's wartime fulminations on the subject (*Lebensgesetzlichkeit in der Geschichte* (Frankfurt 1940) 118–21).

[10] The final sentence of Nicholas Hammond's biography of Alexander (*KCS*² 273), immediately following a quotation of Plut. *Mor.* 329c. See also Hammond's more recent work, *The Macedonian State* (Oxford 1989) 226: 'his ideas on race, nationalism, intermarriage, and religion are, or should be, an inspiration to us today; and the fact that he put them all into effect in a span of thirteen years fills one with hope of what a man of genius may be able to do in our contemporary world'.

[11] So again Hammond, *Historia* 39 (1990) 288. The reference to Plutarch is *Mor.* 328 d; the 'HMIs' (Hammond 279) are the *epistatai* of Plut. *Al.* 47. 6 and Diod. 17. 108. 2, whom I take to have been the regional commandants of the Epigoni. The instruction in Greek letters (Ἑλληνικὰ γράμματα), mentioned by Plutarch (*Al.* 47. 6) may have included literacy as well as oral fluency in Greek, but there is no reason to think that it included the literary classics—any more than Eumenes needed a

historical sources can be enlisted to provide nuggets of fact, which taken out of context buttress the interpretation. There is also the tendency to idolize and idealize success. Alexander is the ultimate winner and so loved by everybody, often endued with the qualities one would like to see in oneself—he is now rational, now visionary, now humanitarian. What is more, consideration of Alexander is usually centred on the moral stratosphere of policies and grand strategy. The turbulent and appallingly violent circumstances in which he actually spent his life (and which, unlike matters of policy, are recorded in detail) tend to be relegated to the periphery and their importance minimized. The result is a sanitized Alexander detached from and unrelated to the carnage he created. My intention is to focus upon precisely that background, and in doing so I feel myself in the unenviable role of Hephaestus in W. H. Auden's fine poem, 'The Shield of Achilles'.[12] You will recall how the goddess Thetis watches the Olympian smith forge the new shield for her son and waits in expectation:

> She looked over his shoulder
> For vines and olive trees.
> Marble well-governed cities
> And ships upon untamed seas.
> But there on the shining metal
> His hands had put instead
> An artificial wilderness
> And a sky like lead.

'A sky like lead'. That takes us appropriately to our first example, set in the late spring of 326 against a background of violent showers, the precursors of the summer monsoon. The scene is Pakistan, the northern Punjab between the rivers Jhelum and Chenab, and the

---

grounding in Aramaic literature to concoct a letter in *Syria grammata* (Diod. 19. 23. 3; Polyaen. 4. 8. 3) or, for that matter, Laomedon for his dealings with Persian prisoners-of-war (Arr. 3. 6. 6). Hammond's entire educational structure rests upon Plutarch's flight of fancy, as does his startling conclusion (287): 'In the history of education Alexander is the outstanding figure in ancient times.'

[12] The poem, not surprisingly, seems a favourite among classicists. It is, for instance, quoted by Oliver Taplin, *G&R* 27 (1980) 2–3: 'Three times Thetis looks to see the scenes she expects because she knows them—or rather we know them—from Homer, and each time she is presented with a scene from a world of militaristic and totalitarian inhumanity.' This is precisely the contrast which I see between the rosy rhetoric of Plutarch and the grim campaign narrative of Arrian.

occasion the battle of the Hydaspes, where Alexander defeated and crushed the army of the Indian ruler, Porus. This battle has been hailed as one of Alexander's greatest military achievements—'among the most brilliant operations of ancient warfare' claimed D. G. Hogarth, approvingly quoted by Major-General Fuller.[13] That opinion was certainly shared by Alexander himself. His coinage commemorated it to an extraordinary degree with a number of unique celebratory issues. The most impressive is a great silver decadrachm, probably struck during Alexander's last year at Babylon. It depicts Alexander on horseback lunging up with the great Macedonian *sarisa* at two riders mounted on a war elephant: Porus in the place of honour astride the neck brandishes a spear defiantly, while his attendant to the rear turns aside in fright.[14] It is a deliberately heroic representation, with the two adversaries locked in a symbolic hand-to-hand conflict which never in fact took place. On the reverse the heroic conflict gives way to victory with Alexander standing in triumph with the thunderbolt of Zeus in his hands and receiving a wreath of victory from Nike herself. The message here is patent. It is less so with a subsidiary series of tetradrachms which commemorate the various units of the defeated army. The elephants, as we should expect, are prominent, depicted with and without their riders; and there is also a war chariot, drawn by four horses, and an Indian archer with a typical composite bow and the characteristic hairstyle, 'twisted back and surrounded with a headband'.[15] This impressive visual record of the defeated army is difficult to explain.[16] The coins seem to emphasize the fighting potential of Porus' army,

---

[13] D. G. Hogarth, *Philip and Alexander of Macedon* (London 1897) 239, quoted by J. F. C. Fuller, *The Generalship of Alexander the Great* 180. For bibliography on the Battle of the Hydaspes see Seibert, *Alexander der Große* 156–60; Bosworth, *HCA* ii. 242–3.

[14] The scene is best described and elucidated by P. Bernard, in *Orientalia Tucci* i. 76–9, proving beyond doubt that the heroic figure at the head of the elephant is Porus himself (*contra* M. J. Price, in *Studia Naster* i. 80). See also Stewart 203–5.

[15] Strabo 15. 1. 71 (719); Arr. *Ind.* 16. 2 = Nearchus, *FGrH* 133 F 11. See further Bernard, in *Orientalia Tucci* 72–4. On the Indian bow see Arr. *Ind.* 16. 6: 'a bow as tall as the archer which they base on the ground and set their left foot upon it before shooting, drawing the bow a long way back.' Cf. Ch. 5 n. 21.

[16] It is the main difficulty in dating the series. Bernard suggested, against the hoard evidence, that the coins were struck after Alexander's death by Eudamus, who commanded Indian troops and elephants during the Iranian campaign of 317/16 (*Orientalia Tucci* i. 83–9). Other scholars (e.g. Price, in *Studia Naster* i. 84; W. Hollstein, *SNR* 68 (1989) 8–14) have placed the issues implausibly early, during Alexander's stay in Taxila. For a more acceptable dating to 325/4 see Stewart 205–6 with Price, *Coinage* i. 452 n. 9.

Fig. 1. The Porus decadrachm and a tetradrachm depicting an Indian archer and elephant

and there must be conscious propaganda at work. Alexander was underscoring his victory.[17] In a manner unique in ancient coinage he was sending a message to people who could never hope to witness an Indian army in the flesh. These were the outlandish and formidable forces which he had faced in battle and crushed. Five years might have elapsed since the Persian grand army was humiliated at Gaugamela, but his army had lost none of its frightful efficiency. The victory over Porus was the proof, and the coinage ensured that its implications were not lost. In the context of the troubles in Greece which followed the Exiles' Decree it would constitute a blunt warning. Beware the consequences of revolt. The army which crushed Porus will easily crush you.

The message of the coinage is paralleled by the literary sources. Porus, Alexander's Indian adversary, is portrayed as a figure of heroic grandeur, his kingdom rich and heavily populated, with some 300 cities.[18] In every respect, it is alleged, he was a worthy opponent of Alexander. There is a famous episode, recorded in every version of the battle, in which Porus, finally defeated and forced to surrender, was brought before his conqueror. Alexander was impressed by his stature (something over 2 metres) and his physical beauty, and asked how he would like to be treated. The answer was a single word, 'like a king' ($\beta \alpha \sigma \iota \lambda \iota \varkappa \tilde{\omega} \varsigma$). When Alexander asked for further details, Porus insisted that everything was comprised in the single word. This episode is very well attested, and Arrian's version of it goes back to contemporaries of Alexander, Ptolemy, and Aristobulus.[19] An interview clearly took place, through the medium of interpreters, who probably imposed some distortion, 'like clear water passing through mud'—as the Indian sage, Dandamis, is made to say by Onesicritus.[20] Porus demanded to be treated in regal style; Alexander took the request in more orthodox terms, for him to

---

[17] The point was made by Curtius (8. 14. 46), commenting on Alexander's magnanimous treatment of Porus: 'his own grandeur would be the more illustrious, the greater the adversaries he had defeated' ('eandem clariorem fore, quo maiores fuissent quos ipse vicisset').

[18] Strabo 15. 1. 29 (698). Other passages suggest no less than 5,000 cities, each larger than Meropid Cos, between the rivers Hydaspes and Hyphasis (Strabo 15. 1. 3 (686), 33 (701); Pliny, *NH* 6. 59; cf. Arr. 6. 2. 1; Bosworth, *HCA* ii. 318–19).

[19] Arr. 5. 19. 2; cf. Plut. *Al.* 60. 13; *Mor.* 181e, 332e, 458b; *Metz Epit.* 61; Themist. *Or.* 7. 88d–89b). Curt. 8. 14. 41–5 has a somewhat different (and highly rhetorical) exchange. For the view that Arrian's version comes from his principal sources see Kornemann 24 n. 26; Bosworth, *HCA* ii. 309 (*contra* Hammond, *Sources* 108–9).

[20] Strabo 15. 1. 64 (716) = Onesicritus, *FGrH* 134 F 17a. See below, Ch. 4 n. 1.

behave as a king, and displayed the appropriate magnanimity. But the upshot was the same. Alexander confirmed Porus in his dominions as paramount ruler subject only to himself, and gradually expanded his realm at the expense of his neighbours. By the time he left northern India, Porus had been recognized as ruler of the whole sweep of lands east of the river Hydaspes (Jhelum), his power in fact vastly increased by grace of his conqueror.[21] Alexander had acted like a king and treated Porus as a king. His adversary had proved his mettle by his resistance, and he could be recognized as viceroy in northern India.

So much for the propaganda. Can we probe beneath it to the historical reality? It is as well to begin with a few crude statistics of geography and population. Porus' dominions were not large. The ancient sources are unanimous in describing his boundaries. His territories were defined by two great rivers, the Jhelum (Hydaspes) to the west and the Chenab (Acesines) to the east.[22] Porus controlled the plain land between them, the so-called Jech Doab, and his sway ended at the Himalayan foothills, where the mountain tribes were independent and perhaps hostile.[23] The total area under his domination now comprises some 15,000 square kilometres. In antiquity the course of the rivers was somewhat different, more to the east, but the area between them cannot have been disproportionately greater. The same applies to the population. At the time of the 1901 census it amounted to 1,500,000, predominantly rural. There were only five towns with populations greater than 10,000 and the vast majority of settlements were villages of less than 1,000 inhabitants.[24] The source picture of a land of great cities is, to put it mildly, a gross exaggeration.

Porus, then, controlled a territory far smaller than Alexander's Macedonia, and he faced an enemy who had the manpower of an empire at his disposal. He also stood virtually alone. His one attested ally—or rather, sympathizer, was Abisares, the ruler of the mountain

[21] Arr. 5. 29. 2; 6. 2. 1. For the earlier grants see 5. 19. 3, 20. 4, 21. 5, 24. 8.

[22] Strabo 15. 1. 29 (698); cf. Curt. 8. 12. 13. Arrian makes it clear that Porus' lands began east of the Hydaspes (5. 8. 4) and ended before the Acesines (5. 21. 2: 'he sent Porus back to his domains').

[23] Arr. 5. 20. 2–4; Strabo 15. 1. 29 (698); Diod. 17. 89. 4–90. 1; Curt. 9. 1. 4. Cf. Bosworth, *HCA* ii. 316–19.

[24] These figures are extracted from the *Punjab District Gazetteers*, which provide census details for the period before 1913. For more detailed references see Bosworth, *HCA* ii. 264.

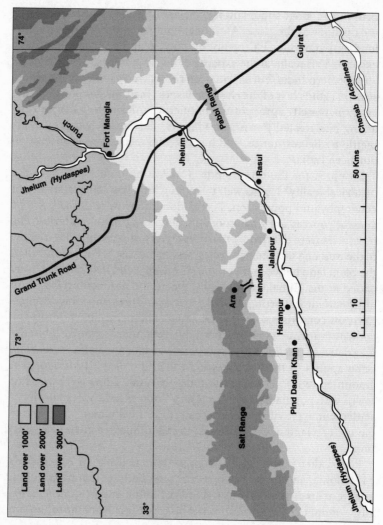

Fig. 2. The modern topography around Jhelum

areas between the Indus and Hydaspes,[25] and against Abisares' very unreliable support could be set the utterly dependable hostility of his nearest neighbours. To the west his enemy, the prince of Taxila, had been one of Alexander's earliest vassals, and had urged the Macedonian to extend his conquests to India at least a year before the actual invasion.[26] To the east his cousin, also named Porus, was at loggerheads with him and submitted to Alexander before the crucial battle.[27] Porus could expect no help from that quarter. He was a small, beleaguered prince, who chose to challenge the most professional army of the ancient world, now swelled by local levies at least equivalent in size to his own forces. It was a forlorn cause from the outset, and Porus could only be overwhelmed if the two armies met at full strength.

There was only one hope, to divert the invader from his territory; and to this end Porus' most potent ally was the weather. When Alexander reached the Punjab, it was early spring, and the Jhelum, fuelled by the melting Himalayan snows, was already beginning to rise.[28] It would soon be swelled by the advent of the monsoon rains to a breadth of up to a mile and provide an impassable barrier until its subsidence in September. Until the waters rose, Porus occupied the main crossing point with the bulk of the army,[29] and his strategy—such as it was—was to keep Alexander fixed on the west bank of the river until exasperation and shortage of supplies forced him

[25] On the location of Abisares' realm see Bosworth, *HCA* ii. 177–8, 260–1. He had previously allied himself with Porus in a campaign against the Cathaei, east of the Hydraotes (Ravi), and he is alleged to have contemplated joining forces against Alexander (Arr. 5. 20. 5, 22. 2; Diod. 17. 87. 3; Curt. 8. 14. 1). Previously he had taken the precaution of approaching Alexander (Arr. 5. 8. 3; *Metz Epit.* 55; Curt. 8. 13. 1), but he allegedly detained the ambassador who was sent to receive the surrender (*Metz Epit.* 56; cf. Berve ii no. 566). His behaviour was quite ambiguous; Porus could not count on his support nor Alexander upon his neutrality.

[26] For the enmity of Taxiles see Arr. 5. 18. 7 ('an enemy of long standing'); Curt. 8. 12. 12; *Metz Epit.* 53. Even Alexander was unable to broker a lasting reconciliation between the two (Arr. 5. 20. 4; Curt. 9. 3. 22).

[27] Arr. 5. 20. 6, 21. 3. Cf. Diod. 17. 91. 1; Strabo 15. 1. 30 (699).

[28] Arr. 5. 9. 4 (this passage is textually defective (see Bosworth, *HCA* ii. 270–2), but the sense is clear). Nearchus and Aristobulus gave a full description of the weather conditions: the rains began in Taxila early in spring 326 (Strabo 15. 1. 17 (691) = *FGrH* 139 F 35), and continued until the rising of Arcturus, late in September. The height of the deluge came at the solstice (Strabo 15. 1. 8 (692) = *FGrH* 138 F 18; Arr. *Ind.* 6. 5). According to Curt. 8. 13. 8 the Hydaspes was already 4 stades wide at the time of Alexander's crossing, well on its way to maximum breadth, which would reach nearly 2 km. (*Punjab District Gazetteers* xxvii.A (Jhelum) 10).

[29] Arr. 5. 8. 4; Curt. 8. 13. 5.

southwards and away from Porus' own domains. But the strategy had a fatal flaw. It depended on Alexander backing away from a challenge, something he had never done in his entire career, as the seven-month siege of Tyre and the recent storming of the supposedly impregnable fortress of Aornus (Pir-sar) had proved beyond cavil. Now the crossing of the Hydaspes in the face of the enemy was an irresistibly intriguing problem, far more so than the earlier crossing of the Danube (again in the face of a hostile army).

An elaborate game of bluff developed. Alexander began to stockpile provisions in highly visible localities, giving the impression that he intended to stay in position until the river reached low water in the autumn. At the same time he split his army into detachments, moving along the entire length of the bank and forcing Porus to divide his own forces to counter him. Alexander seems also to have positioned at least one army group at another relatively distant crossing point,[30] so that the Indian army was separated into at least two segments. He was the aggressor with an overwhelming advantage of numbers, and the strategy of dividing forces was one that Porus could only lose. During the marching and counter-marching the headquarters army with the Indian king was diluted, and the time was ripening for the Macedonian strike across the river. That required a colossal logistical exercise. Alexander had a fleet already built for the pontoon bridge which took his army across the Indus in the early spring. The vessels were built in sections, designed to be dismantled and transported from river to river, so that the army could progress through the Punjab even at the height of the summer monsoon, and there were literally hundreds of them.[31] All were

---

[30] Arr. 5. 9. 2–3. Porus is said to have sent garrisons to defend the most vulnerable crossing points in other areas (Arr. 5. 9. 1), and Alexander presumably sent detachments to counter them. That would explain the fact that the forces attested at his headquarters comprised only a fraction of the army (Bosworth, *HCA* ii. 276–8).

[31] Arr. 4. 30. 4; 5. 3. 5, 8. 4–5; Curt. 8. 10. 2–3. One may compare Cortés' preparations for the siege of Tenochtitlan, between Oct. 1520 and Jan. 1521, when he had a number of brigantines transported in segments nearly 100 km. by land, using a column of 8,000 Indian porters. The basic construction was done in Tlaxcala (although anchors, sails, cables, and tow were brought from Villa Rica (Vera Cruz) on the coast), and the precut timbers were conveyed to Texcoco, by the inland lake (Cortés pp. 165, 183–6; Díaz, pp. 311, 324–5 (Cohen), pp. 450–1, 468–9 (Maudslay); Gómara, pp. 238, 250–1, 262). There they were rebuilt and caulked, under the supervision of the shipwright, Martín López. This was an impressive feat, highly esteemed by Prescott, but it pales into insignificance beside Alexander. Only thirteen brigantines were built, and Cortés himself estimates the distance they were transported as 'some eighteen leagues' (p. 185). The ships were far fewer, the distances shorter, and the time-scale more leisurely.

painfully hauled by ox teams at a snail's pace—a top speed of 2 miles per hour and 10 miles in a day; and the distance to be covered was formidable, 40 miles from the Indus to Taxila and another 120 from Taxila to the Hydaspes.[32] One can only imagine the labour and hardship which went into this gigantic haulage exercise—and it is notable that the marshal in charge, Coenus, went on to supervise the crossing of the Chenab in its summer spate and then voiced the grievances of the troops at the 'mutiny' of the Hyphasis, forcing the king to turn back from yet another crossing.[33] Enough was enough. But the mutiny was a summer and a monsoon in the future. In the spring of 326 over a period of weeks Alexander's fleet gradually materialized by the Hydaspes. It was carefully concealed at his chosen crossing point, at a bend in the river, behind a dense cover of forest and protected by an uninhabited island which provided further concealment,[34] while Alexander ensured that Porus was diverted from this crucial area by manœuvres elsewhere on the bank.

The preparation had been immaculate, and the crossing itself was executed with staggering efficiency. Alexander left a holding force at his main camp and under cover of night took his attack force to the waiting fleet, nearly 20 miles away. It was a select force, the pick of his Macedonian infantry and cavalry, swelled by élite horsemen recruited from the north-east satrapies. All the infantry that could be embarked in the transport vessels began the crossing as dawn broke, while the cavalry followed on great leather floats stuffed with chaff. The surprise was complete, the crossing unopposed, and an army of 5,000 horse and 6,000 foot eventually disembarked on the east bank

[32] The estimates of distance come from the bematists (Pliny, *NH* 6. 62 = *FGrH* 119 F 2a. For statistics of the speed of ox teams see Bosworth, *HCA* ii. 264.

[33] Arr. 5. 8. 4; 21. 1, 4; 27. 1–28. 1. Cf. Heckel 58–64 for an appreciation of Coenus' career.

[34] The area is described by Arr. 5. 11. 1–2 (cf. Curt. 8. 13. 17; *Metz Epit.* 59). Its exact location cannot be determined, despite the valiant efforts of Sir Aurel Stein (*GJ* 80 (1932) 31–46; *Archaeological Reconnaissances* 1–26) and Bernard Breloer (*Alexanders Kampf gegen Poros* 121–47). Both these interpretations rest on the flawed assumption that the course of the Hydaspes was the same in ancient and modern times. Most geographers assume that there has been a considerable shift over the millennia and that the course of the river has gradually moved to the west of the plain of Gujrat, towards the Great Salt Range. Given the considerable 'vagaries of the stream', which were noted in the early 20th century (*Punjab District Gazetteers* xxvii.A (Jhelum) 10), it does seem practically impossible that the modern Hydaspes runs in anything like its ancient course, once it has passed the 6-km. gap between the Salt Range and the Pabbi Hills.

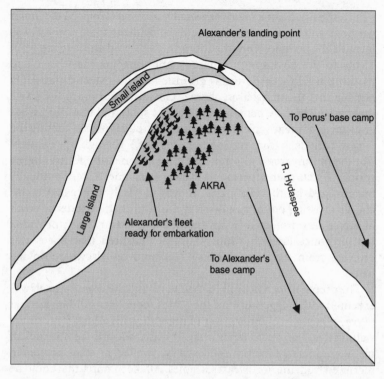

Fig. 3. Alexander's crossing of the Hydaspes, according to Arrian

of the river.[35] It was a fraction of the troops available to Alexander, but it was the cream of his army and—as we shall see—more than sufficient to win the battle without reinforcements. No other crossings are mentioned, and it is hard to see how they could have been effected en masse in the relatively few hours before the battle took place.[36] As our sources make clear, the battle was fought and

---

[35] The figures are supplied by Arrian (5. 14. 1, 18.2), and are consistent with the list of units he gives for the crossing force (5. 12. 2: the cavalry comprised the *agema* and three hipparchies, along with horsemen from Bactria and Sogdiana, and the mounted archers; the infantry consisted of hypaspists, two phalanx *taxeis*, archers, and Agrianians). Even these contingents may not have crossed in their entirety. The vessels available determined the number who crossed, and many troops in the units earmarked for the battle may not have been able to find a place in the transports.

[36] In Arrian's casualty list (5. 18. 2) the infantry that participated in the battle is said to have numbered only 6,000 (they are described as fighting 'in the first engagement', as opposed to the pursuit group headed by Craterus). As for the mercenary forces on

won with the relatively small expeditionary force which crossed with Alexander. That has obvious implications for our estimates of the size of Porus' army.

The first encounter was a foretaste of what was to come. When Porus' scouts reported the appearance of the Macedonian fleet shortly after dawn, he was in a dilemma. Was this the main attack force or a diversion? Accordingly he sent a force of cavalry and war chariots, commanded by one of his sons, to determine the size of the incursion and to attack if the numbers were sufficiently small. They came within sight of the attacking force too late to impede the landing or even the subsequent painful fording of a second channel of the river.[37] The Indian reconnaissance force accordingly made contact with the Macedonian cavalry advancing in marching order, and only saw the mass of horse around Alexander when it was too late to escape battle. The wet conditions caused by overnight thunderstorms bogged their war chariots, all of which were captured,[38] and the cavalry, heavily outnumbered, was routed with heavy losses and with effortless ease. Porus now knew that a substantial army had crossed, but the price was a heavy toll of casualties in the sector of his army (the cavalry) where he could least afford them. He chose to give battle, rather than retreat and fight a guerrilla campaign, and moved away from the river bank to a sandy, level clearing and prepared his forces for defence. His trump card was his war elephants, which he positioned in an extended line, with infantry packed in depth between them. The cavalry massed in two groups on the wings.[39]

the bank between the Macedonian base camp and the crossing point, they were explicitly instructed to cross only when they saw that battle was engaged (Arr. 5. 12. 1), and they duly did so, along with Craterus, at the end of the battle proper (Arr. 5. 18. 1). The fashionable view (Tarn, *Al.* ii. 190–1; Hamilton, *JHS* 76 (1956) 26–7; Hammond, *KCS*² 211) that they reinforced Alexander's army between the crossing point and the battle site is, in my opinion, untenable.

[37] Arr. 5. 13. 1 (reports of the Macedonian crossing). According to Ptolemy (Arr. 5. 14. 6 = *FGrH* 138 F 20) the Indian advance force arrived after Alexander had made his last crossing onto firm ground. Aristobulus (Arr. 5. 14. 3 = *FGrH* 139 F 43) was more dramatic, and claimed that the Indian forces might actually have prevented the crossing. That was a blatant exaggeration of the danger. Arrian was clearly right to opt for Ptolemy's version, which gave a reasonably large reconnaissance force of Indians, strong enough to risk an engagement with the vanguard of Alexander's cavalry (Arr. 5. 15. 2; on the source tradition see Bosworth, *HCA* ii. 287–91). Ptolemy's version is largely supported by Plutarch, who adduces details from a purported letter of Alexander (Plut. *Al.* 60. 7–8; cf. Curt. 8. 14. 2–9).

[38] Arr. 5. 15. 2; Curt. 8. 14. 4–8.   [39] Arr. 5. 15. 4–7; Curt. 8. 14. 9–13.

Porus' dispositions are simple and well attested, but how numerous were his troops? That is the crux, and our interpretation of the battle depends on it. The extant sources give differing figures: the elephants vary between 85 and 200; and there is some agreement on 30,000 infantry and 300 war chariots.[40] Now this data is hard to assess. It is unlikely that reliable figures would ever have been available for the size of Porus' army, and the eyewitness reports of the victors must inevitably have exaggerated the enemy numbers to their own advantage. That happened to a grotesque degree in the reports of Gaugamela, which give figures ranging from 200,000 (Curtius) to 1,000,000 (Arrian) for the Persian infantry. The figures at the Hydaspes are much more sober, but even so they are clearly overestimates. It is attested that Alexander actually had superiority in cavalry,[41] and, more importantly, in the last stage of the battle the Macedonians were able to enclose the entire Indian army in a cordon comprised by the infantry phalanx in close formation and the cavalry.[42] That practically excludes Porus having had as many as 30,000 infantry. Facing a Macedonian line of 6,000, packed 8 deep in close formation, they would need to be massed 40 deep, hardly a feasible proposition for 5,000 Macedonian cavalry to envelop in an unbroken cordon. Porus' infantry may well have outnumbered the attackers, but hardly in a ratio of five to one, and his cavalry was numerically inferior. What mattered was the deployment of the elephants (50 of them spaced at intervals of 20 metres would roughly match the Macedonian frontage). They were intended to trample and disrupt the enemy infantry, and could possibly compensate for Alexander's advantage in numbers and his troops' much greater experience and efficiency.

A defensive strategy was the best Porus could devise, but it was

---

[40] Arr. 5. 15. 4; Curt. 8. 13. 6; *Metz Epit.* 54. Diod. 17. 87. 2 gives somewhat discrepant figures (130 elephants, 1,000 war chariots, 50,000 men), which might represent Porus' total army, not the force which actually fought the battle. On the other hand the figures in Plut. *Al.* 62. 2 are obviously minimized for rhetorical purposes.

[41] 5. 16. 2 (ἅτε ἱπποκρατῶν). Arrian accredits Alexander with 5,000 cavalry (5. 14. 1), whereas Porus disposed of only 4,000 at the battle (5. 15. 4). In Curtius' version 4,000 is the total cavalry in Porus' advance force (Curt. 8. 14. 2), and in Diodorus and Plutarch (see n. 40 above) the figure is even smaller. For all the discrepancies of detail there is unanimous agreement that Porus' cavalry was outnumbered.

[42] Arr. 5. 17. 7: 'Alexander extended his cavalry to encircle the entire Indian formation, and gave orders for the infantry to advance the line, locking shields in the most compact possible array.' See below, p. 19.

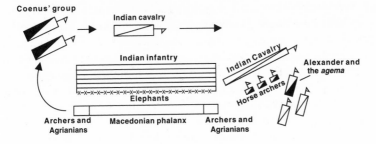

(a) The first phase of the battle

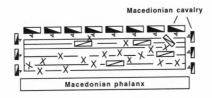

(b) Final stage: the killing ground

Fig. 4. The cavalry engagement at the Hydaspes

woefully inadequate. His battle line was stationary,[43] and therefore vulnerable to Alexander's incomparable cavalry, which far surpassed his own in numbers and expertise. It was divided between the Macedonian wings, matching Porus' dispositions, and comprised the spearhead of the attack.[44] For the moment the Macedonian infantry remained at a distance, while Alexander concentrated his attention upon the enemy left. His horse archers (from the steppes of Turk-menistan) prepared the way, sowing confusion by a series of destructive forays. Alexander himself meanwhile led his cavalry guard in a rapid movement to his right, threatening to attack the enemy force on its flank. To avoid envelopment the Indians ex-

---

[43] Arr. 5. 15. 6–7; Curt. 8. 14. 9–13; Polyaen. 4. 3. 22.

[44] Arr. 5. 16. 2–3; Plut. *Al.* 60. 10–11; Curt. 8. 14. 15–16. Alexander's strategy has been much discussed, many (notably Adolf Bauer and Tarn) seeing an element of surprise in it; but, given his crushing superiority in cavalry, there was no need for elaborate stratagems. The only doubtful issue was whether Porus would transfer cavalry from his right wing to relieve the beleaguered left. For full discussion see Bosworth, *HCA* ii. 295–7.

tended their line leftwards, but, outnumbered as they were, they ran the risk of breaking formation. Unless he resigned himself to the destruction of his left, Porus had no choice but to transfer cavalry from his right wing, to reinforce the defence against Alexander's right. The transfer duly began, but again the superior Macedonian numbers permitted a decisive counter-move. As the Indian cavalry moved leftwards behind its static infantry line, it was followed by its counterpart on the Macedonian side (under the invaluable Coenus).[45] This force kept out of range of the Indian infantry, which could not (or would not) break the integrity of the line, and intervened decisively. The Indian cavalry had united, but, as it did so, it came under attack from front and rear. Overwhelmed by superior numbers it had nowhere to turn other than backwards into the infantry phalanx.[46] That was the critical moment. The influx of cavalry forced the Indian footsoldiers forward into their line of elephants. The beasts were diverted from the Macedonian infantry to face Alexander's cavalry attack, and the carefully ordered Indian battle line was thrown into chaos.[47] The Macedonian infantry engaged immediately.

What followed was sheer horror. The elephant drivers tried to use their beasts as prototype tanks, to trample down their assailants, and they were to some degree successful.[48] But the Macedonians had acquired some experience of elephants over the past year and had clearly been well schooled by their Indian allies. Using their lethal 18-foot pikes (*sarisae*) they lunged up at the mahouts and at the beasts' eyes—there is also some evidence that they had been equipped with a special sickle-shaped cleaver, designed to gash and

[45] Arr. 5. 17. 1; Polyaen. 4. 3. 22; Curt. 8. 14. 17. On the direction of Coenus' movement, *behind* the Indian line, see Hamilton, *JHS* 76 (1956) 29–30; A. M. Devine, *AncW* 16 (1987) 104–5; *contra* G. Veith, *Klio* 8 (1908) 137.

[46] Arr. 5. 17. 2: 'they were dashed back towards the elephants, who served, as it were, as a friendly fortification'. The situation, and the language, is reminiscent of Thucydides' description of the Athenians at Syracuse (Thuc. 7. 6. 3). Other sources describe the Indian line as the equivalent of a fortified city wall, the infantry representing the curtain wall and the elephants the towers (Diod. 17. 87. 5; Curt. 8. 14. 13; Polyaen. 4. 3. 22), but Arrian has developed the imagery, and deliberately superimposed a Thucydidean echo. For the technique see Ch. 2 *passim*.

[47] This critical moment is somewhat understressed by Arrian (5. 17. 3; cf. Plut. *Al.* 60. 11; Curt. 8. 14. 18), who simply states that 'the elephant drivers turned their beasts against the cavalry', not noticing that it destroyed Porus' tactics, as outlined at 5. 15. 6–7. Polyaen. 4. 3. 22, by contrast, lays emphasis on the gaps which occurred in Porus' line and their exploitation by the Macedonians.

[48] Arr. 5. 17. 3; cf. Diod. 17. 88. 1–2; Curt. 8. 14. 22–8.

cripple the elephants' trunks.[49] The elephants inflicted some casualties but were unable to break or seriously disrupt the Macedonian line. On the other hand the Macedonian cavalry, concentrated in a single mass, launched destructive forays against the rear of the Indian line. That created pressure from the back as the Indians, cavalry and infantry intermingled, were driven on to their elephant line; and the beasts themselves under relentless harrying were driven into a panic and trampled their own side.[50] The carnage increased as the mahouts were killed, and the elephants lost direction. Finally they gave up. Arrian has a vivid and immeasurably pathetic picture of them retreating slowly into their line, like warships backing water, no longer charging but emitting a hideous high-pitched squeal. Fortunately there is no modern evidence of elephant behaviour under such duress, and the description cannot be controlled. But it is how elephant experts consider the beasts *would* behave, and the appalling scene would have imprinted itself indelibly on the minds of participants.

Alexander had carefully and deliberately created a killing ground. His phalanx was now united in a single, dense line, shields locked and pikes levelled in a bristling hedge, and the solid mass of cavalry was extended in a continuous cordon around the Indian army, which was now a chaos in which infantry, cavalry, and elephants struggled against each other and did the Macedonians' work of slaughter for them. It was only when Alexander's cavalry line broke that groups of enemy infantry were able to make their escape from the carnage.[51] The rest were trampled down by their own forces or speared by the Macedonians. But even the survivors had little respite. Alexander's forces in his base camp were able to make a crossing and, completely fresh, pursued the Indian refugees until nightfall.[52] This was a massacre, brilliantly planned and ruthlessly executed, and massacre regularly marked the major victories of Alexander. The battle of the Granicus ended with the envelopment and virtual annihilation of the Persian mercenary infantry, while at Issus the pursuit of the vast

---

[49] Arr. 5. 17. 3; Curt. 8. 14. 29. The cleaver is only mentioned by Curtius, but his source was apparently well informed about Indian customs (cf. 8. 14. 10–12), and there is no reason to reject such a circumstantial detail.

[50] Arr. 5. 17. 4–6—our only source for the final stage of the battle.

[51] Arr. 5. 17. 7: 'So it was that the Indian cavalry, all but a few, were cut down in the action; the infantry was slaughtered too, as the Macedonians were now pressing upon them from all sides. At this point, when Alexander's cavalry line parted, they all turned to flight.' [52] Arr. 5. 18. 1; *Metz Epit.* 60.

defeated army over an enclosed, broken terrain resulted in terrible slaughter. The Indian losses at the Hydaspes were comparable. In quantitative terms they may be exaggerated in the sources, but the proportions seem credible: a half or two-thirds of the infantry perished, as did three-quarters of the cavalry.[53] It was a total, crushing victory.

What can we say of Porus' policy and achievement? Heroic it might have been, but it was catastrophic and foreseeably so. Everything depended on his being able to hold the river against a crossing, and he patently did not have the resources to do so. In any case it was a gamble that Alexander would move on rather than attempt the river in its summer spate. If autumn had come and the Hydaspes had sunk to low water, then Porus would have been overwhelmed by Alexander's vastly superior numbers, with the king in embittered mood because of the delay. What is more, Porus knew the risks. Alexander had been in action since the autumn of 327, fighting a campaign above the Khyber Pass which even by his standards was exemplary in ruthlessness. The fighting qualities of his troops hardly needed to be demonstrated, and their numbers were apparent. Alexander may have admired Porus' heroism, but his wretched subjects, decimated by the battle and facing foreign occupation, will have felt that it came at too great a price. And Alexander's admiration may not have been unqualified. He certainly rewarded Porus with a great expansion of territory, but the lands Porus acquired were almost exclusively lands he had attacked in the past or whose rulers were hostile to him. These were likely to resent his domination and prevent him enjoying a united, powerful empire. In fact Porus' sway and its unpopularity may have been the best guarantee Alexander had of keeping his conquests. It is consistent with his appointments elsewhere, where refugees and malcontents were consciously promoted, precisely because they *were* alienated from the populations they governed.[54]

The facts of the battle of the Hydaspes belie the propaganda. It

---

[53] Arr. 5. 18. 2; lower casualties, but in proportion to their lower figure for Porus' army, are given in the vulgate tradition (Diod. 17. 89. 1–2; *Metz Epit.* 61).

[54] Cf. Arr. 4. 22. 8 (the Indian prince, Astis, is replaced by a political enemy), 30. 4 (Sisicottus, the commandant at Aornus, a political exile in Bactria). Similarly Oxydates, Alexander's first satrap of Media, was appointed because he had been out of favour and imprisoned by Darius (Arr. 3. 20. 3; Curt. 6. 2. 11), while in Parthyaea the appointee was Amminapes, who had surrendered Egypt to Alexander and had previously spent a period of exile at the Macedonian court (Arr. 3. 22. 1; Curt. 6. 4. 25).

was no epic struggle of heroes, but a stark massacre, the annihilation of a relatively small and inexperienced army fatefully embroiled in a battle it had no chance of winning. This is hardly an isolated instance. There are many more incongruities of historical fact and report. Let us turn to another field and again invoke W. H. Auden:

> She looked over his shoulder
>   For ritual pieties,
> White flower-garlanded heifers,
>   Libation and sacrifice,
> But there on the shining metal
>   Where the altar should have been
> She saw by his flickering forge-light
>   Quite another scene.
>
> Barbed wire enclosed an arbitrary spot
>   Where bored officials lounged (one cracked a joke)
> And sentries sweated for the day was hot:
>   A crowd of ordinary decent folk
>   Watched from without and neither moved nor spoke
> As three pale figures were led forth and bound
> To three posts driven upright in the ground.
>
> The mass and majesty of this world, all
>   That carries weight and always weighs the same
> Lay in the hands of others; they were small
>   And could not hope for help and no help came:
>   What their foes liked to do was done, their shame
> Was all the worst could wish; they lost their pride
> And died as men before their bodies died.

One does not need to look far in Alexander's reign for parallels to the three stakes. To my mind the most sinister analogue took place in Bactria, a year before the Hydaspes. The victims of 'the mass and majesty of this world' this time were adolescents, boys in their late teens. They were publicly stoned to death—by other adolescents—after first undergoing judicial torture. This was the last act of the so-called Pages' Conspiracy. A group of young Macedonian nobles, attached to the person of the king for personal service and military training, plotted to kill Alexander.[55] The conspirators had arranged for their schedules of duty to coincide and intended to assassinate him in his sleep. According to the sources it was a close-run thing.

---

[55] See below, Ch. 4, p. 112–14.

Alexander only escaped death because he spent the entire night carousing at a symposium, and the plot was divulged immediately afterwards. This is an obscure affair. The conspirators are named for us, and it is attested that the ringleader, Hermolaus, had a personal grievance after being flogged for anticipating the king at a hunt. But the motives of the rest are totally enigmatic. There are indications that Hermolaus' lover and confederate, Sostratus, had his own reasons for enmity and orchestrated the entire conspiracy, but the precise motives are lost. All that we know is that it was a delicate time. The king's experiment with proskynesis, ceremonial prostration, had recently proved a fiasco. It had offended the moral and religious sensibilities of his Macedonians and encountered serious opposition. Now that opposition was compounded by a plot against his life organized by the youngest members of his court. Accordingly he struck hard, in exemplary fashion. All the named conspirators were tortured, so that the full extent of the conspiracy could be determined, and, once condemned, they suffered the regular punishment of stoning.[56]

One should avoid the temptation to be censorious. The Macedonian treason law was savage. In its full rigour it was applicable to all the male family of the accused, and that refinement Alexander regularly waived.[57] Given the series of dynastic murders which constituted the history of the Macedonian ruling house, it is not surprising that law and custom provided the most brutal sanctions, nor is it surprising that the sanctions were enforced when Alexander's own life was at risk. There was no successor designated, and the ever-present danger of civil war if he died.[58] But that is the reality, and a harsh reality. If the king was threatened, the response was immediate and shocking. After the siege of Gaza, when Alexander was wounded by a catapult bolt, the enemy commander was done to death in the most barbarous fashion. The king ordered the execution, and his men clearly approved. They were ready enough

---

[56] Arr. 4. 13. 7, 14. 3; Plut. *Al.* 55. 6–7; Curt. 8. 8. 20. See further, Bosworth, *HCA* ii. 97–9.

[57] Curt. 6. 11. 20; 8. 6. 28, 8. 18. Whether the institution was law or merely custom (cf. Tarn, *Al.* ii. 270–1; Atkinson ii. 242) is immaterial. What Curtius implies is that relatives of regicides had been executed in the past and might have been under Alexander, had he not made a conscious and public decision to waive the practice.

[58] The worries of the army are vividly expressed by Arrian (6. 12. 1–2). See below, Ch. 2, p. 54.

to take reprisals themselves.[59] During the campaign at the gates of India he suffered a similar wound, and when the offending town was captured by storm, 'the Macedonians killed all those they took alive in their anger at the wounding of Alexander'.[60] Not surprisingly, when Alexander received his most serious wound at the Malli town, they killed everybody 'and left neither woman nor child'.[61] An attack on the person of the king and commander was a universal threat and treated with total ruthlessness, even if it meant the torture of adolescents and the massacre of non-combatants.

Let me continue with an instructive anecdote from Aristobulus, a contemporary of Alexander and in later years one of his more eulogistic historians. It is presented as an episode which redounds to the credit of Alexander, illustrating his confidence in one of his professional seers, Peithagoras.[62] However, the background it presupposes exudes a reek of primal terror.[63] It concerns Apollodorus, commander of Alexander's garrison at Babylon since 330, who was summoned to court late in 325, after the king's return from India.[64] There he witnessed Alexander's punishment of delinquent

[59] Curt. 4. 6. 25–9; Hegesias, *FGrH* 142 F 5 (emphasizing the general hilarity at the execution). Cf. Atkinson i. 341–3 (guarded); Hammond, *Three Historians* 124–8. The fact that the atrocity does not appear in Arrian (and was probably omitted by his sources) is no argument against its historicity. The same is true of the mass crucifixions after the fall of Tyre (Diod. 17. 46. 4; Curt. 4. 4. 17). Few things are less conducive to sweetening the temper than a protracted siege, and at Gaza the danger to Alexander was clearly an exacerbating factor.

[60] Arr. 4. 23. 5. Cf. Bosworth, *HCA* ii. 158. According to the vulgate tradition (Curt. 8. 10. 5; Diod. 17 index $\lambda\beta$) Alexander had given explicit instructions not to take prisoners.

[61] Arr. 6. 11. 1; Curt. 9. 5. 20. On the background to this campaign see Ch. 5.

[62] Arr. 7. 18. 1–6 = *FGrH* 139 F 54. Cf. Berve ii nos. 101, 618. The story is repeated by Plutarch (*Al.* 73. 3–5), who claims that information was given *against* Apollodorus; according to Aristobulus he voluntarily confessed. Plutarch follows a tradition different from Aristobulus, in which Apollodorus was actually incriminated (so Hammond, *Sources* 142). The version of the story in App. *BC* 2. 152. 639–40 is an elaboration of Arrian (see now K. Brodersen, *Klio* 70 (1988) 463–4), and naturally adds nothing of substance.

[63] I choose my words deliberately in the light of a frequently quoted essay (W. E. Higgins, *Athenaeum* 58 (1980) 140–52), which argues that there was nothing approaching a reign of terror under Alexander. I base my argument on 'the classic Arrian who seems to offer the best guidance here' (Higgins 152), and focus upon an episode discounted by Higgins ('Undoubtedly some men like Apollodorus were frightened...'). It is the degree of terror that I find instructive. For a general to commission divination on the life of his king (below, n. 66) presupposes a state verging on blind panic.

[64] Arr. 7. 18. 1. It looks as though Apollodorus had been summoned to court at the same time as the Median generals. Although he was not convicted of any crime, he

governors, including at least three of the military commanders in Media, and in understandable insecurity he wrote to his brother, the seer, who was still at Babylon, and asked him to read the entrails on the subject of his own welfare, and the people he most feared, namely the king and his favourite, Hephaestion. The first inspection produced an omen unfavourable to Hephaestion, and Apollodorus received the news the day before Hephaestion died (around October 324). When the second inspection produced omens equally unfavourable to Alexander, Apollodorus had no choice but to reveal the details to his king. It gave him the opportunity for a loyal warning against danger—and also pre-empted any information being laid against him;[65] it could perhaps be argued that by procuring adverse omens he was threatening the king's life.[66] As it happened, he was able to maintain himself in favour, but it was close, and the actions of Apollodorus are an eloquent testimony to the atmosphere of fear and suspicion which prevailed at court during 324 and certainly justify the label of a reign of terror. It underwrites the very unfriendly picture of court life which we owe to the contemporary pamphleteer, Ephippus: 'in his honour myrrh and other kinds of incense were consumed in smoke; a religious stillness and silence held all present in fear. For he was intolerable and murderous, reputed in fact to be melancholy-mad.'[67] This overtly hostile portrait coheres with what may be read from Aristobulus' more encomiastic story, and what emerges is almost wholly black: a court in terror and a king lost in savage brooding. The terror was not always justified, nor was the king invariably merciless, but we can hardly question the prevailing atmosphere.

---

was not, it seems, completely exonerated. He was not reinstated in his command, but remained at court in growing trepidation, as he witnessed the executions of Cleander, Sitalces, Heracon, Orxines, Abulites, and Oxathres. For the details see Badian, *JHS* 81 (1961) 17–18; *CHIran* ii. 476–9.

[65] That is implied by Arr. 7. 18. 3. Plut. *Al.* 73. 3 alleges that Apollodorus was already incriminated, and in his story it is the seer, Peithagoras, who retains Alexander's favour. What is more, Aristobulus stated that his informant was Peithagoras, not Apollodorus (Arr. 7. 18. 5). The protagonist may not have remained in the world to give his version of events. He may have retained Alexander's favour, as Aristobulus stated, but that favour—and Apollodorus—could have been short-lived.

[66] I know of no evidence for the Macedonian period, but in Roman times it was certainly a capital offence to consult an astrologer *de salute principis* (Paulus *Sent.* 5. 21. 3; cf. Tac. *Ann.* 2. 27. 2, 30. 1–2, 32.3).

[67] Athen. 12. 538 A = *FGrH* 126 F 5. The hostile animus of the passage is clear (cf. Pearson, *LHA* 63–4), but that does not invalidate the descriptive detail.

> She looked over his shoulder
>> For athletes at their games,
> Men and women in a dance
>> Moving their sweet limbs
> Quick, quick, to music,
>> But there on the shining shield
> His hands had set no dancing-floor
>> But a weed-choked field.
>
> A ragged urchin, aimless and alone,
>> Loitered about that vacancy; a bird
> Flew up to safety from his well-aimed stone:
>> That girls are raped, that two boys knife a third,
> Were axioms to him, who'd never heard
> Of any world where promises were kept,
> Or one could weep because another wept.

Now is this not an absurd comparison—Alexander the Great and a tearless, loveless urchin? We remember the great scene described by Nearchus in which the king first wept for grief at the loss of his fleet and then for joy when he realized it was safe.[68] We recall too how Alexander responded with tears to the tears his veterans shed at Opis, in an emotional leave-taking before they set out on their homeward journey.[69] A cynic might comment that those tears came only after Alexander had crushed disaffection in his camp and forced those same veterans to submission by summary execution and a dramatic appeal to his Iranian troops, but there is no doubt about Alexander's emotional, passionate reactions which could take him to extremes of generosity or savagery. What, then, is the point of the quotation?

Auden, I think, here epitomizes a casualness of violence, where rape and murder are the norm; and in a very different way casual violence was the norm around Alexander. What is rarely stressed in histories of the reign is the omnipresence of combat with its concomitance of violent death, an omnipresence without parallel before Alexander. Recent studies of hoplite fighting in the classical period have rightly stressed the rarity of pitched battle.[70] During the fifth century the

---

[68] Arr. *Ind.* 35. 4–7 = *FGrH* 133 F 1.

[69] Arr. 7. 12. 3 (δακρύων καὶ δακρύοντας); cf. Justin 12. 12. 7–9.

[70] Thucydides underlines the general inexperience of war among the younger generation before the Peloponnesian War (Thuc. 2. 8. 1; cf. 1. 80. 1). For the Spartiates the Archidamian War hardly proved a learning process. Apart from desultory skirmishes during the invasions of Attica, the only real fighting they engaged in was the abortive attack on Pylos and the minor engagements after the occupation of Cythera (Thuc. 4. 55. 1–2, 56. 1). Many Spartiates will have had no experience of

average citizen soldier might have seen actual combat between hoplite phalanxes a handful of times, perhaps even never, in his lifetime. In the fourth century, when professional mercenary armies were employed, combat was perhaps more frequent. The period before and after Leuctra (371 BC) saw Theban and Spartan armies regularly in action, and the frequency of combat by land was far greater than it had been during the Peloponnesian War. Such sustained conflict, however, was unusual, and even the most professional mercenaries might have little fighting to do. Their expertise and reputation could deter any adversaries from risking a pitched battle. We have interesting data for the Ten Thousand, the mercenaries who fought for the younger Cyrus at Cunaxa and who are often seen as forerunners of Alexander. The record of their march up to Babylon and back again to the Black Sea coast and Byzantium is given for us by Xenophon, a leading actor in the events, and Xenophon makes it clear that their practice under arms had made them especially proficient.[71] However, when we inspect the detailed campaign narrative, there is precious little record of actual fighting. Indeed Xenophon himself states that the seven days of continuous fighting as they passed through the territory of the Carduchi (in the mountains above Assyria) caused more hardship than in the entire previous campaign[72]—and even in those seven days what is attested is a series of skirmishes, arduous certainly but not costly in terms of lives. There was fighting subsequently as the Ten Thousand moved along the Black Sea coast, but it amounted to a mere handful of engagements, and the bulk of the casualties came in Bithynia, close to home, when isolated divisions were attacked by the natives.[73] Apart from Cunaxa there were three minor pitched battles and two brief sieges.[74] A good deal of skirmishing took place, but it rarely resulted in hand-to-hand combat.

The contrast with Alexander's reign is dramatic. There are ad-

actual combat, despite the war, until the Battle of Mantineia (the liberated helots under Brasidas' command in the north were less fortunate). See in general V. D. Hanson, *The Western Way of War* (New York 1989) 25; *Hoplites* 3–5, 125.

[71] Xen. *Anab.* 5. 6. 13: 'expert because of their practice' (διὰ τὴν τριβὴν ἱκανούς).

[72] Xen. *Anab.* 4. 3. 2. Small-scale skirmishes are attested at 4. 1. 10–11, 14, 16–18; 2.7, 11–12, 18, 24–8, none involving any serious casualties but cumulatively exhausting. Later (*Anab.* 4. 3. 31) he comments that the armament of the Carduchi was only appropriate for hit-and-run tactics in the mountains, not for close combat.

[73] Xen. *Anab.* 6. 3. 5–9, 4. 23–4 (500 casualties).

[74] Xen. *Anab.* 4. 7. 2–14; 5. 2. 3–27 (sieges); 4. 8. 8–19; 5. 4. 11–26; 6. 5. 26–32 (pitched battles). The subsequent campaign in Thrace was notable for its lack of military action (cf. Xen. *Anab.* 7. 7. 5–9).

mittedly periods when military action was minimal, the first nine months of 331 and the last eighteen months of his life. But they are more than countered by years on end of almost uninterrupted combat. In 334 the pitched battle of the Granicus was followed by extended sieges at Miletus and (notably) Halicarnassus, and the campaign of Issus around November 333 was followed by seven months of siege activity at Tyre and two months at Gaza. But the most arduous period was marked by the ghastly catalogue of repression beginning with the Sogdian revolt in 329, continuing with the invasion of India, the campaign of the Hydaspes, and the voyage down the Indus. There were interludes of inactivity, the summer of 327 and the autumn of 326 (while the Indus fleet was being built), but the period was otherwise marked by continuous fighting, on a small scale for the most part, but with consistent siege operations, which naturally witnessed the most intense and vicious close combat.[75]

The result of this constant campaigning was to school the veterans of Alexander into the most adept and proficient fighters seen in the ancient world. The Silver Shields, the survivors of Alexander's hypaspists (infantry guard), were reputed to be invincible, 'such was the skill and daring acquired during the unbroken series of their actions',[76] and at the critical battle of Gabiene early in 316 they are said to have routed the entire phalanx of Antigonus, inflicting 5,000 casualties without a single loss on their own side.[77] It is a detail recorded by a contemporary, Hieronymus of Cardia, who was wounded at the battle; and even if exaggerated the story will be substantially correct. It is corroborated by another remarkable story of a handful of prisoners-of-war held in confinement in a fortress in Anatolia after the civil war of 321. Eight of them, in poor shape thanks to their captivity, were guarded by 400 soldiers, 'but they excelled in daring and dexterity because of their campaigning with Alexander'.[78] Accordingly they were able to expel their garrison, occupy the fortress, and with their numbers swollen by accomplices to a total of fifty they held at bay an attacking army of 900 regulars and 3,000

---

[75] See e.g. the analysis of the Malli campaign in Ch. 5. There the intensity of combat was quite staggering.

[76] Diod. 19. 41. 2; cf. Plut. *Eum.* 16. 7 ('war's athletes, as it were, without a defeat or a fall up to that time'); Justin 14. 2. 6.

[77] Diod. 19. 43. 2, again confirmed by Plut. *Eum.* 16. 8–9. On Hieronymus as the source of the information see Hornblower, *Hieronymus* 190–3.

[78] Diod. 19. 16. 1. Cf. R. H. Simpson, *Historia* 6 (1957) 504–5; Hornblower, *Hieronymus* 125–6.

native irregulars. It was sixteen months before they were finally overrun by direct assault.

These men were dangerous and none of them more than Alexander himself. He was no rearguard general. Indeed it could almost be said that where two or three were gathered in his name, there was he in the midst of them. He gloried in battle and killing, and had an awesome proficiency in the technique of slaughter. The picture of Alexander most familiar to his entourage was the sight which terrorized the embassy of the Indian city of Nysa when they found him covered in dust, in full armour complete with helmet and spear—and they prostrated themselves in dumb panic at the apparition.[79] The act of killing meant little, and it can be shown that the level of violence escalated as a direct response to resistance during the grim campaigns in the north-east and India. When the Sogdian campaign began, Alexander gave explicit instructions for the massacre of all adult males in towns taken by storm,[80] and enslavement of non-combatants was the norm. The frightfulness increased as he moved on India. Massacre and enslavement was the policy against settlements which stood siege, but Alexander viewed even refugees as insubordinate and sent his lethal cavalry against populations which took to flight rather than submit. 'Alexander's men kept at the fugitives as far as the mountains and there was great slaughter of the barbarians until they finally reached the harsh terrain and got away.'[81] Behind Arrian's bald words there is a whole volume of horror, and we can hardly mitigate it by claiming that the fugitives were combatants. In other circumstances the massacre of refugees included the sick and wounded who fell behind in the exodus.[82] The climax was reached in 325 as Alexander's fleet and army moved south along the Indus, decimating such communities as the Malli which failed to submit: and rebellion was repressed by massacre and crucifixion.[83] When he ended his voyage, at Patala at the mouth of the Indus, he entered a deserted land as the inhabitants melted away in terror at his coming.

The killing was certainly a dreadful constant in the reign, and with

[79] Arr. 5. 1. 4; Plut. *Al.* 58. 7. On the circumstances see Bosworth, *HCA* ii. 203–4.
[80] Arr. 4. 2. 4; Curt. 7. 6. 16. For analysis and explanation of the policy of terror see below, Ch. 5 *passim.*
[81] Arr. 4. 24. 2. For the background of the campaign see Bosworth, *HCA* ii. 159–67 and below, Ch. 2, pp. 42–7.
[82] Arr. 5. 24. 7. Similar pursuits of refugees are recorded among the Malli (Arr. 6. 6. 6; 7. 2; 8. 3, 8).
[83] See below, Ch. 3, pp. 94–7; Ch. 5, pp. 133–43.

it went a distinct lack of respect for life. Alexander had a short way with horse thieves, at least when his favourite stallion, Bucephalas, was stolen. His love for the animal is not in doubt, nor is his ruthlessness in face of the loss. The culprits, the nomad Mardi of the Zagros, were explicitly threatened with genocide, and Alexander had allegedly begun to implement his threat before the horse was returned.[84] There is also some deterioration in 'the world where promises were kept'. We see it in the treatment of the Indian mercenaries at Massaga, who were apparently guaranteed their safety and then massacred on a trivial pretext once they had left the city.[85] Similarly the last act of the siege of Aornus was not entirely creditable: Alexander led the defenders to believe that he would allow them to capitulate, encouraged them to withdraw and then attacked in the middle of the evacuation.[86] By this stage the enemy which resisted had forfeited the right to honourable treatment, and Alexander himself had fully accepted the doctrine said to have been enunciated by his court philosopher, Anaxarchus of Abdera: everything done by Zeus was done with justice, and so were all acts of his human counterpart, the Great King.[87] Alexander certainly behaved as though he felt no binding moral constraints, and by the end of his reign he was able to revoke one of the foundation clauses of the Corinthian League, a compact sanctioned by his father and himself, and demand by edict the restoration of exiles throughout the Greek world. His sovereignty was the overriding imperative. Its acquisition justified any and every act of violence; resistance to it merited massacre and repression.

We have travelled a long way from Plutarch and his rhetorical creation of Alexander the civilizer. Instead I have emphasized the real conditions of largely unremitting warfare, and outlined some of their consequences. That is not to say that there are no positive features to the reign of Alexander, and as a commander and soldier he can only

[84] Diod. 17. 76. 7–8; Curt. 6. 5. 20; cf. Arr. 5. 19. 6; Plut. *Al.* 44. 4. There is some divergence in the location of the episode, but all sources agree that the tribesmen were threatened with extermination.

[85] The breach of faith is emphasized in the sources (Plut. *Al.* 59. 6–7; Diod. 17. 84. 3; Polyaen. 4. 3. 20; *Metz Epit.* 44), which credit Alexander with a callous cynicism worthy of the darkest moments of the Peloponnesian War (cf. Thuc. 3. 34. 3). Arrian (4. 27. 3–4) is defensive, ascribing the violation of trust to the Indians themselves (cf. Bosworth, *HCA* ii. 174–5). Yet even on Arrian's version the slaughter is hard to justify. It is reminiscent of the nauseating stratagem which the Corcyrean democrats used to dispose of their political opponents (Thuc. 4. 46. 4–47. 3).

[86] Arr. 4. 30. 2–4; cf. Diod. 17. 85. 7; Curt. 8. 11. 21–3.

[87] See below, Ch. 4 *passim.*

command the mixture of awe and terror which he inspired in the men of Nysa. But my theme is the underside of victory, the huge unjustifiable cost in human life of a war of imperial annexation and the horror of killing which it entailed. The concomitant squandering of resources is another story again. It imposes the reflection that the history of Alexander is the history of waste—of money, of forests stripped for siege works and navies, and above all of lives. That perspective cannot be lost. The price of Alexander's sovereignty was killing on a gigantic scale, and killing is unfortunately the perpetual backcloth of his regime.

> The thin-lipped armorer,
>   Hephaestos, hobbled away,
> Thetis of the shining breasts
>   Cried out in dismay
> At what the god had wrought
>   To please her son, the strong
> Iron-hearted man-slaying Achilles
>   Who would not live long.

2

Windows on the Truth

FEW subjects are more paradoxical than the source tradition of Alexander's reign.[1] The extant histories are late, ranging from three to five centuries after the king's death; yet they are based for the most part on early material, deriving from the first generation of the age of the Successors. In bulk they are relatively abundant, and sometimes provide a day-by-day narrative of events. However, the interests of the extant authors are very different from those of their primary sources and, for that matter, modern historians. Rhetoric tends to prevail: vivid and uninformative battle descriptions, which focus upon the gruesome and sensational, elaborate set speeches written with all the stock devices of Roman imperial literature, and supposedly pertinent apophthegms, smart comments often quoted without the necessary explanatory context. The rhetoric of the extant sources is complicated by bias in their primary material. The host of contemporaries who described their experiences under Alexander, whether notables such as Ptolemy and Nearchus or comparative nonentities such as Aristobulus, all had their individual perspectives. Their experiences coloured and warped their reportage. Past and present enmities and friendships determined what they omitted or included, and influenced their shaping of events.[2] Even if there was no obvious malice or intention to misrepresent, it was inevitable that they would stress the actions in which they were prominent or had direct experience, downplay the successes of people they disliked, and interpret the events of the period according to their interests at

[1] For a deliberately schematic description of the sources for the reign see Bosworth, *Conquest and Empire* 295–300. A more extended introduction to the problems is provided in *From Arrian to Alexander* 1–15. For a very different approach to the extant histories and their presumed sources one may consult the two monographs by N. G. L. Hammond (*Three Historians; Sources*).

[2] Recent debate has focused on Ptolemy and Nearchus. On Ptolemy see particularly the contrasting essays of Errington, *CQ* 19 (1969) 233–42 and Roisman, *CQ* 34 (1984) 373–85; and for Nearchus see the classic article of Badian, *YCS* 24 (1975) 147–70, with modifications of detail by Bosworth, in *Zu Al. d. Gr.* i. 541–67.

the time of writing, sometimes (as with Aristobulus) decades afterwards.[3] This secondary agenda is often not merely hidden but
unconscious; and it is practically impossible for the modern reader
to penetrate to underlying biases which may not have been recognized by the authors themselves.

In the face of this welter of uncertainty there has been a simple,
almost Cartesian principle. Find the infallible criterion of truth, or
at least a source which is uniformly preferable to all others.[4] Then we
have a yardstick for establishing the credibility of the rest of the
tradition. Fortunately Arrian provides us with a starting point. His
preface, unlike that of Curtius, survives and reveals his principles for
choosing between the multitude of different sources. Autopsy is the
main criterion. He selects writers who were actually on the campaign
and who wrote after Alexander's death, beyond the influence of fear
or favour.[5] That applied to his main sources, Ptolemy and Aristobulus (and, for that matter, Nearchus, who emerges almost as a third
narrative source in the latter books of the Alexander history and
dominates the monograph on India).[6] However, it also applied to
most of the first-generation historians, with the notable exception of
Callisthenes, who wrote very much under the influence of Alexander. Even Cleitarchus may have had some experience of the
campaign, and was certainly close enough in time, had he wished, to
interview survivors in the manner of Thucydides.[7] The principle of

---

[3] Aristobulus wrote after the Battle of Ipsus of 301 BC (Arr. 7. 18. 5 = *FGrH* 139
F 54), and he allegedly claimed in his preface that he began his history in his eighty-
fourth year ([Luc.] *Macr.* 22 = *FGrH* 139 T 3). For a brief characterization of his work
see Bosworth, *HCA* i. 27–9; fuller treatments in Pearson, *LHA* 150–87 and Pédech,
Historiens compagnons 331–405.

[4] I attacked this approach twenty years ago in my early paper 'Arrian and the
Alexander Vulgate', *Entretiens Hardt* 22 (1976) 1–9, with some success. However, the
belief that Arrian and Ptolemy were based on an original archive dies hard (below, n.
9), and there is still some reluctance to abandon the limpid prose of Arrian for the
rhetorically shaped material in Curtius or the garbled précis of a Diodorus or Justin.
The literary dressing can distract attention from the factual material.

[5] Arr. *Praef.* 2. On the frequency of the topos in historical literature see G.
Avenarius, *Lukians Schrift zur Geschichtsschreibung* 46–54: Bosworth, *HCA* i. 43–4. By
Arrian's time it was almost a platitude.

[6] On Arrian's use of Nearchus see now Bosworth, *HCA* ii. 361–5 and below, p. 54.

[7] On Cleitarchus' date, between Theopompus and Theophrastus, see particularly
Pliny, *NH* 3. 57–8 = *FGrH* 137 F 31, with Bosworth, *From Arrian to Alexander* 87–9. He
seems to have been active in the first decades after Alexander's death, when there was
an abundance of firsthand information. There is an outside chance that Cleitarchus
witnessed the last years of the campaign in person (Diod. 2. 7. 3 = *FGrH* 137 F 10, with
Badian, *PACA* 8 (1965) 1–8), but he was certainly able to question survivors. Diodo-

selection is in effect no principle at all. In the face of this dilemma the standard reaction has been to adopt some variant of Arrian's second principle of selection, the explanation of his choice of Ptolemy as his primary source: he was not merely a participant but a king, and 'it would have been more disgraceful for him to lie than for anybody else'. Arrian does not go so far as to claim that there were no lies in Ptolemy (and he *is* occasionally uncomfortable with what he reports),[8] but he certainly implies that Ptolemy's account was the most truthful. Most modern historians of Alexander have endorsed his view, and buttressed Arrian's rather naïve moral verdict with the more sophisticated premiss that a king is in the best position to verify what he records. Hence the once universal assumption that Ptolemy's history was based on a Court Journal, the supposed archive kept by the chief secretary, Eumenes of Cardia, which supposedly gave a detailed day-to-day record of the public events at court.[9] That gave Ptolemy's work a double cachet of authenticity; he was an eyewitness, and used original, archival material.

Whether this theory is correct (it almost certainly is not) is irrelevant to my present discussion. What matters is the underlying assumption that an official source is necessarily a reliable or informative one. The theory of the Court Journal was excogitated in the nineteenth century by scholars such as Droysen and Wilcken, who wrote under the (largely) benevolent autocracy of the Prussian monarchy, when it was fashionable to characterize the official record as fact, albeit fact determined by the ruler. Another German (or rather, Austrian) scholar, Fritz Schachermeyr, had a very different view of officialdom, coloured by his experience of a very different autocracy (which he had, to a large extent, supported). For Schachermeyr the

---

rus' detailed reports of the defence of Halicarnassus have often been claimed to derive from *Söldnererinnerungen* in Cleitarchus (so explicitly Schachermeyr, *Al.*[2] 180 n. 188; cf. 202 n. 222); even Tarn (*Al.* ii. 71), who denied Cleitarchus' authorship, ascribed the material to contemporary recollections, his infamous 'mercenaries' source'.

[8] At 4. 12. 7 he is carefully noncommittal about Callisthenes' involvement in the Pages' Conspiracy, implicitly rejecting Ptolemy's (and Aristobulus') bold assertion that he was the instigator (Arr. 4. 14. 1 = *FGrH* 135 F 16; cf. Bosworth, *HCA* ii. 90), and at 4. 14. 3 he complains about the conflict between Ptolemy and Aristobulus on a matter as notorious as the death of Callisthenes. One of the two, it followed, was in error, if not guilty of falsehood. For other reservations see below, pp. 42, 64.

[9] For the history of the theory see my discussion in *Entretiens Hardt* 22 (1976) 3–6. The most complete exposition in recent years is that of Hammond (*GRBS* 28 (1987) 331–47; *Historia* 37 (1988) 129–50; *Sources* 200–5). For sceptical criticism of the 'Diaries' see Badian, in *Zu Al. d. Gr.* i. 610–25; Bosworth, *From Arrian to Alexander* 157–84.

official record can be a deliberate façade, created to obscure the truth on sensitive issues, and he attacks the bureaucratic tendency to view it as authentic and unassailable.[10] From this perspective the archive is an instrument of concealment, and one might add that a king has more to conceal than anybody else. An official diary is therefore suspect when its authority has something to hide. It is also selective. What is singled out for record need not be the events of real significance. One recalls the entry in Louis XVI's diary for Bastille Day—'Rien'.

The search for a criterion of truth is delusive. All sources are to some degree unreliable, including, particularly including, those of an 'official' nature. One can therefore operate only by cross-comparison, painstakingly isolating common material, identifying and explaining variants, and arguing from general probability, that is, the appropriateness of the recorded details to the overall historical context. I can best illustrate this by an example from a very different period which provides more sources but a simpler tradition and which allows more precise explanation of context and method than is possible with the historians of Alexander. The episode is a small part of the dramatic and tragic story of the reconquest of Mexico by Hernán Cortés and his Indian allies, and dates to April 1521. On the course of his march to besiege the Mexican capital of Tenochtitlan Cortés attacked and captured two rock fortresses. The type of operation is strongly reminiscent of Alexander's operations in Sogdiana and Swat, and the source tradition is comparable. There are three accounts. The first is what we might term the 'official' version, the Third Narrative Letter ('Carta de Relación') written by Cortés himself. It was sent from Mexico on 15 May 1522, within a year of the action, and its authenticity is guaranteed by three signatories.[11] The second also derives from Cortés, in that it was written by his secretary, Francisco López de Gómara, and published

---

[10] See the trenchant discussion in the introduction to the second edition of his monograph (*Al.*² 14–15), where he defends his abandonment of the traditional 'Ptolemaios-Kult': 'nur zu häufig die Offiziellen die eigentlich grossen Lügner sind'. Schachermeyr's attitude to the sources is not as unique as he would have us believe; in his tolerance of the vulgate tradition he was preceded by Georges Radet. However, his indictment of the official record is memorably passionate. For an appreciation of Schachermeyr's work, see my forthcoming essay in the *American Journal of Ancient History*.

[11] These personages include the royal treasurer, Julián de Alderete, and they state that they have no need to report on the recent events, 'as all this is described in great detail here in this letter, and is the truth as we ourselves would have written it' (*Hernán Cortés: Letters from Mexico* 281). Could anything be more 'official'?

in 1552, five years after the death of the Conquistador (hence, in Arrian's terms, without fear or favour). Gómara had no personal experience of Mexico, and was largely dependent upon the verbal and written reminiscences of Cortés, which he developed in a self-conscious literary style.[12] Our third account is the eyewitness record of one of Cortés' junior followers, Bernal Díaz del Castillo, who began his narrative at the age of 76, in 1568, nearly half a century after the stirring events of his youth, and only completed his work when he was 84.[13] We have, then, the 'official' version of the primary actor, the polished literary version of a non-combatant, and the avowedly non-literary reminiscences of a junior participant towards the end of a long life. Ptolemy, Cleitarchus, and Aristobulus spring to mind as the counterparts from the Alexander period—the protagonist, the litterateur, and the aged memorialist. For all the differences in detail the basic analogy is valid.

The context of the attack is simple. Cortés set out for the siege of Tenochtitlan. From the town of Chalco he moved to a smaller village (Chimaluacan),[14] where he was joined by many thousands of Indian allies. He then invaded enemy territory, and reached 'a very high and steep rock' occupied by warriors and a refuge for women and children. Cortés considered it strategically impolitic to disregard the challenge they presented,[15] and organized a three-pronged assault, which failed because the defenders released a virtual avalanche of boulders. A second rock fortress was discovered some 7 km. distant, less strongly defended and with a supply of water (which proved illusory). After a miserable night the Spaniards began a reconnaissance, and noticed two hills which overlooked this second fortress. Cortés accordingly concentrated his army in an assault on

---

[12] *Historia de la Conquista de México* (Saragossa 1552), most conveniently consulted in the translation by L. B. Simpson, *Cortés: The Life of the Conqueror by His Secretary, Francisco López de Gómara* (Berkeley 1965). The capture of the citadels comes at ch. 128, pp. 255-8.

[13] Bernal Díaz del Castillo, *Historia Verdadero de la Conquista*, ch. 144. One may consult the classic translation of A. P. Maudslay, *The Discovery and Conquest of Mexico* (London 1928), chs. 103-4, pp. 487-95, or the more recent abridged version of J. M. Cohen, Bernal Díaz, *The Conquest of New Spain* (Harmondsworth 1963) 332-8.

[14] The name is supplied by Díaz (p. 488 Maudslay); Cortés (p. 193) merely refers to a village.

[15] 'it would be cowardly to pass by without giving them a lesson, and our allies might think we were afraid' (Cortés p. 194). The motivation would have been appreciated by Alexander (cf. Arr. 4. 21. 3; Plut. *Al.* 58. 2 ('nothing is impregnable for the daring, nothing safe for the cowardly'); Curt. 7. 11. 4).

the enemy stronghold, and the threatened attack drew the Indian defenders from the higher elevations to protect the main citadel. At that Cortés sent a small company of men with crossbows and arquebuses to occupy the higher of the hills, while he himself led the attack on the fortress proper. Once he reached the level of the defenders they surrendered, and sent an embassy to the first rock, which was promptly surrendered in its turn.

So far I have used Cortés' letter, which is expressed in a deceptively straightforward style. The details, however, are not as straightforward as would first appear. It is perhaps significant that the five subordinate commanders who led the abortive attack on the first rock are singled out by name. They fail by no fault of their own, but they fail none the less, and only survive because Cortés recalls them when he sees that they have reached the limits of their endurance.[16] By contrast, when it comes to the successful attack on the second rock, Cortés is the only commander mentioned by name. It is his achievement in reaching the level of the defenders ('which had seemed an impossible thing to do') which breaks the spirit of the enemy, not so much the outflanking party. What is more, the success of Cortés' diplomacy is underscored. The Indians are guaranteed impunity if they become vassals of the Spanish Crown,[17] and their generous treatment ensures the surrender of the first rock, which had successfully resisted attack. Here one glimpses the delicate political atmosphere in which the letter was composed. In December 1521 a royal official, Cristóbal de Tapia, had arrived in Mexico to assume the government of the new province (and to depose Cortés).[18] Tapia had been prevailed upon to depart, but Cortés' position, despite his crowning success in recapturing Tenochtitlan, was still insecure, and his enemies represented him (rightly) as the insubordinate agent of the governor of Cuba. Hence the stress on Cortés' qualities of leadership and his direct responsibility for the military success. Hence too the scrupulous attention to winning

---

[16] 'When I saw they could do no more…I ordered the captains to withdraw' (Cortés p. 195).

[17] 'it has always been my intent to persuade these people that we wish them no harm, no matter how guilty they may be, especially if they wish to become Your Majesty's vassals, and they are so intelligent a people that they understand this very well…' (Cortés p. 196).

[18] Tapia's arrival is mentioned by Cortés in highly contentious terms at the end of the letter (Cortés pp. 274–5). On the background see Elliott's introductory essay in *Hernán Cortés: Letters from Mexico*, pp. xxix-xxx.

vassals for the Crown and the alacrity with which the natives supposedly accepted their new state of vassalage.

The version of Gómara is clearly based on Cortés. The figures for the Spanish forces and their allies are identical, and the details of the attack on the first rock are very similar. What differences there are are minor. Gómara agrees on the names of the commanders involved in the triple attack, but divides them in a slightly different way and gives different strengths for their units.[19] More significantly he emends Cortés' statement of motive. Cortés stated that it was madness to try to take the fortress by siege, and so he decided on a direct assault, ordering his men to triumph or die. For Gómara the madness was to storm the fortress; the attack was a bluff, to test the resolution of the enemy.[20] Here there is no prescient Cortés, who recalls his troops to save them from annihilation. It is a trial which fails, and the Spaniards retreat without intervention from Cortés.

The difference in perspective is more marked in the attack upon the second fortress. Here Cortés' own participation is minimal. He takes advantage of the Indians' confusion to occupy the elevated crag overlooking the fortress. However, it is the small occupying force which does the damage; the crossbow and arquebus fire demoralizes the Indians, who immediately surrender. There is a passing reference to the frontal attack led by Cortés, but it is virtually ignored, eclipsed by the success of the flanking party.[21] The message is reinforced in the next sentence, when the Indians accept Cortés' invitation to treat with the defenders of the first rock. They duly persuade their compatriots to surrender, emphasizing the mildness of the Spaniards' terms and adding that 'they were equipped with wings to fly wherever they wished'. This last comment has no parallel in either Cortés or Díaz, and it is clearly Gómara's insertion. It is easy to see his motive. He was deliberately drawing a parallel between Cortés and Alexander's celebrated capture of the rock of Ariamazes in 328. That rock was surrendered largely through bluff,

[19] Both versions agree that Cristóbal del Corral led the main group (with 60 men in Cortés, 70 in Gómara), but the division of commands at the second and third faces is quite different; Gómara has support groups which have no counterpart in Cortés.

[20] 'To storm such a strong point would have been madness...to learn whether [the enemy] would yield from fear or hunger, Cortés attacked...' (Gómara pp. 256–7). Cf. Cortés p. 194: they should ascend, and triumph or die.

[21] Gómara p.257: 'Cortés...told all his men to follow him, and began the ascent.' This is almost a feint. It has the effect of drawing the defenders from the neighbouring hills so that the artillery can occupy its strategic positions.

when a small company of Macedonian pioneers scaled the heights above the defenders and demoralized them into surrender.[22] It was a response to the natives' taunt that he would need 'winged soldiers' to defeat them, and the turning point of the siege was Alexander's demonstration that he had found winged men.[23] Gómara had the advantage of a classical education at Salamanca and ten years' residence in Italy.[24] He was possibly acquainted with Arrian (at least in Facius' translation),[25] and must have known the work of Curtius, who was extraordinarily popular during the Renaissance.[26] At all events the comment which drives the defenders to surrender ('pinnas habere ait milites Alexandri') is almost a mirror image of Gómara. It must be the inspiration for his literary shaping of the episode. Just as Alexander's pioneers force Ariamazes' men to surrender, so the small force of Cortés' artillery drives the Indian defenders to capitulation; they 'frightened rather than harmed the Indians, who at once threw their arms to the ground.'

Gómara's work, then, shows him operating within a framework provided by Cortés, but reshaping the details for encomiastic reasons and adding a literary allusion, which he probably expected his readers to recognize. The commander is implicitly assimilated to Alexander, his men to the Macedonian élite, and the rash attempt to take the first rock by storm is deliberately softened; Cortés' attack was bluff, an anticipation of the successful tactics the following day. If we now turn to Bernal Díaz, we encounter a work of a very different flavour. This 'untutored child of nature', as Prescott called him, displays a

---

[22] Arr. 4. 18. 4–19. 4; Curt. 7. 11. 1–29; *Metz Epit.* 15–18; Polyaen. 4. 3. 29; Strabo 11. 11. 4 (517).

[23] Arr. 4. 19. 3–4: the natives are 'astounded at the unexpectedness of the apparition'; Curt. 7. 11. 25: 'it was this which…prompted the barbarians to surrender.'

[24] Cf. Simpson (above, n. 12) p. xx, citing H. R. Wagner, 'Francisco López de Gómara and His Works', *Proceedings of the American Antiquarian Society*, October 1948.

[25] For Latin translations of Arrian, see P. A. Stadter, in *Catalogus Translationum et Commentariorum* iii (Washington 1976) 1–20. The most widely used appears to have been Gerbelius' edition of Facius, printed by Robert Winter in Basle (1539).

[26] Between 1471 and 1545 there were no less than 17 editions of Curtius, and at least 2 Spanish translations (by J. Varela de Salamanca (Seville 1518) and Gabriel de Castañeda (Seville 1534)). Simon Hornblower has suggested to me (by letter) that Gómara's recollection of Curtius may have been subconsciously reinforced by the familiar vulgate text of Psalm 139. 9–10: 'si sumpsero pinnas aurorae, et habitavero in extremis maris, etiam illuc manus tua deducet me'. If so (and it is very likely), the reference to Alexander had secondary, religious overtones. Not only did Cortés' men find wings; they had divine guidance as well.

very shrewd talent for self-promotion, reminiscent of Xenophon's *Anabasis* with its simple, quasi-autobiographical narrative. Díaz, like Gómara, agrees with Cortés on the contextual setting, although his figure for the allied forces is considerably less. His Cortés also attacks the first rock in order to strike at Indian morale, and expresses himself trenchantly on the subject.[27] However, Díaz has no reference to a three-pronged assault. In fact he implicitly excludes it, claiming that there was a single access route which all the attackers took.[28] Few names are mentioned. The standard-bearer, Cristóbal del Corral, is described leading the assault, and Pedro Barba, a captain of cross-bowmen, plays a role; but both act as foils to Díaz himself. Corral is wounded in the hail of rocks from the defenders and refuses to go on, while Barba, full of braggadocio, stings Díaz into clambering even further up the rock, and is promptly wounded himself. At this juncture, when Díaz has reached the highest point of the attack, Corral sends down word to Cortés, and Cortés recalls the assault party, later expressing wonder that the boulders had not destroyed the entire force. The whole description revolves around the person of Díaz. Superficially modest, he manages to highlight his heroism, and the two captains whom he identifies by name come off relatively poorly. Cortés hardly does better. He orders the attack almost out of bravado, and the eight Spanish dead are represented as a significant loss. Díaz returns to the episode towards the end of his work, and he is more forthright in his criticism. The assault on the rocks was a prime example of Cortés' obstinacy, comparable with his calamitous march to Honduras; it was an imprudent attack against the advice of his men, and it almost brought disaster.[29] There must have been considerable dissatisfaction at the time, and Cortés was wise to minimize the losses in his narrative letter.

As for the second rock Díaz agrees with Cortés on its location, a league and a half distant, but he claims that it was 'even stronger' than the first,[30] and that it was impregnable by direct assault. He

[27] 'It seems that all these Mexicans who shut themselves up in fortresses make mock of us so long as we don't attack them.' (Díaz p. 488 (Maudslay), 334 (Cohen)).

[28] 'there was no other place where it was possible to climb up, for it was all steep rock' (Díaz p. 489, (Maudslay), p. 334 (Cohen)).

[29] Díaz ch. 204 (translated in Maudslay's Hakluyt edition, v (London 1916) 216). I owe this reference to Sir John Elliott, who suggests that Cortés' account was pre-emptive; he was giving his own version of the episode before his enemies could turn it into a catastrophe.

[30] Díaz p. 492 (Maudslay), p. 336 (Cohen). Cf. Cortés p. 195: 'this one was not so strong as the other'. So Gómara p. 257 'not so strong as the first'.

mentions the outflanking party and the crag overlooking the fortress, and (unlike Cortés and Gómara) he names the commanders. However, although the crag is occupied, the resulting barrage is comparatively ineffectual; it 'just succeeded in hitting the enemy, killing some and wounding others'. The main assault force is even less successful, pinned down in mid-ascent. Even so, after half an hour the defenders capitulate, and Díaz adds the highly pertinent comment: 'The reason was that they had no water' ('y fue por causa que no tenían agua ninguna'). He then describes the negotiations with the defenders of the first rock, who (it now transpires) had no water either, and continues with another autobiographical reminiscence. He had been in the party which received the surrender there, and he describes from memory the parlous state of the defenders, on an exposed flat rock with twenty dead and not a drop of water.[31] Díaz's autopsy comes like a ray of light, illuminating the brute fact which the other versions obscure. Both citadels were indefensible because of inadequate water. For Cortés the lack of water emerges once only, as a difficulty for the Spaniards which he managed to surmount.[32] There is no hint that the defenders were hard pressed. Instead of a lengthy, abortive attack against hopeless resistance he describes a brilliantly improvised diversion and a heroic assault which was sufficient in itself to break the morale of the defenders. Gómara also mentions water once only, as one of the reasons which *might have* induced the defenders of the first rock to surrender,[33] and he clearly implies that it was not the decisive reason. In Díaz's case his autopsy had beneficial effects. He was not, it seems, a major actor in the assault on the second rock, and he can depict it as the rather desultory affair it must have been. He was also able to witness at first hand the effects of thirst at the first citadel, and emphasized the crucial factor of the shortage of water at the second. Elsewhere his reminiscences may not have been so happy. He has probably laid too much emphasis upon his experiences at the first rock and ignored the other two assault groups.

This has been a long and detailed investigation, but its results, I

---

[31] Díaz p. 494 (Maudslay): 'there was a great breadth of meadow land all crowded with people, both warriors and many women and children, and we found many dead men and many wounded, and they had not a drop of water to drink.'

[32] Cortés p. 195: 'we endured considerable hardship and privation for we found no water there, and neither we nor the horses had drunk all day.'

[33] Gómara p. 258: 'For these reasons, or for lack of water, or because they wanted to go home in safety, the men of the rock came at once to surrender to Cortés.'

think, are worthwhile. Our three versions share a common framework, agreeing on the rough topography of the actions and the general sequence of events. Within that framework there is considerable variation and scope for narrative distortion. As we have seen, Cortés' account highlights his talents as general and his disinterested loyalty to the Spanish Crown; Gómara constructs an elaborate literary echo of Alexander's campaigns, while Díaz subtly makes himself the focus of the narrative. All the versions manipulate the facts to some degree, and the earliest 'official' account is not necessarily the most reliable. The basic truth that the Indian fortresses were ultimately indefensible emerges virtually by accident as a casual, almost throw-away statement by Díaz. Otherwise it is deliberately obscured for propagandist or encomiastic reasons.

The principles we have observed may easily be applied to the Alexander historians. One obvious analogy is the triple attack which Alexander launched against a concentration of Aspasian refugees in modern Bajaur. Here we have a single source, Arrian, who demonstrably used Ptolemy's description of the episode,[34] but all the elements present in the Mexican narratives come into play. The military situation is simple. As the Macedonian army moved from valley to valley, the inhabitants vacated their settlements, and took refuge in the mountains. In his pursuit Alexander encamped by the fringes of a prominent mountain, probably the Kohimor, and sent out scouting parties to detect the main groups of refugees. The major discovery came from Ptolemy, who sighted a large number of camp fires, 'more than in the camp of Alexander'. Despite his reservations (which proved unfounded) about the size of the enemy concentration, Alexander took forces 'which appeared sufficient for what was reported',[35] and divided the army into three assault groups. The

[34] Arr. 4. 24. 8–25. 4. The extract ends with a named citation of Ptolemy (*FGrH* 138 F 18), and there has never been any doubt that the entire episode derives from Ptolemy. Cf. Pearson, *LHA* 200–1; Hammond, *Sources* 238 ('Ptolemy added the incident from his memory to a short entry in the Royal Journal'). For detailed commentary see Bosworth, *HCA* ii. 163–7.

[35] Arr. 4. 24. 9: ἀναλαβὼν ὅσοι ἀποχρῶντες ἐς τὰ ἀπηγγελμένα ἐφαίνοντο. This force is immediately shown to be 'small' and insufficient (Arr. 4. 25. 1). The king, it is implied, should have taken Ptolemy's first report at face value. So Seibert, *Ptolemaios* 21, *contra* Tonnet i. 192, ii. 148, n. 83. This interrelation of narrative detail is a strong indication that Ptolemy is the basis of the account. He might well have reminded his readers that he, Ptolemy, had provided the reports of enemy numbers which his king thought exaggerated. He contrasted Alexander's mistaken belief with the reality of the situation, and emphasized the fact that the troops which were thought adequate were in fact insufficient.

enemy was attacked from three sides, and was defeated with heavy losses. An immense booty of humans and animals fell into Macedonian hands.

Within this simple narrative there are several complexities. Ptolemy's work is an eyewitness account like that of Díaz, but it is written from the political perspective of a dynast of the age of the Successors. Like Díaz he stresses his contribution to the victory, but he goes much further. He represents himself as the real architect of the triumph. His information did not simply locate the enemy. It provided a realistic estimate of the Aspasian forces, which Alexander chose to disregard. As a result the Macedonian expeditionary group was inadequate, and it was unnecessarily imperilled when the enemy realized the paucity of the attackers. Ptolemy's information is ultimately vindicated by the vast booty: 40,000 prisoners-of-war and no less than 230,000 cattle. The figures are apocryphal, and Arrian himself casts doubt upon them by ascribing their authorship explicitly to Ptolemy. He was not prepared to guarantee their authenticity. Rightly so. In the nineteenth century the entire population of Bajaur, an area of some 13,000 sq. km., amounted to no more than 100,000,[36] and if it was comparable in Alexander's day, it is most unlikely that 40 per cent of the district were cooped up in a single refuge. Still more unlikely are the 230,000 cattle. The mind boggles at the amount of fodder they would have required, concentrated in the mountains after the end of summer. The figures must be enormously exaggerated, partly to vindicate Ptolemy's original report of the enemy numbers, partly to underscore the vast booty which he was able to obtain for the Macedonians at large.[37] As a material benefactor he came second only to Alexander himself.

Ptolemy also displays the limited perspective of the eyewitness. He notes the division of Alexander's forces, and names the three commanders: the king, Ptolemy himself, and Leonnatus the Bodyguard. However, there is a distinct concentration upon the contingent commanded by Ptolemy. Its constituent components are named: hypaspists, light infantry, Agrianians, archers, and half the cavalry. Leonnatus' contingent (a phalanx *taxis* and javelin men) is also spelled out,[38] but there is nothing about the composition of

[36] For figures at the turn of the century see the *Imperial Gazetteer of India* vi (Oxford 1908) 219–20.

[37] On the importance of booty and the war economy in general see M. M. Austin, *CQ* 36 (1986) 454–61, 464–5.

[38] Arr. 4. 24. 10. On the units listed see Bosworth, *HCA* ii. 164–5.

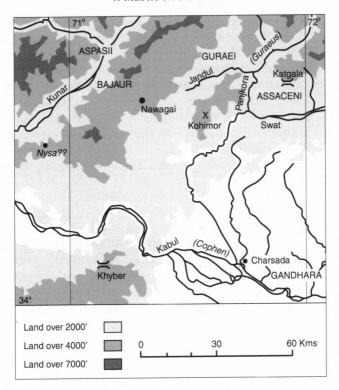

Fig. 5. Alexander's campaign in Bajaur

Alexander's command force, which was presumably the largest, and was directed against the largest enemy concentration. The omission may be Arrian's own, but it is hard to see why he should have listed the specific units under the command of Leonnatus and Ptolemy, only to lose interest when he came to the central figure of his narrative. It is more likely that Ptolemy made a deliberate decision not to record the units with Alexander. One can see why. Given that Alexander took the largest of the assault groups, it must have comprised at least one phalanx *taxis* (that of Coenus), as well as a large force of hypaspists, cavalry, and light armed. If one consults the list of units actually with Alexander in Bajaur,[39] it would appear that the

[39] Arr. 4. 24. 1. Alexander is represented with the hypaspists, archers, Agrianians, the battalions of Coenus and Attalus as well as the *agema*, four hipparchies of Companions and the mounted archers. That is a partial list, and does not include

king took the vast majority of his forces with him to attack the enemy concentration, leaving only a small contingent to guard his camp below Kohimor. In that case he hardly discounted the size of the enemy encampment, as Ptolemy alleged, nor could the natives have despised the attacking forces as derisorily small. Ptolemy, it would seem, faced a narrative dilemma. He wished to emphasise the size and importance of his own command, but at the same time to convey the impression that the attacking force as a whole was inadequate for its task. If he spelled out the contingents under his own leadership, it was necessary to leave Alexander's command as an undifferentiated mass.

The description of the engagement proper focuses upon Ptolemy. Alexander, it is stated, won his victory without effort, and there is a postscript that Leonnatus was also victorious.[40] In between comes Ptolemy's description of his own action, which involved hard fighting. Arrian shapes his narrative to contrast the ease of Alexander's victory with Ptolemy's hard-won success, and some of the antitheses are probably his own. However, the material for his rhetoric was provided by Ptolemy, who stressed that Alexander's fighting took place on level ground, whereas his own objective was to capture a hill densely occupied by the enemy.[41] The difficulties of the terrain exacerbated the fighting, and Arrian adds that Ptolemy's adversaries were the most warlike of the local population—the most warlike *by far*.[42] There is a hint of apologetic here. Arrian's account omits the whole issue of casualties, but the clear implication of his narrative is that Alexander's (and Leonnatus') victory was comparatively bloodless, whereas Ptolemy sustained losses. The body of the narrative gives the explanation; he was attacking a particularly difficult position, and its defenders were particularly formidable.

---

some of the light infantry. However, it must be substantially complete; at least two battalions of infantry (the *taxeis* of Polyperchon and Alcetas) remained with Craterus in the Alingar valley (Arr. 4. 23. 5; cf. Bosworth, *HCA* ii. 158–9), and roughly half the army was operating with Hephaestion and Perdiccas in the Cophen valley to the south (Arr. 4. 22. 7, 23. 1; cf. Bosworth, *HCA* ii. 152–3, 154–5). It seems certain that the troops Alexander took to investigate Ptolemy's report represent almost the whole of the force with him in Bajaur.

[40] Arr. 4. 25. 1 (οὐ ξὺν πόνῳ ἐνίκα Ἀλέξανδρος); 25. 3 (ἐνίκων γὰρ καὶ οὗτοι).

[41] Arr. 4. 25. 1–2: 'they [the Indians]...descended to the plain; a fierce battle followed. However, Alexander defeated them without effort, whereas Ptolemy's men had not taken their position on level ground—for the barbarians had occupied a hill'...

[42] Arr. 4. 25. 3: ἀλλὰ πολὺ δή τι ἀλκιμώτατοι τῶν προσχώρων. The superlative is emphatically underscored; for an exactly comparable expression, see Arr. 3. 29. 3.

Ptolemy leaves us in no doubt that the success of the operation was primarily due to himself. He located the enemy concentration, and gave a true impression of its huge size, so huge that Alexander could not be blamed for doubting his report. The upshot of this royal scepticism was that an unnecessarily small force went into action and experienced unnecessarily stiff resistance, the brunt of which was borne by the indispensable Ptolemy. This strongly recalls Cortés at the rock citadels. The achievements of others are not ignored, but they are used to underscore the outstanding contribution of the narrator, who is invariably in the right place at the right time. The same providential attributes appear a paragraph earlier, where Arrian describes another of Ptolemy's exploits.[43] The context is the grim harassment of Aspasian refugees who had deserted their city in the Kunar valley. There was a bloodbath in the plain until the survivors reached the shelter of the mountains. Ptolemy represented himself leading a small troop of horse at the head of the pursuit. Catching sight of the local ruler and his bodyguard, he dismounted and rushed up to the foothill which the Aspasians had occupied, his minuscule force grossly outnumbered. A single combat ensued in which Ptolemy pierced the thigh of the Aspasian commander, killed him, and stripped his body. At that reinforcements poured down from the adjoining mountains, and there was a struggle over the corpse, which lasted until Alexander brought up the entire infantry, and finally gained possession.

The colouring of this little episode is unmistakably Homeric. Arrian's account follows a classic formula. The hero receives a spear cast, which his cuirass deflects,[44] and responds with a fatal throw. The thigh wound which Ptolemy inflicts has its counterparts in Homer,[45] but there is a peculiarity. Death seems to come immediately, as Ptolemy downs and strips the Aspasian chief in a single

---

[43] Arr. 4. 24. 2–5, printed as a fragment of Ptolemy by Jacoby (*FGrH* 138 F 18). Discussion and bibliography in Bosworth, *HCA* ii. 161–3.

[44] Arr. 4. 24. 4. For the Homeric 'near-miss descriptions' see B. Fenik, *Typical Battle Scenes in the Iliad* (Wiesbaden 1988) 196–7. Simon Hornblower observes that this passage of Arrian comes close to the counterfactual 'if not' situations in Homer, where the hero would have perished but for some deity averting the danger (e.g. *Il.* 5. 22–4; 15. 459–60; the instances are compiled and discussed by Irene J. F. de Jong, *Narrators and Focalizers* (Amsterdam 1989) 68–81). Here, it is implied, Ptolemy would have died, had his cuirass not withstood the blow. The critical situation is vividly underscored (de Jong 78–9).

[45] Cf. Hom. *Il.* 4. 146–7; 5. 660–2, 694–6; 11. 583–4, 829–30, 844–6; 16. 27–9. In none of these cases is the wound fatal, or even serious. On the other hand Aeneas' thigh wound (5. 305–12) *would* have killed him, had not his divine mother intervened.

action. That corresponds to one of the most famous encounters in the *Iliad*, in which Patroclus begins his *aristeia* by transfixing the thigh of Areilycus, as the latter wheels round to face him (just as the Aspasian and his guard turn back to face the onslaught of Ptolemy),[46] and Areilycus immediately collapses on his face, presumed dead. The two passages are almost exact copies, and Arrian, acutely conscious of the epic atmosphere, breaks into dactylic sequence with a near-perfect hexameter.[47] He has clearly enhanced the Homeric flavour of the original, and he may have added a heroic echo from another source. One word he uses in the description of the thigh wound (διαμπάξ, 'right through') is slightly unusual. It is a favourite with Arrian, who employs it seven times,[48] but there are few occurrences in classical prose. In fact there is one attestation before Plutarch, in Arrian's model, Xenophon, and it occurs in the context of a thigh wound, suffered, we may add, by a commander, none other than Agesilaus' son, the future King Archidamus.[49] On that occasion Archidamus survived, but his bodyguard was decimated in the epic struggle to save him.[50] Arrian clearly transferred the colouring and vocabulary from Xenophon, and expected his readers to be aware of the allusion. It heightened the heroic atmosphere already present in Ptolemy.

The primary inspiration for the narrative was undoubtedly Ptolemy himself. He provided the 'facts' of the single combat for Arrian to embellish. As we have seen, the description of the thigh wound and its devastating effect was intended to recall Patroclus'

[46] Hom. *Il.* 16. 308: αὐτίκ' ἄρα στρεφθέντος Ἀρηιλύκου βάλε μηρὸν ἔγχεϊ ὀξυόεντι, διαπρὸ δὲ χαλκὸν ἔλασσεν ('then as Areilycus turned about, he struck his thigh with the sharp spear-head and drove the bronze right through').

[47] Arr. 4. 24. 5: ὡς δέ τὸν ἡγεμόνα σφῶν κείμενον οἱ ἀμφ' αὐτόν. If one allows the hiatus without correption in the fifth foot, one has a nice hexameter with third foot caesura. Given the context this can hardly be fortuitous. For similar metrical passages in Herodotus and Thucydides see Simon Hornblower's observations, in *Greek Historiography* (Oxford 1994) 66–9, with his observation: 'it is a noticeable feature of such echoes that they often avoid strict metricality' (note also the critique of Demetr. *eloc.* 112–13). One may compare the elevated encomium at Arr. 7. 29, where the barrage of superlatives produces dactylic and iambic runs, but no complete line. That makes the rogue hexameter at 4. 24. 5 all the more striking.

[48] Elsewhere at 2. 3. 7, 27. 2; 3. 30. 11; 4. 4. 4, 23. 3; *Tact.* 40. 6.

[49] Xen. *Hell.* 7. 4. 23: ἐτέτρωτο τὸν μηρὸν διαμπάξ. In the *Anabasis* Xenophon twice uses the epic διαμπερές (never used by Arrian), once in the context of a thigh wound (*Anab.* 7. 8. 14; cf. 4. 1. 18).

[50] Xen. *Hell.* 7. 4. 23 (no less than 30 deaths, including Polyaenidas and Archidamus' brother-in-law, Chilon); cf. Arr. 4. 24. 5 (the Aspasian chief's entourage first flee but are reinforced from the mountains, and a fierce struggle develops).

killing of Areilycus, the only instance in Homer of a fatal spear thrust right through the thigh. Any educated reader would recall the famous passage of *Iliad* 16 and immediately think of Ptolemy as Patroclus. He rather than Hephaestion (so the narrative implied) should be considered the favourite of the Macedonian Achilles, and he had performed exploits appropriate to the role. Its heroic nature is emphasized in the sequel. The fighting over the body is so furious that it requires the intervention of Alexander and the infantry to drive the defenders back into the mountains. That highlights the initial achievement of Ptolemy in killing their champion. The picture is extremely flattering, and the self-promotion had political importance in an age when commanders, at least Macedonian commanders, were expected to risk their persons in a crisis. Ptolemy later placed himself at the centre of the fighting against Perdiccas, and led the defence of the Fort of Camels by the Nile, personally disabling the elephant at the head of the attack.[51] That was exemplary action, as was his single combat against the Aspasian chief. Ptolemy did not merely lead; he could personally dispose of the enemy commander, a feat which Alexander himself had never achieved.[52]

What truth underlies the description we cannot say. This was an event which had few witnesses, and it was easy for Ptolemy to take the credit from one of his men. If the Indian leader had been felled by a javelin which came from the ruck of the attacking party, Ptolemy could later claim that it was his own cast, and construct a Homeric picture of single combat, a picture which it was impossible, or impolitic, to refute. However, the story could well be true more or less as it stands. Ptolemy had the expertise to kill his man, and the heroic colouring may simply reflect the reality. But, true or false, the description had a political dimension. Ptolemy deliberately portrayed himself as a second Patroclus, comparable in military valour and in intimacy with his royal master.

[51] Diod. 18. 34. 1–2. Such episodes were, if not *de rigueur*, at least not infrequent in the age of the Successors. Compare the equally epic combat between Eumenes and Neoptolemus at almost the same moment as Ptolemy's act of daring (Diod. 18. 31. 2–5; Plut. *Eum.* 7. 7–12), and Justin's remarks on the mettle of Lysimachus and Seleucus at the Battle of Corupedium (Just. 17. 1. 8–12).

[52] His coinage, in particular the Porus decadrachm, stresses the heroics, and clearly implies a single combat, which never in fact took place (see above, p. 6). Such fictitious combats became part of the historiography of the reign (Plut. *Mor.* 341c; *Al.* 20. 8 = Chares, *FGrH* 125 F 6; Arr. 5. 14. 4; Luc. *Hist. Conscr.* 12 = *FGrH* 138 T 4; cf. E. Mederer, *Die Alexanderlegende* 15–34). Dr. E. Baynham draws my attention to Curt. 3. 11. 7 (cf. Atkinson *ad loc.*); there (at Issus) Alexander in his charge for Darius is implicitly compared with a Roman general after the *spolia opima*.

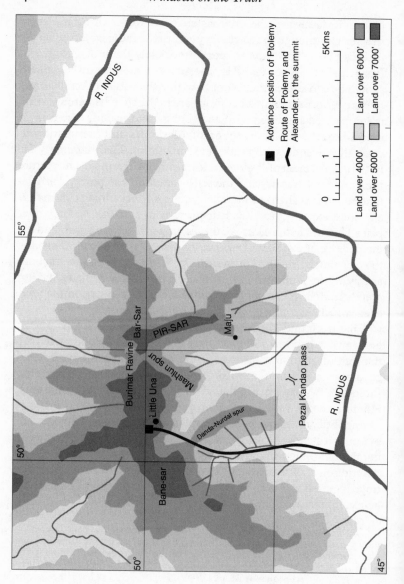

So far we have examined Ptolemy's account solely through Arrian, considering its literary presentation and political implications. There has been no control source to provide the different perspective which Díaz supplies for Cortés. That emerges in the next scene in which Ptolemy was a major actor, the dramatic siege of Mt. Aornus. This site, almost certainly identifiable with the plateau of Pir-sar,[53] lay in a bend of the Indus, well to the east of Alexander's operations against the Assaceni in the Swat valley. Because of its remoteness it was used as a sanctuary by refugees from the fighting, and Alexander decided to capture it, as the ultimate proof that there was no escape from his dominion. That presented him with a complex tactical problem. Pir-sar itself is a spur, a level plateau nearly 3 km. long and 100 to 200 metres broad, and even in recent times it was covered with wheat fields. It was an ideal citadel, protected on three sides by steep slopes and divided from the rest of the plateau to the north-west by a deep ravine. To attack the refugees Alexander had to occupy a position high on the shoulder of the plateau (the Little Una), and then bridge or fill the ravine to reach the defenders of Pir-sar. The first, and crucial act of the siege was therefore the occupation of the forward position far up on the mountain side. It effectively imprisoned the defenders on their plateau, and served as a base for the elaborate siege mound which eventually was to break the will of the defenders. We have two very different descriptions of the occupation of this forward base, and here there is an independent, if highly erratic control upon Ptolemy.

According to Arrian it was Ptolemy who led the advance party, an élite group of hypaspists, Agrianians, and light infantry, the troops best fitted for mountain work.[54] The occupation of the position was accomplished apparently without incident, as native guides took Ptolemy on a 'harsh and difficult' path up the mountain. He fortified the position, using timber from the heavily wooded slopes, and announced his success to the army below by firing a beacon (Arr. 4. 29. 2). Alexander made an attempt to take up the main army, but failed, thanks to enemy action; and Ptolemy was left to fend off a full-blooded assault on his camp (4. 29. 3). During the next night he

[53] The identification was made in the classic work of Sir Aurel Stein (*On Alexander's Track to the Indus* 113–54; cf. *GJ* 70 (1927) 417–39, 515–40). His views have recently been challenged, but Pir-sar remains the most plausible location of Aornus (see the review of the problem in Bosworth, *HCA* ii. 178–80).

[54] Arr. 4. 29. 1–6. See in general Seibert, *Ptolemaios* 21–3; Tonnet i. 192–3 and, for the route, Stein, *Alexander's Track* 144–5.

received a message ordering him to take the offensive and attack the
Indians from his camp, while the main force made its way upwards.[55]
The following day Alexander's army did indeed reach the heights,
but it was a hard struggle, and the ascent lasted until evening (4. 29.
6). Ptolemy may well have attacked from the summit as he was
instructed, but there is no record of it in Arrian, who makes it clear
that Alexander had to cope with harassment throughout the climb.
If there *was* action by Ptolemy, it had no dramatic effect. However,
Arrian stresses his successful occupation of the advance position, his
stubborn defence of the position once occupied, and Alexander's
instructions to risk his forces for the common good. All this no doubt
derives from Ptolemy himself, and underlines his contribution to the
ultimate victory.

   The capture of Aornus figured prominently in the historical
tradition outside Ptolemy and Arrian. The so-called Vulgate is here
represented by Diodorus and Curtius Rufus, who provide us with
overlapping narratives.[56] What interests Diodorus is the revelation
of the route to the forward position. He expatiates on the background of the local guides, an impoverished old man and his sons,
but is extremely brief about the siege proper. The actual occupation of the advanced base is mentioned, as are the subsequent
siege works, but with such extreme brevity that we are left completely in the dark about the details of the ascent.[57] What is clear
is that in this version of events Alexander had no difficulty in
reaching the level of the enemy. Curtius gives much the same
impression, but, as usual, there are complications. If Diodorus is
excessively compressed, Curtius is hopelessly confused, and regales
us with one of his most incompetent contaminations, grafting to-

---

[55] Arr. 4. 29. 4. Alexander's instructions, 'not to content himself with merely
defending the position' (μηδὲ ἀγαπᾶν ἐν φυλακῇ ἔχοντα) have been interpreted as
criticism of Ptolemy's action, which Ptolemy recorded (Seibert, *Ptolemaios* 22; Brunt,
Arrian i. 439 n. 1). However, in Ptolemy's account it is hard to see how his defence
could be faulted. The terminology which might imply criticism (μηδὲ ἀγαπᾶν) is
Arrian's, not Ptolemy's, and may have been chosen for an echo of Xenophon (*Hell.*
3. 1. 5), where Thibron wisely avoids endangering a comparatively small force (ἠγάπα
δὲ εἰ...τὴν χώραν ἀδήωτον διαφυλάττειν). For Alexander the situation is so critical that
he is prepared to sacrifice the advance force, if he can bring the rest of his army to the
summit.
   [56] Diod. 17. 85. 4–6; Curt. 8. 11. 3–19.
   [57] Diod. 17. 85. 6: 'he first occupied the pass leading to the Rock, and since there
was no other way of egress, he imprisoned the barbarians in a blockade which could
not be raised.'

gether two quite incompatible accounts of the siege.[58] The first is essentially the version of Diodorus with the elderly informant, the ascent to the forward position, and the seven days of operations to fill the ravine which barred access to the plateau. The party which first occupied the heights is described, as it is in Arrian, as light-armed, but there is no record of Ptolemy in command. The leader is a certain 'Mullinus', a royal secretary.[59] Now, 'Mullinus' seems an important individual. Without doubt he is the Myllenas, son of Asander, who is honoured in a decree of Eretria alongside Tauron, son of Machatas, commander of the archers at the Battle of the Hydaspes.[60] Myllenas was of the same calibre as Eumenes, Alexander's chief secretary, who held at least one independent cavalry assignment before he succeeded, in late 324, to the permanent command of Perdiccas' hipparchy,[61] and then developed into one of the subtlest strategists of the post-Alexander period. It is quite credible that Myllenas commanded the light-armed troops assigned to the ascent of Aornus, and in Curtius he has the role that Arrian gives to Ptolemy.

That is only part of the problem. Having reached the construction of the siege mound, Curtius suddenly transfers to another source, and his narrative abruptly switches to the first stage of the operation.[62] Alexander is at the foot of Aornus, sending out the first ascent group: archers, Agrianians, and thirty chosen youths from his personal cohort (the hypaspist *agema*). This is more or less the composition of the advance group in Arrian, but here again there is no reference to Ptolemy; the leaders are named as Charus and Alexander (a royal namesake).[63] In the highly rhetorical sequel Charus and Alexander scale the heights with their group, and die

---

[58] As briefly noted by Eduard Schwartz, *RE* iv. 1877 = *Gr. Geschichtschreiber* 164: see also Hammond, *Three Historians* 149, arguing that Curtius has conflated the accounts of Cleitarchus and Chares.

[59] Curt. 8. 11. 5: 'leviter armatis dux datus est Mullinus, scriba regis.'

[60] *IG* xii. 9. 197. The identification is accepted by Berve ii. no. 542; see also Heckel 338. The name probably recurs in the trierarch list in Arr. *Ind.* 18. 6, which records a 'Mylleas, son of Zoilus, of Beroea' (however, the different patronymic excludes identification with the son of Asander honoured at Eretria).

[61] Arr. 5. 24. 6; Plut. *Eum.* 1. 5; Curt. 9. 1. 19 (mission after Sangala); Plut. *Eum.* 1–5, Nepos *Eum.* 1. 6 (hipparchy). Cf. Heckel 346–7; Bosworth, *HCA* ii. 335.

[62] Curt. 8. 11. 9: 'Within seven days they had filled in the caverns, and the king now ordered the archers and Agrianians to scale the steep cliffs.'

[63] Curt. 8. 11. 9–10. The story recurs briefly in Plutarch (*Al.* 58. 5), who mentions only Alexander. For their identification as hypaspists see Heckel 295–6.

fighting off an Indian attack in a manner deliberately reminiscent of
the episode of Nisus and Euryalus in the ninth book of the *Aeneid*.
In both cases the elder of the pair rushes to avenge his companion,
and dies over his body; and the Vergilian vocabulary is consciously
echoed.[64] Rhetoric here runs away with sense. Alexander has begun
the ascent, reaching a position from which retreat would be ruinous,
but none the less, once he learns of the death of Charus and his own
namesake, he sounds the retreat—and the enemy lets him go. The
king is now in a state of despair, contemplating abandonment of the
siege, but Curtius saves the day by switching to his earlier narrative
source. Without a word of explanation he continues the Diodoran
tradition, and has Alexander advance his siege towers along the
access ramp, which is miraculously completed.[65]

From this intricate source tradition there appear three strands,
comparable to the variant accounts of the storming of the Mexican
rock citadels. We have a common framework. All sources stress the
need to occupy the high shoulder and cut off the refugees on
Aornus; and it is agreed that the position was occupied by stealth,
thanks to a force of hypaspists, Agrianians, and light-armed, so that
Alexander subsequently took up the main body of his army and
began operations in earnest. Within that framework there are considerable differences. The amount of Indian resistance varies. The
vulgate account common to Diodorus and Curtius suggests that
Alexander had no real difficulty reaching the heights, whereas both
Arrian and the second version of Curtius have an initial unsuccessful
attempt, foiled by Indian harassment. In what (for the sources) is the
most important matter, the command of the advance group, there
is total divergence—or rather, one should say, the spotlight falls in
different places. Curtius' first tradition stresses the services of
Myllenas at the head of the light-armed, while his second source
dealt with the leaders of the hypaspist group, who died impressively
heroic deaths. These are not invented figures. They probably did
participate in the occupation of the forward position, and distin-

[64] Verg. *Aen*. 9. 438–45: 'at Nisus ruit in medios solumque per omnis Volcentem
petit...tum super exanimum sese proiecit amicum confossus'. Curt. 8. 11. 15–16: 'Ergo
Alexander...confossus undique obruitur. quem ut Charus iacentem conspexit, ruere
in hostem omnium praeter ultionem immemor coepit...super amici corpus procubuit
exanimis.'

[65] Curt. 8. 11. 19: 'although there is no hope of capturing the Rock', Alexander gives
the appearance (*speciem ostendit*) of continuing the siege. He orders the roads blocked,
siege towers to be moved, and attacks to be made in relays. By the end of the sentence
the supposedly hopeless siege is in full cry.

guished themselves doing so. Myllenas may have been the first to the top, and Charus and Alexander were the main casualties of the fighting when the Indians attacked the advanced encampment. That leaves Ptolemy in a somewhat unromantic role. He must have been the overall commander of the advance group. Its importance justified a Bodyguard taking charge, and Ptolemy could hardly invent an appointment so public and well attested. However, like Cortés at the second rock, he mentioned none of his subordinates by name, and (if Arrian's account is not systematically misleading) he implicitly took credit for the success. His leadership preserved the camp, and Alexander was only able to make the ascent after instructing him to expose his small assault group and counter-attack the Indians. The more colourful details of the involvement of Myllenas and the deaths of the two youthful hypaspists probably derive from other eyewitness reports, which infiltrated the tradition and took the limelight away from Ptolemy himself. It is just possible that his autobiographical account was a conscious attempt to redress the balance, but the relative chronology of the strands of the tradition is impossible to establish. All that can be said is that we have three sharply different perspectives. They focus on quite separate aspects of the action, but they are complementary. They presuppose the same topographic and strategic context, and permit a reconstruction which does justice to them all.

I wish now to tackle a more extended episode in which we can probe the veracity of eyewitness reports and trace the influences upon their literary shaping. This is the famous scene, based on Nearchus, in which Alexander's men agonize over the prospect of his dying from the wound at the Malli town, and salute him enthusiastically when, against all expectation, he appears alive before his fleet. The episode receives extended treatment from Arrian, and Curtius gives a comparable account from a different source, emphasizing different aspects of the incident.[66] Both authors treat it as a display piece, and the question immediately arises of how far one can assume that the original material is accurately presented. Does the literary encrustation distort the sense of the original report?

Arrian's narrative (6. 12. 1–13. 5) maintains a striking unity of scene. It is recounted from the perspective of the fleet and the land army, which had split away from Alexander before the invasion of

<hr>

[66] Arr. 6. 12. 1–14. 1; Curt. 9. 5. 30–6. 26.

the Malli and taken a waiting position at the confluence of the rivers Acesines and Hydraotes.[67] These men had not witnessed Alexander's wound, and were perturbed by rumours of his death. Even news that he was alive was received with a scepticism which verged upon cynicism.[68] The deep despondency was succeeded by manic delight when Alexander appeared in person, first greeting the troops on shore with a wave of the hand and then mounting a horse to prove his fitness (6. 13. 2–3). Arrian continues with an extract explicitly ascribed to Nearchus; the king first glowers at the justified criticism which his friends directed against his culpably reckless behaviour at the Malli town, but is consoled by an elderly Boeotian, who reminds him that suffering is the price of glory. There follows the formal surrender of the surviving Malli, again at the confluence.

The narrative is self-consistent, and there can be little doubt that it derives from Nearchus.[69] It is written from the perspective of the fleet, which Nearchus commanded, and it is reminiscent of other passages securely attributed to Nearchus. The brilliant description of the noise of the army's acclamation resounding off the banks and nearby hills is a recapitulation of the more famous account of the voyage down the Hydaspes with the beat of the oars echoing from the river banks.[70] This earlier passage is almost universally assigned to Nearchus,[71] and it has Aristotelian overtones suitable in an ex-

---

[67] Arr. 6. 5. 6–7. 1, 13. 1, 14. 4.

[68] Cf. Arr. 6. 12. 3, where the men suspect that the reports of Alexander's recovery were a concoction, deliberate deceit by his Bodyguard and generals. The same suspicions recur in the reports of the king's last days (Arr. 7. 26. 1; Plut. *Al.* 76. 8).

[69] The definitive discussion is that of Strasburger, *Studien* i. 131. Kornemann 85 considered that the whole passage came from Ptolemy, but that Ptolemy directly borrowed from Nearchus (in other words Arrian's contribution was zero!). Other scholars (e.g. Schwartz, *RE* ii. 913 = *Gr. Geschichtschreiber* 123; ii. 1239 = *Gr. Geschichtschreiber* 143; Hammond, *Sources* 269) argue (or rather state) that Nearchus' contribution is limited to the named citation and that the rest comes from Aristobulus.

[70] Arr. 6. 13. 3: 'the entire army beat upon its shields with a prodigious clashing' (that I take to be the force of ἐπεκτύπησαν (cf. Ap. Rhod. 1. 1136; 2. 1081); it was the regular Macedonian mode of greeting for a general (Plut. *Eum.* 14. 11)); 'and the banks and neighbouring glens threw back the echo'. Cf. 6. 3. 3. Curt. 9. 9. 26 describes a similar scene after Alexander's return from the Ocean; the echo effect must have been impressive. The description may have enjoyed a vogue beyond purely historical literature. Simon Hornblower reminds me of the famous scene in Vergil (*Georg.* 4. 527), where the laments from Orpheus' disembodied head echo off the banks of the Hebrus. If Vergil used a Greek model here, one might infer that Nearchus' description of the Indus was absorbed into the mainstream of Alexandrian poetry.

[71] Cf. Jacoby, *FGrH* ii. D 467; Strasburger, *Studien* i. 130. See, however, Hammond, *Sources* 262–5 (but even on Hammond's analysis Arr. 6. 3. 3 and 13. 3 can be ascribed to the same source, if not Nearchus).

student of the master.[72] Nearchus was clearly impressed by the remarkable echo effect, and referred to it on at least two occasions. Arrian has reproduced Nearchus' description in his own words, as he does a few lines later, when he describes the troops showering their king with ribbons and flowers. That is an act of rejoicing which occurs twice in the account of Nearchus' ocean voyage[73] and in no other context in the Alexander literature. Nearchus must surely be the source for this detail. The conclusion is virtually inescapable. When Arrian comes to refer to Nearchus by name (at 6. 13. 4), he does so to isolate a detail in the general narrative which he finds particularly striking, in this case the exceptional and justified criticism by Alexander's friends.[74]

Arrian, then, reproduces a highly charged section of first-hand narrative from Nearchus. It deals first with the army's grim forebodings about its future with Alexander dead (6. 12. 1–3), continues with the exhilaration when the forebodings were proved ungrounded (6. 13. 1–3), and finally concentrates upon the propriety of Alexander's consistent courting of death (6. 13. 4–5). This dramatic script is deliberately enhanced by Arrian, who superimposes vocabulary reminiscent of one of the most famous passages of Xenophon's *Anabasis*. That is the scene after the execution of the generals of the Ten Thousand, when the survivors ponder what to do. Their first thought is for the hostile peoples surrounding them and the difficulties of the return with the many impassable rivers blocking their journey home.[75] Both considerations recur in Arrian, and are expressed in vocabulary directly borrowed from Xenophon.[76] The coincidences are remarkable, and cannot be a matter of chance. One word

[72] Arr. 6. 3. 3 follows Aristotle in attributing the echo effect to the rebounding of the air in a confined space (Arist. *de Anim*. 419^{b}26), and has the bare glens above the river banks act as the smooth reflecting surface necessary to produce the echo (Arist. *de Anim*. 420^{a}1–3; *Probl*. 11. 899^{b}19–20). On Aristotelian theory in Nearchus see Bosworth, *Topoi* 3 (1993) 413–21.

[73] Arr. 6. 13. 3: οἱ δὲ ταινίαις ἔβαλλον, οἱ δὲ ἄνθεσιν. Cf. *Ind*. 36. 3, 42. 9. In both cases it is Nearchus who is honoured, exactly like a victorious athlete (Plut. *Per*. 28. 5; Thuc. 4. 121. 1).

[74] Arr. 6. 13. 4: 'and in my opinion (καί μοι δοκεῖ) Alexander *was* irked by these criticisms, because he realised they were justified and that he was liable to censure...'

[75] Xen. *Anab*. 3. 1. 2–3. The echo in Arrian was noted long ago by Krüger (212). There may be an earlier echo in Coenus' speech at the Hyphasis, where the reference to the Macedonian yearning (πόθος) for parents, wives, and children has its exact counterpart in the agonizing of the Ten Thousand (*Anab*. 3. 1. 2).

[76] Xen. *Anab*. 3. 1. 2: κύκλῳ δὲ αὐτοῖς πάντῃ πολλὰ καὶ ἔθνη...ποταμοὶ δὲ διεῖργον ἀδιάβατοι ἐν μέσῳ τῆς οἴκαδε ὁδοῦ. Arr. 6. 12. 2: τοσούτων μὲν ἐθνῶν μαχίμων περιειργόντων σφᾶς ἐν κύκλῳ...ποταμῶν τε ἐν μέσῳ ἀδιαβάτων.

in particular (ἀδιάβατος, 'uncrossable') occurs on this one occasion in Arrian, and in classical prose it is found only in the work of Xenophon.[77] Arrian must be drawing upon his stylistic model. The atmosphere may well be continued in the story of the Boeotian's intervention. There is another quirk of vocabulary (βοιωτιάζοντα...τῇ φωνῇ) which is attested almost exclusively in Arrian and Xenophon, and in Xenophon it comes in the same context of the deliberations of the Ten Thousand.[78] There the speaker is a 'false Boeotian', who opposes the eminently sensible suggestions of Xenophon, just as Arrian's Boeotian nullifies the justified reproaches of Alexander's friends—and was rewarded and promoted, not dismissed in ignominy as was the speaker in Xenophon.

This brings us to the crux. Arrian has superimposed the context of Xenophon. By the language he uses he invites his readers to draw an analogy between Alexander's men and the leaderless Ten Thousand. To what extent is it rhetorical imagination? Did Arrian invent the worries of the army, or adapt the terminology of Near-chus to suggest the parallel with the Ten Thousand? Here the account of Curtius Rufus provides a control. Curtius, or his source, shows little interest in Alexander's reunion with his men. Whereas Arrian covers the episode from the perspective of the fleet, Curtius keeps the narrative focus upon Alexander. He mentions the anxiety of the troops after the operation, but he implies that it was soon allayed, and makes no comment on the news of the king's recovery reaching the main camp.[79] What concerns him is the danger of native unrest, which forced Alexander to leave his base before his wound was properly scarred over. He accordingly appeared on a canopy supported between two boats—and Curtius adds the pertinent comment that the rest of the fleet kept its distance so as not to disturb the king's sleep (Curt. 9. 6. 1–2). After four days' progress Alexander picked a site suitable for convalescence (for himself and his troops), and it was here that his friends reproached him for his recklessness.

The two traditions present us with an interlocking pattern of events. It is agreed that Alexander received surgery at the Malli

[77] Besides this passage, at *Anab.* 2. 1. 11 (similar context) and *Hell.* 5. 4. 44.

[78] Xen. *Anab.* 3. 1. 26–30; cf. Arr. 6. 13. 5. The only other occurrence of the phrase is D. Chrys. 43. 5, referring to an apophthegm of Epameinondas.

[79] Curt. 9. 5. 30: Alexander is watched by the army under arms, until he lapses into convalescent sleep. At that point they were able to report more optimistically to the base camp ('hinc certiorem spem salutis eius in castra rettulerunt').

town, moved to his main base, and after a brief convalescence resumed his voyage for a more protracted rest four days' journey downstream.[80] Within the framework there are different emphases. Nearchus concentrated his account at the base camp, whereas Curtius' source spread the events over a longer stretch of the river journey. But what Curtius reports is intrinsically credible. The detail is circumstantial, and one passing observation, that Macedonian custom required the royal Bodyguard to sleep by the king's bedroom at times of illness, is confirmed by the detailed narrative of Alexander's last days.[81] What is more, the two spokesmen for Alexander's friends, Craterus and Ptolemy,[82] had been separated from the assault force for the Malli campaign, and were only now able to remonstrate. Curtius, then, has the proper context for his set debate, and the theme of the debate echoes the narrative in Arrian. Craterus tactfully reproaches the king for his rashness, and is answered by a longer rhetorical outburst by Alexander. The initial speech is crafted to elicit a reply, and seems to embody material already in the tradition. Craterus begins with Alexander's indispensability. While he is alive, the Macedonians can scorn the threat from any number of hostile forces by land or sea, but that immunity would end with his death (9. 6. 7–9). Next, they have come to the far east under Alexander's leadership, and their only hope of return is for him to return with them.[83] These are two of the dominant themes for Arrian's Macedonians, the concern over revolt and the difficulties of return; 'everything appeared hopeless and intractable if they were bereft of Alexander.'[84] That is the burden of Craterus' exordium,

---

[80] The two accounts are compatible. Curtius omits the grand reception at the base camp at the confluence, while Arrian has nothing about the convalescent camp four days downstream. Instead he uses the confluence as a basic reference point, locating there a large number of transactions (6. 15. 1–3) which probably took place over a period of time. He also (6. 14. 4) begins the voyage before the confluence. Presumably Alexander (or perhaps a deputy) returned to the vicinity of the Malli and embarked his expeditionary force, which he transported by shipboard to the river bank below the confluence.   [81] Curt. 9. 6. 4; cf. Arr. 7. 25. 6; Plut. *Al.* 76. 6.

[82] For Craterus' movements see Arr. 6. 5. 6–7, 13. 1 with Heckel 122–3. Ptolemy explicitly stated that he was elsewhere at the time of Alexander's wound at the Malli town (Arr. 6. 11. 8 = *FGrH* 138 F 26 a; Curt. 9. 5. 21 = F 26 b; cf. Bosworth, *From Arrian to Alexander* 80–2).

[83] Curt. 9. 6. 9: 'eo pervenimus auspicium atque imperium secuti tuum unde, nisi te reduce, nulli ad penates suos iter est' ('following your auspices and your command we have reached a point so distant, that unless you lead us back, nobody can find his way home').

[84] Arr. 6. 12. 2. The language is highly evocative. The combination of ἄπορος and ἀμήχανος occurs ironically in the speech of Tissaphernes immediately before the

which Curtius expresses with even more hyperbole ('quis enim tibi superstes aut optat esse aut potest?'). There would seem to be a common tradition of anxiety, which Arrian has elaborated to suggest the comparison with the Ten Thousand, but it is superficial elaboration, taking over the sense of the original and dressing it in highly evocative language.[85] The troops' worries about native revolt are eminently justified, and they are coupled with equally justifiable worries about competition for pre-eminence among the surviving generals. Nearchus must have given a vivid picture of insecurity, as the Macedonians agonized over the prospect of a divided command and the spectre of general insurrection, and it is hardly surprising that Arrian evoked the parallel of the Ten Thousand in crisis.

Craterus' speech in Curtius continues with a sermon on the perils of incurring unnecessary risks. The capture of an obscure village was not worth the danger to the king's life: 'we demand for ourselves the dangers that bring no fame, the battles that bring no glory: but *you* save yourself for those which are appropriate to your greatness.'[86] That is precisely the thinking behind the reproaches of Alexander's friends in Arrian/Nearchus. His actions are those of a common soldier, not a general. This seems a favourite expression of Arrian's. It recalls his earlier commendation of Porus at the Hydaspes, who played the part not merely of a general but of a gallant soldier.[87] In

murder of the generals (Xen. *Anab*. 2. 5. 21; cf. Hdt. 5. 3. 1); and the combination of ἔρημος and the genitive, a favourite with Xenophon, is reminiscent of Clearchus' appeal to his men (who are his country, friends, and allies; cf. Arr. 1. 12. 5): bereft of them he would be helpless (*Anab*. 1. 3. 6: ὑμῶν ἔρημος ὢν οὐκ ἂν ἱκανὸς οἶμαι εἶναι κτλ.).

[85] Compare the new papyrus fragment of the History of the Successors (*PSI* xii 1284; cf. Bosworth, *GRBS* 19 (1978) 227–9), where Eumenes' threat to the Silver Shields ('he would bar them from provisions...even if they considered themselves altogether invincible, they would not square up against famine for long') recalls Tissaphernes' identical threat to the Ten Thousand (Xen. *Anab*. 2. 5. 19): 'we will set famine against you, which you would not be able to combat, even if you were altogether valiant.' The shaping and vocabulary is virtually identical (and Xenophon's λιμὸν...ἀντιτάξαι more or less guarantees Bartoletti's restoration in the papyrus: λιμῶι...ἀντιτάξαιντο).

[86] Curt. 9. 6. 14: 'temet ipsum ad ea serva, quae magnitudinem tuam capiunt.'

[87] Arr. 5. 18. 4; cf. 6. 13. 4. The phrasing is striking, but I know of no instance before Arrian. The usage inspired his younger contemporary, Appian, who described a comparable event in the career of Caesar in terms deliberately reminiscent of Arrian on Alexander. After rashly committing himself to the wintry Adriatic Caesar was reproached for his deed 'becoming a soldier, not a general' (ὡς στρατιώτῃ πρέπον...οὐ στρατηγῷ App. *BC* 2. 58), a formulation which occurs in no other report of the episode (Plut. *Caes*. 38. 7; Dio 41. 46. 4; Lucan 5. 680–99; cf. M. Gelzer, *Caesar: Politician and Statesman* (Oxford 1968) 228–9). Appian was surely echoing Arrian, exactly as Arrian had echoed Xenophon.

both cases the involvement of the general in the fighting is at issue, but Arrian commends it in Porus and explicitly criticizes it in Alexander. It is Curtius who provides the necessary commentary, and places it in the context of ancient strategic thought. What matters is the importance of the engagement. If victory in a crucial battle is at stake, then the general must sway the issue by his personal involvement and, at the worst, die in defeat. That even Polybius agrees to be the duty of the commander.[88] But to risk one's life when defeat was not irretrievable was dereliction of duty. Alexander's career could thus be represented as a series of acts of irresponsibility, and the tradition here throws into high relief an element of the campaign which is often overlooked. Alexander's behaviour caused chronic anxiety throughout the army, and it was felt to be reprehensible. It was only after he had been weakened by his wound that his officers had the courage to confront him with the consequences of his actions and demand a change.

In Curtius the officers' intervention is followed by a bombastic speech, in which Alexander evades the question and preaches a sermon on the paramount importance of glory, stressing that fame comes at a price and echoing the choice of Achilles: a short and glorious life rather than a long but obscure existence.[89] The theme is developed by Curtius with all the pyrotechnics of imperial rhetoric, but its nucleus is exactly the message of Arrian's Boeotian. In Arrian the sentiment is conveyed with more pithiness and unashamed machismo ('these are the deeds of men').[90] He goes on to paraphrase an iambic line to the effect that suffering is the price of action. The verse is not quoted directly (a practice Arrian tends to avoid), and he gives no indication of either author or context. However, the line was carefully chosen, and, like Cleitus' pointed quotation of Euripides'

---

[88] Polyb. 10. 32. 7–12 is the *locus classicus*, reproving Marcellus for his unnecessary death ('he acted more like a simpleton than a general': ἀκακώτερον ἢ στρατηγικώτερον). See also 10. 3. 7 with Walbank's commentary. The duty of the good general to go down with his army is stressed in memorable language at 11. 2. 9–10. On the principles at stake see Everett L. Wheeler, in *Hoplites* 150–4.

[89] Curt. 8. 6. 18–19. In Arrian the theme is embroidered in Alexander's speech at the Hyphasis (Arr. 5. 26. 6), and emerges prominently in the narrative of the action at the Malli town (Arr. 6. 9. 5).

[90] Arr. 6. 13. 5: "ταῦτα", φάναι, "ὦ Ἀλέξανδρε, ἀνδρῶν τὰ ἔργα." The punctuation, suggested by Boissevain, must be correct. Elsewhere Arrian tends to begin a quotation with the demonstrative (e.g. 1. 13. 6; 4. 8. 7; 5. 19. 2), and the verb of speaking is embedded within the direct speech. The quotation summarised the entire debate and gave it a highly charged bias.

Andromache,[91] it was intended to be understood in a particular dramatic context. Unfortunately what is paraphrased by Arrian is a tragic truism, ascribed both to Aeschylus and to Sophocles,[92] and we cannot place it in a meaningful setting in either author. However, there was at least one play of Euripides, the *Archelaus*, in which the theme of glory won by effort was particularly prominent. 'A young man must always show daring; for no man achieves glory through slackness; rather suffering (οἱ πόνοι) is what engenders manliness (εὐανδρία).[93] That is one apophthegm. Compare the rhetorical utterance also quoted by Stobaeus: 'Is it not right for me to labour? Who has achieved fame without labour? What coward has aspired to the highest achievements?'[94] Now, the *Archelaus*, which propagated the lineage of the Macedonian royalty, will have been a play very familiar to Alexander, and he was deeply attuned to the thinking which depicted suffering as the price of glory. The Boeotian's quotation may not have come from Euripides, but it had pregnant associations and will have reminded Alexander of the traditional aspirations of Macedonian royalty. It *was* the role of his line, and of Homeric kingship in general, to sacrifice life itself in the pursuit of glory, and the quotation brought home a whole literary topos with considerable force. There is an interesting parallel in the career of Cortés. Díaz records a cryptic exchange between the Conquistador and his lieutenant, Alonso Hernandez Puertocarrero, at the time of his landing at San Juan de Ulúa, when Cortés was contemplating a break with the governor of Cuba and acting in the name of the king alone.[95] Puertocarrero made an apposite quotation from the Castilian ballad of Montesinos, who was urged to escape his enemies

---

[91] Plut. *Al.* 51. 8; Curt. 8. 1. 28–9. On this, see my forthcoming discussion in 'Alexander, Euripides and Dionysos', *Transitions to World Power, 360–146 BC: Studies in Honor of E. Badian*, ed. R. W. Wallace and E. M. Harris (Norman, Okla., 1996).

[92] Aesch. F 456 (Nauck, Radt) = 665 (Mette); Soph. F 209 (Nauck) = 223b (Radt) τὸν δρῶντα γάρ τι καὶ παθεῖν ὀφείλεται. The tag is platitudinous, and could well have occurred independently to both authors. The quotation in Sophocles is closer to Arrian's wording, and it is assigned to a satyr play, *Heracles at Taenarum*. If so, the context could be mock heroic, but if it was placed in Heracles' mouth, it was singularly appropriate for Alexander.

[93] F 237. The *Archelaus* is best consulted in the recent monograph by A. Harder, *Euripides' Kresphontes and Archelaos* (Leiden 1985), which contains full text and commentary. Cf. p. 222: 'The idea of gaining fame by efforts was apparently rather prominent in the *Archelaos*.'

[94] F 240: τίς δ' ἄμοχθος εὐκλεής; τίς τῶν μεγίστων δειλὸς ὢν ὠρέξατο; The theme is also found in F 236 and 238–9. See also Euripides' *Erechtheus* F 364 (Nauck).

[95] Díaz ch. 36 = p. 84 (Cohen). Cf. V. Frankl, *Saeculum* 13 (1962) 13–14; J. H. Elliott, in *Hernán Cortés: Letters from Mexico* p. xvi.

by taking service with the crown, and Cortés responded with an equally apt reference to the Paladin Roland, praying for comparable success. The Castilian ballad has the same function as the Greek iambic. It alludes obliquely to a line of argument fully expounded in the body of the work. The speaker has no need to explain himself, and the context gives the message a positive charge. It has all the authority of a recognized classic.

Arrian and Curtius address an important issue and an important moment in the campaign. Arrian followed Nearchus in describing the intervention of the anonymous Boeotian, which reinforced Alexander in his determination to continue the pursuit of glory at all costs. He used verbal colouring which evoked Xenophon's portrait of the foolish pseudo-Boeotian, Apollonides, and underlined his disapproval of the encouragement of Alexander's recklessness. At the same time he dealt very cursorily with the tragic quotation which Nearchus may have treated more expansively. What he does make clear is that Nearchus placed considerable emphasis upon his Boeotian, and it is somewhat curious that Nearchus (so Arrian explicitly attests) did not provide his name. Perhaps this was conscious imitation of Herodotus, who twice refrains from naming delinquents and refers to them by their ethnics alone.[96] Nearchus, it appears, had little love for the man whom he saw as confirming Alexander in his foolhardiness, and reduced him to an anonymous cipher. In this case the withholding of information conveys a very pointed message. The scene as a whole is a nice piece of eyewitness reporting by a man who, as commander of the fleet, must have been present at the scene, supported the representations of the generals, and felt chagrin when they were undermined. This complex scenario is considerably simplified by Curtius, who turns the encounter into a rhetorical exchange of views between Craterus and Alexander. The Boeotian flatterer disappears, and was presumably passed over by Curtius' source; but his not-too-subtly encoded message on the price of fame is developed at length in the mouth of Alexander. However, on the basic matter Arrian and Curtius are in agreement. The worries shared by staff and rank-and-file came to a head when Alexander received his wound. The officers demanded less risk-taking, and the king refused to co-operate. According to Nearchus Alexander chafed at his friends' reproaches, but was confirmed in his attitude by the

---

[96] Hdt. 1. 51. 4 (the Delphian who inscribed the Spartans' name upon Croesus' dedication); 4. 43. 7 (the Samian who appropriated the treasure of Sataspes).

literary allusion of the Boeotian courtier, while for Curtius' source the king has no regrets, and calmly rebuts the criticism. Once more the variation of detail takes place within an agreed framework.

The material which Arrian takes from Nearchus is largely based on autopsy, and he makes the most of what was a lively and highly coloured description. Its highlight seems to have been the king's reception at camp and the gradual explosion of joy, as he first stretched out his arm to the troops ashore, and then, once on land, ordered a horse to be brought, and mounted it, apparently without assistance. At that the entire army raised a din of acclamation, which echoed from the river banks, while Alexander rode to his tent and dismounted, proving that he was able to walk (Arr. 6. 13. 2–3). For all its colour the description contains one highly suspicious detail. Alexander was in the first stages of recovery from a supposedly devastating wound, a matter of days after critical surgery. Yet he can rise from his stretcher and mount his horse. The implausibility increases once one refers back to Arrian's description of the wound at the Malli town. He cites Ptolemy explicitly for the dramatic escape of air from the wound along with the blood.[97] In other words, as most modern scholars have assumed, the lung was perforated,[98] and the surgery later enlarged the perforation. In that case, when Alexander came to mount his horse, he had a collapsed lung, as well as huge loss of blood and post-operative shock. He could only have mounted his horse if he was physically hauled onto its back by his entourage,[99] and that would hardly have relieved or enthused the watching army. If the lung wound is a reality, then the story of Alexander mounting his horse is sheer fantasy. So much for the reliability of the eyewitness!

Another line of argument is possible, indeed essential. Ptolemy's description is at odds with the rest of the tradition, which has the Indian arrow lodge in Alexander's breastbone,[100] and the surgical procedure which follows, deliberate enlargement of the wound to

---

[97] Arr. 6. 10. 1 = *FGrH* 138 F 25.

[98] This was observed long ago by Friederich Schmieder, and the lung wound has been enshrined in modern accounts (e.g. Droysen i². 2. 184; Schachermeyr, *Al.*² 455; Lane Fox, *Alexander the Great* 381–3; Hammond, *KCS*² 225). Few scholars (Green 420–1 is an exception) have seriously addressed the vulgate account.

[99] I am deeply indebted to Dr John Papadimitriou, Professor of Pathology at the University of Western Australia, for advice on the medical aspects of this episode.

[100] Plut. *Al.* 63. 6 (cf. *Mor.* 327b; 341c; 344c); Diod. 17. 99. 3 (under the breast); Curt. 9 . 5. 9, 22 (above the breast).

permit extraction of the barbed arrow head,[101] is precisely the technique advocated by medical writers—if no vital organ lies in the way.[102] Such a procedure would have been dangerous enough if there were no penetration of the lung, but, if the lung was already perforated, it would surely have been fatal. Ptolemy's description of the wound must be erroneous. He was not, so he explicitly stated, present at the siege when Alexander was wounded, and may have picked up highly coloured and exaggerated reports from participants. But we cannot assume that he was naïvely credulous. Ptolemy will have had experience of lung wounds in the course of his military career, and will have been well aware that the common run of mortals could not behave as Alexander did subsequently, defying the hardships of the Gedrosian desert at the head of his cavalry and leading his army into siege warfare within weeks of the wound.[103] It is hard to avoid the impression that he deliberately exaggerated the wound's seriousness in order to suggest that Alexander had superhuman qualities. His flatterers had compared his blood to ichor, the fluid in the veins of the gods,[104] and Ptolemy implied that he could recover at short notice even from a lung wound. If so, his recuperative powers rivalled those of Ares in *Iliad* 5,[105] and justified the claims

---

[101] Arr. 6. 11. 1; Curt. 9. 5. 22–8; Plut. Al. 63. 11–12. On this procedure Friedrich Lammert, *Gymnasium* 60 (1953) 3–5, is fundamental, proving that the tradition of a chest wound must be accepted. However, he attempts to save Ptolemy's credit by arguing that the πνεῦμα which escaped from the wound was not air, rather the life force which was thought to permeate the body. This is a desperate hypothesis. By its nature the 'life force' is invisible and indetectable, whereas Arrian (6. 10. 2) describes the πνεῦμα as forcing the blood out: 'it poured out prodigiously and in a gush (ἀθρόον) since it came out with the πνεῦμα.' What is at issue is the air from the lungs, which is represented as driving the haemorrhage. This can only be a description of a lung wound.

[102] See particularly the *Epitomae medicae* by Paulus of Aegina, which devotes an entire chapter to the extraction of missiles from wounds, 'one of the most vital branches of surgery' (Paul. Aeg. 6. 88 = *CMG* ix. 1–2). It specifies (6. 88. 4) that when the arrow is barbed (cf. Curt. 9. 5. 23–4) one must enlarge the wound by excision (cf. Cels. *Med.* 7. 5. 1c) and adds the procedure is only possible if no vital organ is in the way. In the case of a perforation of a whole set of organs (including the lung) the physician will avoid intervention 'so that we may avoid the situation, where, in addition to doing no good, we provide the layman with a pretext for abuse'. If Curtius (9. 5. 25, cf. Plut. *Mor.* 345a-b) is right, Critobulus was nervous enough about the *prospect* of internal damage. Had the wound been oozing the bloody foam characteristic of a perforation of the lung, it is unlikely that he would have proceeded, even in the face of a direct command.

[103] Arr. 6. 16. 1–2; Diod. 17. 102. 5; Curt. 9. 8. 11–15; Strabo 15. 1. 38 (701).

[104] See below, p. 114.

[105] Hom. *Il.* 5. 900–4; cf. 416–17 for the healing of Aphrodite and 447–8 for Aeneas' miraculously swift resuscitation at the hands of Leto and Artemis.

to divinity which were made for him. The lung wound in that case was a propagandist falsehood, and Arrian suggests as much when he attaches Ptolemy's name to the story. It was an item which he found suspicious and was not prepared to endorse on his own authority.

On the other hand the more popular tradition of a chest wound, with the arrow lodging in the breastbone, makes perfect sense. The painful and difficult operation to remove it was well within the capacity of contemporary field surgery. It produced an immediate haemorrhage and loss of consciousness,[106] so that there were immediate fears that Alexander had died. With recovery of his senses the fears were allayed in his immediate entourage, and within a few days he could be shipped downstream to the base camp, where he proved to the assembled forces that the rumours of his death were greatly exaggerated. The mounting and dismounting would have required considerable effort, but it was just feasible. Nearchus' description, as it is elaborated by Arrian, can therefore be accepted as a vivid and authentic description of what was obviously a supremely exciting event.

The results of this investigation can give us some reassurance. The information in our extant sources has undergone an intricate process of transmission, with the possibility of distortion at every stage. Eyewitness reports may overemphasize the perspective of the observer, or be deliberately framed to enhance the achievements of the narrator and serve his personal interests. At another level the extant secondary literature is overlaid by rhetoric; and subtle analogies and moral commentary may be built into the historical narrative. However, the literary shaping can be detected and analysed. Arrian in particular based his style upon the classic historians, and his models are largely extant. His allusions can be identified, and by and large they can be seen to enhance the narrative by adding an emotive charge, like the echoes of Thucydides' account of the Syracusan disaster which punctuate the description of Porus' defeat at the Hydaspes.[107] They add depth and colour to the exposition without detracting significantly from the factual narrative. The distortions in the primary authors are more intractable, and many must remain undetected for all time. However, the sources for the reign of Alexander are rich enough for cross-comparison. The framework of agreed 'fact' can be constructed, and

---

[106] Arr. 6. 11. 2; Curt. 9. 5. 28; Plut. *Al.* 63. 12.
[107] Bosworth, *HCA* ii. 300–1, 306 (cf. 275, 280 for other echoes).

within that framework the variations can be subjected to comparative criticism. The more probable version can often be identified, and reasons for bias may sometimes be apparent. What emerges starkly is that there is no single window to the truth. The sources present several perspectives, all of them fallible, but from them emerges a body of agreement and sufficient comparative material to weed out obvious fallacies. What remains is, of course, a lacunose and unsatisfactory coverage, and many of the vital questions we wish to ask of the evidence must remain unanswerable. However, in comparison with many periods of ancient history, where we are at the mercy of a single source (and that includes the Peloponnesian War), the reign of Alexander stands out as an oasis of illumination.

3

Information and Misinformation

TOWARDS the beginning of the Julian year 324 Nearchus left Harmozeia (Old Hormuz) on the final stage of his Ocean voyage. His first port of call was the richly wooded island of Oaracte (modern Qeshm), where he was entertained by the Persian governor, Mazenes.[1] The reception he received was clearly sumptuous, as befitted the friend of the new despot of the east, and at this provincial court was an exotic refugee. Mithropastes was the son of the disgraced satrap of Hellespontine Phrygia, who had committed suicide after Alexander's first victory at the Granicus.[2] The father's failure blighted the prospects of the son, who was exiled to the Persian Gulf, the traditional oubliette for fallen members of the Achaemenid court.[3] After the death of Darius he found his way to Oaracte and applied himself to winning the favour of his new masters, in the hope of reinstatement in civilized lands. With that in mind he recounted strange local traditions which he considered would excite the curiosity of the visitors. In particular he told of the tomb of the eponymous king of the area, a certain Erythras, who was interred at a remote island, some 2,000 stades distant in the ocean, and he claimed to have firsthand knowledge of it. It would seem that

---

[1] Nearchus' account is excerpted by Arr. *Ind.* 37. 2–4 and Strabo 16. 3. 5–7 (766–7) = *FGrH* 133 F 27–8. Arrian's version is excessively contracted, and he has erroneously drawn the conclusion that Erythras' tomb was on display at the satrapal centre of Oaracte (Qeshm). It is clear from Strabo's more extended digest that the tomb was reported on the more distant island of Ogyris, 2,000 stades from Oaracte. Pliny, *NH* 6. 153 also gives the name of the island, which he reports 1,000 stades from the mainland (cf. Mela 3. 79; Dion. Per. 606–7). Curtius 10. 1. 13–14 also mentions the story, which he presumably took from Cleitarchus (cf. Diod. 17. 106. 6–7), and provides two supplementary details which could also come ultimately from Nearchus. The fullest modern treatment of the episode is P. Goukowsky, *REG* 87 (1974) 111–37, esp. 120–3. See also Pédech, *Historiens compagnons* 196.

[2] Arr. 1. 16. 3. Cf. Bosworth, *HCA* i. 111–13; Berve ii. 82, no. 151.

[3] Cf. Ctesias' story of Megabyzus, satrap of Syria under Artaxerxes I, who fell into disgrace and narrowly escaped the capital penalty. Instead he was relegated to Cyrtaea, a city on the Persian Gulf (*FGrH* 688 F 14. 43; Steph. Byz. s.v. Κυρταία), where he languished for five years. See also Hdt. 3. 93. 2; 7. 80.

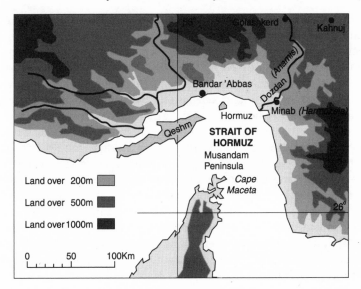

Fig. 7. The Strait of Hormuz

Mithropastes succeeded in his intentions and was restored to civilization, for Nearchus duly recorded his personal history and the antiquarian details he provided, and the material was picturesque enough to be excerpted by Strabo and Arrian.

The details are picturesque indeed. They are also paradoxical. Mithropastes, a Persian, was giving a typically Greek rationalization of a Greek geographical term. The business was the explanation of the *Greek* nomenclature of the Persian Gulf, the 'Red Sea' (Ἐρυθρὰ θάλαττα). This nomenclature was purely Greek. From time immemorial the inhabitants of Mesopotamia had referred to the Persian Gulf as the 'Lower Sea',[4] and the Persian kings had adopted the terminology. 'Red Sea' was a Greek term, first attested in the mid-fifth century BC in the works of Aeschylus and Pindar,[5] and by the fourth century its origins were an enigma. Ctesias explained it by

[4] See the convenient compilation by W. Heimpel, *ZA* 77 (1987) 22–91, and the *mise au point* by D. O. Edzard, 'Meer', in *Reallexikon der Assyriologie* viii. 1 (Berlin 1993) 1–5. For the Egyptian terminology ('Great Green', 'Great Sea of the Circling Water') see A. B. Lloyd, *Herodotus Book II* (Leiden 1976) Commentary 50.

[5] Pind. *Pyth.* 4. 251 (462 BC); Aesch. F 192 (Radt) = Strabo 1. 2. 27 (33). Aeschylus seems to apply the term to our Red Sea; Herodotus (1. 180. 1, 189. 1) seems the first to refer to the Persian Gulf by that name.

reference to a spring discharging red-coloured waters into the sea,[6] but, like most of Ctesias' reports, it lacked conviction with later generations. However, curiosity had been aroused, and Nearchus, once in the confines of the 'Red Sea', was eager to question his hosts about the origins of the name. He received an answer, and it was an answer couched in Greek terms. There was an eponymous hero, named Erythras, who left an indelible mark on the area. His memory persisted at the time of the first Greek penetration of the sea, and so the Greeks (but not the locals) named the sea after him. This was an attractive explanation, excogitated by a Persian with recent experience of the satrapal court of Dascylium, in close contact with the Greek intellectual milieu. Mithropastes was familiar with the Greek mania for eponyms and devised an appropriate rationalization of the Greek name. What he actually saw on the island of Ogyris we shall never know. Presumably there *was* an immemorially old sanctuary and a local cult, but the name Erythras looks like the product of Mithropastes' fertile imagination.[7] If his visitors wished for an explanation, he would provide one that was attractive to them and appeal to what he knew of their modes of historical interpretation.

As it happened, Mithropastes was successful beyond his wildest dreams. Nearchus presumably restored him to his homeland. He also recorded his explanation of the 'Red Sea' and his description of the tomb of Erythras, so that it became a curiosity reported in most of the derivative accounts of Alexander's reign. Erythras was then absorbed into Greek mythology. Deinias of Argos claimed that he was a son of Perseus, engendered during his father's stay in Persia,[8] and in the second century BC Agatharchides of Cnidus questioned a Hellenized Iranian resident in Athens, a certain Boxus, 'who had

---

[6] Ctesias, *FGrH* 688 F 66 = Strabo 16. 4. 20 (779); 'Ctesias of Cnidus reports a spring of reddish, ruddle coloured water discharging into the sea.' Strabo took his information from Artemidorus of Ephesus, who in turn drew upon Ctesias' fellow-countryman, Agatharchides. Agatharchides, it is clear (cf. Phot. cod. 250: 442b20–22), explicitly addressed and rebutted Ctesias, as (it seems) did at least one of the Alexander historians. Curtius (10. 1. 13) also rejects Ctesias' view, and the rejection could come ultimately from Cleitarchus.

[7] Goukowsky (above, n. 1) 123 regards the whole story of the localization on Ogyris as a fabrication: a mythical version of a 'historical' tradition which placed Erythras' tomb at the heart of his kingdom. This reconstruction takes Arrian and Strabo as independent excerpts of different passages of Nearchus, which is highly unlikely. The shorter version of Arrian must surely be distorted through excessive contraction (so Jacoby, *FGrH* ii. D 460).

[8] Agatharch. *De m. rubro* 1. 4 = *FGrH* 306 F 7. For Perseus' legendary role as the eponymous hero of Persia see Bosworth, *HCA* i. 270.

become Greek in language and thought'. For Boxus Erythras was the inventor of navigation, who built a raft to pursue his fugitive mares from Carmania to an offshore island (Qeshm) and then populated the coast on either side of the Persian Gulf.[9] The eponym has now been given a cultural context and a historical persona. How far Boxus exploited native Iranian tradition we cannot say.[10] What matters is the expansion of the myth. For Mithropastes and Nearchus the question was the origins of a problematic name, and Mithropastes drew on his local experience to provide a conveniently named eponym. That was all. It was left to the invention of subsequent generations to find an appropriate background to the name. Deinias gave it an acceptable Greek pedigree, whereas Boxus integrated it into local Iranian tradition, identifying the eponym as an indigenous culture hero.

This is an intriguing episode, and an interesting cultural interaction. Nearchus, we know, had an intense interest in current scientific questions, an interest which probably dates from his student days with Aristotle. In India he noticed the flooding of the rivers in the aftermath of the monsoon rains of 326, and inferred that the same conditions applied in Egypt. The empirical evidence from the Punjab confirmed the Aristotelian hypothesis that the cause of the Nile floods was the summer rainfall in Ethiopia.[11] The nomenclature of the 'Red Sea' was another conundrum, and Nearchus was ready enough to accept the eyewitness testimony of a prominent Persian refugee, testimony which appealed to Greek rationalism. If Atlas had given his name to the western Ocean,[12] then it was a priori likely that the first Greeks in the Persian Gulf had named the sea after a local dynast; it was, then, not the 'Red Sea' but the sea of Erythras. We

---

[9] Agatharch. *De m. rubro* 1. 5. This is now most conveniently found, in translation with explanatory notes, in S. M. Burstein, *Agatharchides of Cnidus: On the Erythraean Sea* 43–5. The relationship between Boxus and Agatharchides is reminiscent of another famous literary association, that between Herodotus and Zopyrus, another Persian resident at Athens (Hdt. 3. 160. 2: see now E. Badian, *From Plataea to Potidaea* 35–6).

[10] See the erudite and ingenious discussion of Goukowsky (above, n. 1) which identifies 'Erythras' as the mythical founder of the ancient kingdom of Makkan (124–8) and finds evidence of an age-old trade route between the Persian Gulf and southern Pakistan.

[11] Strabo 15. 1. 25 (696) = *FGrH* 133 F 20; cf. Arr. *Ind.* 6. 6–7. See further Bosworth, *Topoi* 3 (1993) 417–20.

[12] The name is already used in Herodotus (1. 202. 4), and was perhaps suggested by the Homeric description of Atlas (*Od.* 1. 52–4), who 'knew the depths of every sea'.

can easily understand Nearchus' enthusiasm for a new and exotic derivation. What is more surprising is that it was a derivation provided by a *Persian*. Mithropastes knew enough about Greek culture and literature[13] to provide an explanation which the visitors found intellectually satisfying; he gave them what they were predisposed to accept. This is a situation which typifies the acquisition of knowledge during Alexander's reign. Mithropastes and his host Mazenes needed to ingratiate themselves with Nearchus and so gain a passage to Susa and the Persian heartland. And the patronage of the friend of the new world ruler was an incalculable asset. Accordingly the information which accrued was distorted to accommodate the prejudices of the enquirer. The age-old tumulus on the island of Ogyris was duly reported,[14] but its occupant was given a Greek name—or at least a name which a Greek audience would accept as an eponym. Whether Nearchus actually believed the explanation we cannot say. He may simply have named his source, and retailed the information in Herodotean style, without committing himself to an endorsement of it. But the combination of enthusiastic enquirer and over-compliant informant was a dangerous one, and the combination must have been frequent during the Asian campaign. Equally dangerous was the interpretation of local data according to Greek categories. The questions asked tended to be posed from a Greek perspective, and it was fatally easy to select facts which would buttress one's presuppositions.

A classic instance was Alexander's discovery of growths of sacred lotus along the river Chenab (Acesines).[15] He and his staff were familiar with the plant from their stay in Egypt, where it had been introduced, probably by the first Achaemenids, and became known

---

[13] Hardly surprising if he had spent some years in the satrapal capital of Hellespontine Phrygia, surrounded by Greek *poleis* of long standing.

[14] I am assuming that the island of Ogyris actually existed and was Mithropastes' initial place of exile (so Berve ii. 263–4, no. 528). That makes identification peculiarly difficult. One cannot find an appropriate island in the Ocean (Strabo 16. 3. 5); the favourite candidate, Masirah (O. Stein, *RE* xvii. 2080–1; H. Schiwek, *BJ* 162 (1962) 75), is close to the coast of Oman and well outside the writ of the Achaemenid king; and there is no obvious island out to sea. It may well be that the whole of Mithropastes' story was a fanciful concoction; both the eponymous hero and his burial place could be imaginary.

[15] Strabo 15. 1. 25 (696) = Nearchus, *FGrH* 133 F 20; Arr. 6. 1. 2–6. Both Strabo and Arrian give complementary digests of Nearchus, as is generally accepted (cf. Jacoby, *FGrH* ii. D 467; Hammond, *Sources* 262–3, is to my knowledge the only dissentient voice). For detailed discussion of the subject-matter see my article (above, n. 11) 413–17.

to the Greek world from Herodotus onwards as the Egyptian bean.[16] The lotus was an exotic curiosity, found in scattered places in the Greek world, notably Torone,[17] and its appearance in India excited speculation. The speculation had historical precedents. According to Herodotus Darius I was intrigued by reports of crocodiles in the Indus and sent an expedition under Scylax of Caryanda to determine the course of the Indus.[18] Scylax had found his way to the southern Ocean and back to the west, but even so speculation persisted that the Indus and Nile might be interconnected. One branch at least of the Indus might loop to the south of the ocean (conceived as an inland sea) and join the Nile. Artaxerxes III is said to have made enquiries, still puzzled by the elusive crocodiles found in India and Egypt but apparently nowhere else.[19] Alexander was, it seems, familiar with the controversy, and considered for a brief, heady moment that he had discovered the upper reaches of the Nile. The appearance of the sacred lotus was analogous to the crocodiles, suggesting that the Nile and the Indus were one and the same. On this occasion, however, local investigation exploded the theoretical construct. The natives reported that all the Punjab rivers coalesced in a single stream, which discharged into the Ocean.[20] There was no subsidiary channel veering east and south away from the sea. On the contrary all the rivers of the Indus plain ended in the sea to the south. There could be no linkage between the Nile and the Indus. Empirical research refuted a fashionable hypothesis.

The source for the episode, Nearchus, is not much interested in the process of discovery, and Alexander's informants are anonymous. Most probably Nearchus gives us the distillation of more general geographical enquiries. When questioned, the natives told

---

[16] Herodotus (2. 92. 4) is in fact the first evidence for Egypt (cf. Lloyd (above, n. 4) 372–5). Theophrastus, *HP* 4. 8. 8, gives a careful description, on which one may consult the indispensable Budé edition by S. Amigues (pp. 266–7).

[17] Theophr. *HP* 4. 8. 8. Phylarchus, *FGrH* 81 F 65, attests the appearance of a growth in Epirus (*c.*260 BC) which caused such excitement that a royal guard was installed to protect it.   [18] Hdt. 4. 44. 1–2 = *FGrH* 709 T 3.

[19] The source is the Aristotelian treatise on the flooding of the Nile (*FGrH* 646 F 1. 4; cf. D. Bonneau, 'Liber Aristotelis de inundatione Nili', *Études de papyrologie* 9 (1971) 4–5). This work is of dubious authenticity. Most recent scholars (e.g. S. M. Burstein, *GRBS* 17 (1976) 135–46) accept that it is derived from an actual work of Aristotle, but for a sceptical view see my article (above, n. 11) 417–20.

[20] So Arr. 6. 1. 5. Strabo notes that Alexander was told that *all* Indian rivers discharged into the Ocean. In that case even outside the Indus system there was no river which could provide the desired connection with the Nile.

what they knew of the rivers of the region, just as (at a later stage) they gave precise and factual information about the prevailing winds in the Indian Ocean.[21] The status of these informants was relatively humble. They were presumably the counterparts of the Gedrosian native, Hydraces, who volunteered his services at the harbour of Mosarna.[22] On Nearchus' description Mosarna was a small remote outpost, inhabited by fishermen,[23] and Hydraces was obviously of fairly humble status, not to be compared with Mithropastes and Mazenes in Qeshm. What recommended him would have been his linguistic expertise. Presumably he had some knowledge of Persian or even Aramaic and was able to communicate with the Phoenicians in Nearchus' fleet without the elaborate machinery of three inter-preters, which Alexander had found necessary in India.[24] Hydraces was only one of a set of local guides whom Nearchus consulted at critical stages in the voyage, on the habits of whales or the magical island of Nosala, where all who landed disappeared.[25] The latter report Nearchus treated with a hard-headed scepticism, forcing his reluctant crew to land with him on the island. When he and they remained in the visible world, the magic island was revealed as a local myth, or worse, the product of his informants' imagination. Once more the episode is instructive. Local informants were a valued commodity, enlisted and rewarded for their services, but the information they gave was treated with proper caution when it was unpalatable to the recipients. Nearchus did not wish his crews panic-stricken when they landed on unfamiliar islands, and took pains to have the fantasy publicly exploded.

If Nearchus had the benefit of information (or misinformation) at the hands of local guides, the same was true of Alexander, but to a

---

[21] Arr. 6. 21. 1–2; cf. *Ind.* 21. 1, 12; 23. 3; 24. 1.

[22] Arr. *Ind.* 27. 1. Hydraces is not attested elsewhere. Nearchus clearly made a point of his adhesion to the fleet, and, although he was not the only pilot (see below), he was the most esteemed and presumably the most informative.

[23] Arr. *Ind.* 26. 10. For its conjectural identification as the modern Ras Pasni see Strasburger, *Studien* i. 492 n. 4; Schiwek, *BJ* 162 (1962) 49. It is termed a 'harbour', smaller even than the 'little *polis*' of Cyiza (*Ind.* 27. 6). If, as Arrian's phrasing implies, Hydraces was the first local guide to be acquired, more were pressed into service at Cyiza, which was totally at Nearchus' mercy (see below, pp. 184–5). Hydraces could transmit their information.

[24] Hydraces may indeed have been the interpreter who collaborated with Nearchus in the treacherous seizure of Cyiza (*Ind.* 28. 3, 5).

[25] Arr. *Ind.* 30. 3; Strabo 15. 2. 12 (725)—whales: *Ind.* 31. 2–3 (cf. Strabo 15. 2. 13 (726)—Nosala).

much higher degree. When he began his voyage down the Hydaspes
in late 326, it is stated that he had the prodigious number of 120,000
fighting men in his entourage.[26] The total is presumably inflated, but
the numbers must have been comparatively huge, and a large
proportion comprised Indian auxiliaries with local knowledge.
Accordingly Alexander was forewarned about the rapids at the
confluence of the rivers Hydaspes and Acesines. He therefore took
pains to ensure that the vessels in the fleet kept carefully measured
distances apart, to minimize collision—and only one collision is in
fact reported in the rapids.[27] A significant hazard—and despite the
sensational colouring of Arrian's narrative[28] significant it must have
been—had been surmounted without serious loss, and the local
information clearly contributed much to the success. The same could
be said of Alexander's devastating attack on the Malli immediately
after he forced the rapids. He deliberately took the most difficult
route, across the waterless waste between the Acesines and the
Hydraotes (the Rechna Doab, cursed for its unpleasantness by
British administrators of the nineteenth century).[29] Not only did he
march through the night; he appeared at day-break outside one of
the largest Mallian cities, chosen for its remoteness as a haven for
refugees, and took its inhabitants totally by surprise. Even before this
city was stormed he sent off a second detachment under Perdiccas
to blockade another city in the vicinity and prevent news of the
invasion spreading. He also knew the location of the main ford
across the Hydraotes, and was able to go directly there, again by
night.[30] Given that he was entering terrain totally unknown to him,
without the benefit of modern staff maps, the pin-point accuracy of

[26] Arr. *Ind.* 19. 5; cf. Curt. 8. 5. 4; Plut. *Al.* 66. 5.

[27] Arr. 6. 4. 4 ('this had been reported in advance by the local inhabitants'). The
careful spacing of the fleet is described at 6. 3. 2 and the limited damage at the
confluence at 6. 5. 2–3. Many of the oared vessels were damaged, but only two of
them sank, with the loss of many (but by no means all) of their crew.

[28] The details (difficult eddies, heavy swell, noise of rushing water, terror of crews
who drop their oars) are reminiscent of Odysseus' approach to Charybdis (Hom. *Od.*
12. 201–5). Echoes of the *Odyssey* have been detected elsewhere in Nearchus
(Pearson, *LHA* 134–6; Badian, *YCS* 24 (1975) 148, 161–2), and this is a nice addition
to the repertoire.

[29] Arr. 6. 6. 1–2. For a detailed description of the area a century ago see *Punjab
District Gazetteers* xxii.A Jhang District (Lahore 1910) 2–5: 'probably unrivalled in the
world for its combination of the most disagreeable features a landscape is capable of
affording.'

[30] Arr. 6. 6. 4, 6 (Perdiccas); 6. 7. 1 (Hydraotes).

the invasion speaks volumes for the quality of his local information and the expertise of his guides.

So far the information we have been dealing with is local in scope. The informants were transmitting facts within their experience, and where there was a multiplicity of reports available it is hardly surprising that precise and detailed knowledge accrued. One would expect that accuracy diminished as distance increased. Alexander had subjugated the neighbours of the Malli[31] and could impose sanctions if their information proved incorrect. Under those conditions his informants had every inducement to be helpful and correct. As the distance increased, the constraints were less immediate, and the knowledge of the informants was necessarily less detailed. The evidence for such long-range reconnaissance is, of course, limited, but there is one important episode which sheds considerable light on the quality of the geographical and political information available to Alexander. This is the famous episode in the vulgate tradition where Alexander inquires about conditions beyond the river Hyphasis (Beas).[32] The enquiry is placed immediately before the so-called mutiny of the Hyphasis, when Alexander's men refused to continue the campaign across the river. Its results are alleged to have been catalytic. The armies of the east, so it was reported, were huge, boasting unparalleled numbers of elephants of exceptional ferocity. It was not an enticing prospect for the monsoon-weary Macedonians, and they were unmoved by their king's harangues and his prolonged sulking withdrawal to his tent.

Alexander's informants are named for us. The bulk of the report came from Phegeus, a local prince who ruled the land immediately proximate to the Hyphasis[33] and should have had detailed knowledge of conditions beyond the river. His report was confirmed by Alexander's favourite, Porus, who added scandalous details about the king of the eastern Indians. The report is precise: a journey of twelve days through desert country to the Ganges, a river 30 stades (6 km.) broad and the deepest in India. Beyond it were the

---

[31] Arr. 6. 4. 2, 5. 4; Diod. 17. 96. 2–5; Curt. 9. 4. 1–8; Justin 12. 9. 2.

[32] Diod. 17. 93. 2–4; Curt. 9. 2. 2–10; *Metz Epit.* 68–9; cf. Plut. *Al.* 62. 2–3; Justin 12. 8. 9–11 (garbled). For discussion of the source tradition and its relation to the somewhat different version in Arrian (5. 25. 1–2) see Appendix below.

[33] Diod. 17. 93. 1–2; Curt. 9. 1. 36–2. 1; *Metz Epit.* 68. Phegeus is not mentioned by Arrian, who moves directly from the siege of Sangala to the Hyphasis mutiny, but (*pace* Tarn ii. 280–4) there is no reason to doubt his historicity.

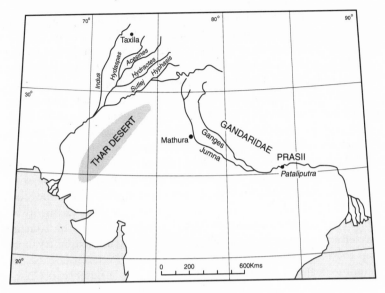

Fig. 8. India East of the Hyphasis

Gandaridae and Prasii,[34] under the rule of King Xandrames, who mustered an army of 20,000 horse, 200,000 foot, 2,000 war chariots, and no less than 4,000 war elephants, all fully equipped. The geographical data can be controlled. Twelve days' journey is consistent with the distance of 250 km. which separates the Hyphasis from the Ganges river system. The first river to be crossed was the Jumna (as Megasthenes later noted)[35] but it would not be surprising if Alexander's informants did not differentiate the two great branches of the Ganges. The river system itself certainly was twelve days' journey to the east, and travellers advancing to the capital of Pātaliputra would need to make a crossing. At all events the eastern

[34] The names are preserved in all sources. Diodorus consistently uses the spelling Gandaridae (see also 2. 37. 2–3: at 18. 6. 1 the name is rendered 'Tyndaridae'—an obvious corruption), while Plutarch refers to them as 'Gandaritae' (*Al.* 62. 3) or 'Gandridae' (*Mor.* 327b). On the other hand the Latin authors, notably Curtius and Pliny (*NH* 6. 65), use the form 'Gangaridae', and may have been subconsciously (or consciously) affected by Vergil (*Georg.* 3. 27). The poet coined a name which suggested the river Ganges and led naturally to the invocation of the Nile in the following lines (3. 28–9). The conceit affected the Latin authors, whereas Greek authorities reproduced the Hellenistic spelling.

[35] Arr. *Ind.* 8. 5 = *FGrH* 715 F 13: Megasthenes appears to have visited Mathura and knew of the cult of Krishna/Heracles there.

kingdom was conceived to lie to the east of the Jumna, where Alexander's troops would first impinge on the Gangetic plain. What is more, the peoples named by Phegeus are attested elsewhere. Megasthenes, who visited Pātaliputra soon after Alexander's death, reported that the Prasii lived around the capital (near modern Patna),[36] and the Gandaridae are independently attested in the Ganges plain. All this is consistent with Phegeus' report, and even the inflated numbers given for the eastern armies have some credibility. Megasthenes was to report at first hand that the military camp of the Indian king contained 400,000 souls (presumably non-combatants included).[37] The figure he provides may be a guess, with little intrinsic credibility, but it is a guess compatible with Phegeus' report. The army of the great eastern monarchy might reasonably be expected to be many times greater than that raised by Porus from his much smaller kingdom—and Porus is credited with an infantry force up to 50,000 strong.[38] As for the elephants, Plutarch (*Al.* 62. 4) comments that the number was no exaggeration: in later years Chandragupta was able to present Seleucus with no less than 500 war elephants. The figure of 500 is well attested and virtually confirmed by Diodorus, who records that Seleucus had 480 elephants with him in Asia Minor during the autumn of 302.[39] The eastern monarchy, it may be concluded, disposed of a prodigious number of elephants, and the report of Phegeus for all its exaggeration truly reflects the fact. The war elephants east of the Ganges far outmatched those of the west.

The additional information given by Porus is at first sight dubious. The eastern king was unpopular, the son of a barber, who had seduced the queen, murdered the previous king, and usurped the throne.[40] But despite the scandalous details there is some corrobora-

---

[36] Arr. *Ind.* 10. 5; Strabo 15. 1. 36 (702) = *FGrH* 715 F 18. On the date of Megasthenes' visit to Pātaliputra see Bosworth, *HCA* ii. 242–4 and the fuller exposition in 'The Historical Setting of Megasthenes' *Indica*', *CPh* 91 (1996), 113–27.

[37] Strabo 15. 1. 53 (709) = *FGrH* 715 F 32 (the Loeb translation wrongly renders the figure as 'forty thousand').

[38] Diod. 17. 87. 2. This refers to the total forces of the kingdom. The army at the Hydaspes was somewhat smaller (cf. Bosworth, *HCA* ii. 292–3).

[39] Diod. 20. 113. 4. The number of elephants which fought at Ipsus in 301 is said to have been 400 (Plut. *Demetr.* 28. 6). For the 500 elephants ceded by Chandragupta see Strabo 15. 2. 9 (724), 16. 2. 10 (751); Plut. *Al.* 62. 4. See further L. Schober, *Untersuchungen zur Geschichte Babyloniens und der Oberen Satrapien* 183–6, *contra* Tarn, *JHS* 60 (1940) 84–6.

[40] Diod. 17. 93. 3; Curt. 9. 2. 6.

tion. An anecdote of Plutarch has the great Chandragupta declare that his predecessor was contemptible in morals and birth.[41] This is not in itself conclusive, for one might argue that Plutarch's source was influenced by the Alexander vulgate. However, there is striking independent corroboration from Indian sources. The Brahman-inspired *Purānas* describe the Nandas, the ruling dynasty at the time of Alexander, as base-born, from the lowest, *śūdra*, caste, and ruling by usurpation.[42] The only difference from Phegeus' report is that the Nandas last for nine generations instead of two. Jain tradition, represented by the *Pariśistaparvan* of Hemachandra, actually describes the first Nanda king as the son of a barber (by a courtesan).[43] The evidence is comparatively late, from the fifth and twelfth centuries AD, but it represents a tradition quite separate from that of the Alexander historians. There is no possibility that Cleitarchus' work could have infiltrated Indian literature of such different persuasions. It seems rather that we have a rare case of authentic historical fact transmitted through separate, independent conduits. The Nandas *were* usurpers, of low birth, and the founder of the dynasty *was* reputed to be a barber. The slander gleefully retailed by Porus infiltrated the Brahman and Jain traditions, and there can be no doubt that it was current in Alexander's day. Once more there are far-reaching conclusions. What Porus recounted was no figment of Hellenistic historiography. It was authentic Indian tradition, and its independent transmission in Greek and Indian literature suggests a substratum of truth. Porus, then, had some knowledge of conditions in the eastern kingdom. He gave a colourful version of the foundation of the current dynasty, no doubt embellished by creative slander but ultimately based on fact. If, then, he knew of the history of the ruling house of Pātaliputra, it is also likely that he knew of its location and the extent of its dominions. The information Alexander received seems so far surprisingly accurate.

There is, however, one exception. Phegeus claimed that the twelve days' journey to the Ganges passed through a desert. That cannot, as it stands, be correct. The land between the Hyphasis (Beas) and Jumna was and is well-watered and populous. The Thar desert

---

[41] Plut. *Al.* 62. 9 (cf. *Mor.* 542d).

[42] The material from the *Purānas* is conveniently digested by R. K. Mookerji, *Chandragupta Maurya and his Times*[3] 7–8.

[43] Ibid. 14; cf. J. J. Schwarz, in F. Altheim and R. Stiehl, *Geschichte Mittelasiens in Altertum* 271.

occurs further south, covering a vast area some 650 km. from north to south and 350 km. from west to east.[44] It ends south of Feroze-pore, well below Alexander's crossing point on the Hyphasis, and there is no direct route from the Hyphasis which would have taken him through the desert. Some conflation has taken place. Phegeus gave a general aperçu of the lands between the Indus and Ganges. He mentioned the desert to the south as well as the less problematic, verdant route between the Hyphasis and Jumna, and presumably gave a reasonably full description, which was contracted by Cleitarchus. The twelve days' journey and the desert crossing have come together instead of being separated. Without a doubt the error is the work of Cleitarchus, for it occurs in all three derivatives of the vulgate,[45] but it is a relatively easy error. The reports he received of Phegeus' data were at best second hand, and there were many opportunities for confusion. The information was transmitted through the medium of interpreters to Alexander's staff and through Cleitarchus' informants to his historical record. It is hardly surpris-ing that reports of a northern journey across the plains and a southern transit of the desert were ultimately conflated. What is less likely is that the reports are the product of Cleitarchus' imagination, or gleaned retrospectively after Megasthenes' *Indica* provided a firsthand description of the Gangetic plain.[46] In the latter case Megasthenes, who visited Pātaliputra in person, is hardly likely to have written of a desert due east of the Hyphasis. The error of fact points to a distortion of original information provided by the local dignitaries of the Punjab. Some of their reports became warped in the complex process of dissemination, but much of what survives is remarkably accurate: the distance to the Ganges, the composition of the eastern army, and, above all, the history of the Nanda dynasty.

Thanks to his local informants, Alexander received a reasonably

---

[44] For a brief geographical survey see D. Kienast, *Historia* 14 (1965) 180–8, esp. 186–7. The terrain is well described by H. Lambrick, *Sind: A General Introduction* (Hyderabad 1964) 6–14.

[45] Curt. 9. 2. 2 ('per vastas solitudines'); Diod. 17. 93. 2; *Metz Epit.* 68.

[46] See the speculations of Kienast (above, n. 44) 188, arguing that Cleitarchus gained information about the Ganges plain in the early period of the Successors, from informants who used the southern route through the Thar. Like Niese and Tarn before him he discounted the possibility that Alexander obtained accurate reports of conditions in the east, and his scepticism has been reinforced in a recent article by T. R. Robinson, *AHB* 7 (1993) 84–99. The method of doubt is here taken to extremes and evidence is destroyed rather than utilized. See below, Appendix.

full description of the Gangetic plain—its distance, resources, and political status. What is surprising is the comparatively late date at which the information accrued. Phegeus' report came only when Alexander was in the eastern Punjab. At the Hyphasis he was informed of the existence of a great kingdom to the east, and the news so surprised him that he turned to Porus for corroboration.[47] That suggests that his expectations had hitherto been somewhat different, and indeed there is good reason to believe that Alexander's concept of the eastern extension of India was severely limited. The received opinion, quoted by Aristotle, was that India was relatively narrow. The Indus itself was acknowledged as the largest of all rivers, with a prodigiously long course to the south, but the eastern ocean was conceived to be close—within view when one has crossed the Hindu Kush (Parnassus).[48] Accordingly, when Alexander commissioned his river fleet after the Battle of the Hydaspes, he planned for it to be ready after his return from the eastern limits of India.[49] Once more the information comes from the vulgate tradition, and it is consistent. It accredits Alexander with limited aims, limited in the sense that he believed the eastern Ocean close at hand and easily accessible, but modified when he discovered that there was another great plain and a great kingdom to the east. This is an interesting process of discovery. At first Alexander's Indian hosts did not disabuse him of his preconceptions. Taxiles at least had a material interest in encouraging him to move east and crush his local rival,[50] and, if the

[47] Diod. 17. 93. 2: 'distrusting what was said by Phegeus, he sent for Porus'; Curt. 9. 2. 5 ('incredibilia regi omnia videbantur'); *Metz Epit.* 69 ('id rex usque eo non credidit, donec a Poro').

[48] Arist. *Mete.* 1. 350ᵃ19–23. Aristotle here takes his information from standard gazetteers (*periodoi*), no doubt including the standard work of Eudoxus of Cnidus. See my article (above, n. 11) 408, 421–2.

[49] So Diod. 17. 89. 5 (see Goukowsky's note *ad loc.*). Curt. 9. 1. 3 writes of a return to the sea after traversing the whole of Asia, while *Metz Epit.* 63 has a full statement that Alexander 'wished to reach the furthest bounds of India with the intention of sailing down to the Persian Gulf and Atlantic Ocean *after his return*'. That is foreshadowed in Justin 12. 7. 4, who has Alexander enter India with the intention of 'making the Ocean and the furthest Orient the limit of his empire'. The tradition is unitary, and there is no doubt that Alexander first commissioned his fleet at this juncture (see my article (above, n. 11) 422). See the detailed discussion by F. Schachermeyr, *IBK* 3 (1955) 126–8 = G. T. Griffith (ed.), *Alexander the Great: The Main Problems* (Cambridge 1966) 140–2.

[50] For his enmity to Porus, of long standing, see Arr. 5. 18. 7, 20. 4. Porus had recently presented a military threat to his neighbours through his alliance with Abisares (Arr. 5. 22. 2; cf. Bosworth, *HCA* ii. 328), and Taxiles could be forgiven for bending the truth to procure his downfall.

proximity of the Ocean was a potent lure, he would hardly wish to dispel the illusion. Accordingly, when Alexander questioned Phegeus, he expected to hear that the sea was close at hand, and the news of another plain and a great empire came as a surprise. For him it was an inspiring challenge, but for his troops it came as the last straw, a promise of misery without end,[51] and their refusal was absolute. But Alexander's enquiries had brought the Gangetic kingdom into the ambit of Greek geographical knowledge, and in the next decade Megasthenes was to visit the eastern court in the interest of his master, Sibyrtius, the satrap of Arachosia.[52] The diplomatic overtures followed hard on the heels of Alexander's campaign and exploited the information he elicited.

In India, as we have seen, there is a distinct possibility that Alexander's geographical misconceptions were encouraged by the local rulers whose interests they served. Something very similar had happened two years earlier, in Sogdiana. When Alexander paused at Maracanda, in the middle of the campaigning year of 328,[53] he was approached by delegations from the outlying Saca peoples whom he had contacted through emissaries the previous summer. Among them was the ruler of Chorasmia, the kingdom centralized in the upper reaches of the river Oxus, just to the south of the Aral Sea. At various times the territory had been subject to Achaemenid rule,[54] and the Chorasmian king now considered it prudent to offer his respects to the successor to Achaemenid power. He met Alexander, bringing an entourage of 1,500 cavalry, and pledged his co-operation. It is unlikely that he surrendered unconditionally, for Alexander granted him the rare privilege of alliance ($\xi\upsilon\mu\mu\alpha\chi\dot\iota\alpha$), a privilege otherwise extended only to communities outside his Empire.[55]

---

[51] See the vivid and rhetorical account of Arrian (5. 25. 1–2); cf. Strabo 15. 1. 27 (697); Diod. 17. 94. 2–3.

[52] Arr. 5. 6. 2. There is no evidence for the standard doctrine that Megasthenes acted as the envoy of Seleucus Nicator.

[53] I here accept the chronology of Curtius 8. 1. 7–9, where the episode is more related to the historical context. In Arrian (4. 15. 1–6) it resumes the narrative after the long digression on Cleitus and *proskynesis* and is very loosely anchored to events at Bactra (cf. 4. 7. 1–2) in early spring 328. See further, Bosworth, *HCA* ii. 45–7, 51–2.

[54] Arr. 4. 15. 4. Chorasmia (*Uvārazmish*) occurs regularly in the Achaemenid satrapy lists of the 5th century (W. J. Vogelsang, *The Rise and Organisation of the Achaemenid Empire* 97–9, 192–3). No Chorasmian contingent fought at Gaugamela, and Alexander's conclusion of an alliance (see below) indicates that he considered the region outside his empire proper (see, however, Vogelsang 232–3).

[55] Arr. 4. 15. 5. Apart from the treaty with the 'European Scyths' (4. 15. 2) the only alliance (other than the Corinthian League) recorded by Arrian is that with the Celts

Alexander was fully occupied with the Sogdian revolt and already had the enticing vista of Indian conquest in his imagination. There was little profit in a push through the desert to the lower Oxus, and Chorasmia could be left to its own devices. That, however, did not suit the Chorasmian ruler, who offered his services if Alexander chose to campaign to the west of his kingdom. He was envisaging Macedonian subjugation of his neighbours, a process from which he, the conqueror's ally, could only benefit. To that end he provided information which would attract Alexander's interest, and tailored his report to Greek interests.

The drawcard was the Amazons, who were a lasting obsession for the Greeks. There seem to have existed female warrior bands among the Sacan nomads, one of which, it seems, encountered Alexander in Hyrcania.[56] For the troops of Alexander they were Amazons, led by their queen from their homeland near Trebizond on the Black Sea, and the rumour soon evolved that their leader was attracted by his fame and set on conceiving a child by him.[57] What is certain is that Amazons were a reality for the Macedonian army, and they were disposed to find them among the female warriors of the Sacae. Pharasmanes, the Chorasmian ruler, was well aware of this.[58] He was also aware that the Macedonians considered themselves relatively close to home. The great river Syr-Darya, locally named Iaxartes, was identified with the European river Tanais (Don).[59] Stands of

of the Adriatic coast, who, like Pharasmanes, lay outside Alexander's planned path of conquest (Arr. 1. 4. 8). For the alliance with Cyrene, again outside the empire proper, see Diod. 17. 49. 3; Curt. 4. 7. 9.

[56] This famous story was denounced in antiquity as a fiction (Plut. *Al.* 46. 1–2; Strabo 11. 5. 4. (505), both probably derived from Eratosthenes). It was certainly omitted by Ptolemy and Aristobulus, and there is no trace of it in Arrian, who has a keen interest in Amazons (cf. *Peripl.* 15. 3; *Bithyn.* F 48–51 (Roos)). However, what was denounced as fiction is far from clear. From Strabo's criticism of Cleitarchus (*FGrH* 137 F 16) it would seem that it was the implausibility of the journey from the Black Sea that raised hackles. The Amazonian extraction of Alexander's visitors was questioned. It certainly cannot be excluded that female warriors did encounter the army in Hyrcania. If so, the tendency to identify them as Amazons must have been irresistible. See further Bosworth, *HCA* ii. 102–3.

[57] Diod. 17. 77. 1–3; Curt. 6. 5. 24–32; Justin 12. 3. 5, 42. 3. 7.

[58] As, it seems, was Atropates, Alexander's satrap of Media, who is alleged to have presented a troop of female warriors to Alexander under the guise of Amazons. This is a unique detail, found in neither Aristobulus nor Ptolemy nor indeed any reliable authority (Arr. 7. 13. 3; cf. Bosworth, *From Arrian to Alexander* 65–7). Again we may have a superimposition of 'Amazon theory' by Greeks predisposed to view all female warriors as Amazons. Something very similar took place in Pompey's much later Albanian campaign (App. *Mithr.* 103. 482–3; Plut. *Pomp.* 35. 5–6; cf. Theophanes, *FGrH* 188 F 4).

silver fir, believed unique to Europe, had been discovered on its banks in 329,[60] and, still more strikingly, ivy, which could not be made to grow in Asia, was discovered north of the river during the campaign of 329.[61] If the Syr-Darya was the Don, then its mouth in the Sea of Azov could not be too far distant, nor could the homeland of the Amazons on the south-east corner of the Black Sea. Alexander had sent out embassies from the Syr-Darya in the high summer of 329 to tribes named 'Scyths of Europe', whom he thought to be domiciled close to the Cimmerian Bosporus (at the mouth of the Sea of Azov).[62] These ambassadors had moved in the direction of Chorasmia, and, when they returned, the Chorasmian king also arrived to greet the new world conqueror. He had clearly entertained Alexander's envoys and had learned from them. He knew of the curious geographical views of the invaders and their interest in female warriors, and now he declared to Alexander that he had Amazons as his neighbours and that his territories in fact bordered on Colchis (on the east coast of the Black Sea).[63]

Pharasmanes' motives were patent. He disingenuously suggested that Alexander might campaign towards the Black Sea, in which case he would direct the expedition and supply provisions. Alexander, he hoped, would subjugate his western neighbours, and he would profit from the exercise. For all his painstaking homework, Pharasmanes' overtures failed to bear fruit. The summer of 328, when revolt was still endemic in western Sogdiana, was not the proper season for a prolonged campaign to the west, and, as Alexander himself ob-

---

[59] Bosworth, *HCA* i. 377–8 and *Topoi* 3 (1993) 409; *contra* G. Huxley, 'The Sogdian Tanais and Aristobulus', *BASP* 22 (1985) 117–21.

[60] On the silver fir see Strabo 11. 7. 4 (510) = Polycleitus, *FGrH* 128 F 7; Theophr. *HP* 4. 4. 1 (accepting the MS reading, as in the Budé edition). It was later found south of the river (Arr. 4. 21. 3) and also, as Eratosthenes sarcastically noted, it abounded in India (Strabo 11. 7. 4 (510); cf. Diod. 17. 89. 4). That was conceded by Aristobulus (Strabo 11. 7. 2 (509) = *FGrH* 139 F 19), who observed that the silver fir was non-existent in Hyrcania but prolific in India. Alexander's conviction that Europe began north of the Syr-Darya was shaken by subsequent discoveries, but in 328 it seems to have been intact.

[61] Curt. 7. 9. 15 (cf. *Metz Epit.* 12). Theophrastus describes the phenomenon at length at *HP* 4. 4. 1.

[62] Curt. 7. 6. 11–12 with Arr. 4. 1. 1–2; Curt. 8. 1. 7–8 with Arr. 4. 15. 1–3. Cf. Bosworth, *HCA* ii. 13–15.

[63] Arr. 4. 15. 4. In Stalinist times this passage was taken seriously and formed a basis for the theory of a 'Greater Chorasmia', straddling Central Asia from the Aral to the Black Sea (cf. S. P. Tolstov, *Auf den Spuren der alchoresmischen Kultur* (Berlin 1953) 119–20, followed by Altheim and Stiehl (above, n. 43) 187).

served, India was a more immediate concern. The overtures of Taxiles and the princes of the Cophen valley were more seductive,[64] and Pharasmanes had to content himself with a vague promise of invasion from west once Alexander had completed his conquest of Asia. This is an exotic episode, but it is retailed as fact by Arrian and derived from his narrative sources, Ptolemy and Aristobulus. What it attests beyond cavil is the interest the natives had in their invaders and their willingness to exploit their preconceptions. If the Macedonians wanted Amazons, then Pharasmanes would supply them in abundance. The price was military action to promote his own interests.

So far we have examined adaptations by the locals, who informed themselves of the interests of their conquerors and provided facts to satisfy or exploit those interests. In the hands of Pharasmanes deliberate misinformation could become a political tool. However, the misinformation might operate at more mundane levels. There was clearly a profitable trade in the skins of exotic animals, which the natives of the Punjab and Sind marketed in the Macedonian camp. Nearchus mentioned that he saw a tiger skin, but not the living animal, and cited local reports of the size and ferocity of the beasts.[65] These reports were exaggerated, implying that tigers had little difficulty disposing of elephants, but they were not without some factual basis—in that tigers can and do attack grown elephants. However, the same cannot be said of the 'ant' skins which Nearchus claims were brought into the Macedonian camp. These were the result of curious Macedonian enquiries about the sensational gold-digging ants, which according to Herodotus provided the Indians with their wealth. These fabulous beasts were somewhat larger than foxes and possessed an amazing turn of speed.[66] Not surprisingly the Macedonians made enquiries about them, not expecting to see live specimens, for Herodotus had located them in the extremities of

[64] Arr. 4. 15. 6. The vulgate tradition (Diod. 17. 86. 4; cf. Curt. 8. 12. 5; *Metz Epit.* 49) confirms that Taxiles had made overtures while Alexander was still in Sogdiana.

[65] Arr. *Ind.* 15. 1–3 = *FGrH* 133 F 7. Megasthenes was equally impressed by the size and aggressiveness of the Indian tiger (Strabo 15. 1. 37 (703) = *FGrH* 715 F 21a). On the accuracy of Nearchus' statement see Pearson, *LHA* 124 and H. H. Scullard, *The Elephant in the Greek and Roman World* (London, 1974) 54, both citing J. H. Williams, *Elephant Bill* (London 1955) 68.

[66] Hdt. 3. 102. 2. On the various modern rationalizations of the story, which fortunately do not concern us here, see K. Karttunen, *India in Early Greek Literature* 171–7.

India, in a vast northern desert. The Indians were unexpectedly obliging, and produced an array of hides which purported to be those of the outsize ants, spotted like leopard skins.[67] What Near- chus thought of these objects is beyond conjecture, but neither Arrian nor Strabo suggests that he doubted their authenticity. Megasthenes at least reported the mining operations of the ants in largely Herodotean terms,[68] and he seems to have considered Hero- dotus' account vindicated by Alexander's discoveries. The material evidence of the ant skins guaranteed the truth of the mining opera- tions, and the ants were recognized as a reality, no more exotic and incredible than the Indian tiger.

This is a relatively uncomplicated process. Alexander's men had certain fixed ideas and preconceptions which determined the ques- tions they asked of the peoples they encountered, and the interest of the locals lay in providing the answers most acceptable and attractive to the invaders. A more complex and interesting question is the invaders' interpretation of the cultures they encountered, in particu- lar the most alien and variegated culture of them all, that of India. Even from the limited evidence at our disposal it is clear that the Alexander historians described Indian society from their own perspective. They did not attempt to reproduce local terminology for the political and social institutions but provided Greek equivalences and clearly envisaged the society in Greek terms. The explanatory models used were Greek, and several of the most authoritative authors, notably Onesicritus and Megasthenes, were acquainted with current philosophical debate and tended to view India as a laboratory for social investigation. Current Indian social practices could be seen as exemplifications of Greek theoretical models. The model became a filter through which the raw observational data were selected and interpreted, and the literary record has inevitable Greek overtones.

Few subjects display this better than the question of Indian slavery in the time of Alexander. It seems clear from Indian sources that there was a broad spectrum of chattel slavery in India, ranging from forms of voluntary enslavement and debt slavery[69] to a type of rural slavery, in which slaves (*dāsas*) and semi-servile labourers (*karma-*

---

[67] Arr. *Ind.* 15. 4; Strabo 15. 1. 44 (705) = *FGrH* 133 F 8.

[68] Arr. *Ind.* 15. 5–7; Strabo 15. 1. 44 (706) = *FGrH* 715 F 23. Megasthenes at least admitted that his information was only hearsay (*Ind.* 15. 7).

[69] Details of the complicated system and the numerous categories may be found in the *Arthaśāstra* 3. 13. See further D. R. Chanana, *Slavery in Ancient India* 87–102.

karas) formed a common agrarian workforce.[70] However, slaves as such are not mentioned in the records of Alexander's campaigns, and there is even some suggestion that the Indians did not maintain slaves. Onesicritus considered the absence of slavery a peculiarity of the princedom of Musicanus in Upper Sind. Musicanus' capital was visited by Alexander in the spring of 325, and the king purportedly admired what he saw in the city and country.[71] Alexander's very temporary admiration was shared by Onesicritus, who described Musicanus' realm as a type of Utopia: its people enjoyed remarkable longevity and good health and lived in an egalitarian community.[72] Nature was sufficiently abundant in her gifts for Musicanus' people to enjoy the independence and wealth which Greek political theorists could only dream of. Accordingly they could live in a state of ideal bliss, and the absence of slavery was one of the standard features of the age of Cronus, that golden infancy of humanity.[73]

Onesicritus seems to have devoted some care to the remarkable phenomenon and described the forms of service in Musicanus' happy land. Unfortunately we have only Strabo's brief digest of his account,[74] and it is contracted to the point of unintelligibility. In fact he appears to have conflated two distinct institutions, one a tradition of the young assisting the old in domestic service and the other a form of rural serfdom comparable to that in Crete and Sparta. The first phenomenon was thought common to primitive societies. For Herodotus the daughters of the archaic Athenians had to draw

[70] R. S. Sharma, *Śūdras in Ancient India* 138–42; R. Thapar, *Aśoka and the Decline of the Mauryas*² 73, 89; U. Chakravarti 'Of Dasas and Karmakaras', in *Chains of Servitude: Bondage and Slavery in India* (ed. U. Patnaik, M. Dingwaney: New Delhi 1985) 35–75.   [71] Arr. 6. 16. 6–7; Diod. 17. 102. 5; Curt. 9. 8. 8–10.

[72] Onesicritus, *FGrH* 134 F 24. The fullest discussion is by T. S. Brown, *Onesicritus* 54–61. See also Pearson, *LHA* 102–3; Pédech, *Historiens compagnons* 114–23; A. Zambrini, *ASNP*³ 15 (1985) 839–41.

[73] There is a convenient review of evidence in J.Vogt, *Ancient Slavery and the Ideal of Man* (Oxford 1974) 26–38.

[74] Strabo 15. 1. 34 (701): Onesicritus made it one of the features of the land of Musicanus 'that they employ young men in their prime instead of slaves, as the Cretans make use of the Aphamiotae and the Spartans of the Helots'. The absurdity of the statement has been noted (e.g. Pearson, *LHA* 103 'The comparison...is not quite clear'; Pédech, *Historiens compagnons* 118): the Helots and Aphamiotae were not exclusively young men in their prime. The text has clearly suffered from abridgement. Onesicritus described two categories of quasi-slavery: young men were used in the place of slaves *and* there were rural serfs such as the Helots. These two categories have been conflated into a single comparison. Strabo may simply have been careless, but it is probably better to assume that a few words have dropped from the text: i.e. 'instead of slaves they use their young men ⟨and agrarian labourers⟩.'

water, because there were no domestic slaves, and, according to
Timaeus, the practice of youths performing domestic service for
their elders persisted in the backward areas of Phocis and Locris
until the fourth century BC.[75] This was quite distinct from rural
serfdom, which Onesicritus also purported to find in the land of
Musicanus. The analogies he draws from the Greek world, those of
the Aphamiotae in Crete and the Helots in Sparta, both representatives of the semi-servile groups classed between slaves and free.[76] In
Crete in particular the serfs had a restricted status in law, with some
access to the law courts, and no less an authority than Aristotle
commented that Cretan 'slaves' had the same rights as their masters,
apart from being excluded from the gymnasium and the profession
of arms.[77] The context of Aristotle's remark is instructive. It comes
in his critique of Plato's *Republic*, which raises the inherent difficulty
of keeping the agrarian mass of the population under control. That,
Aristotle argues, is impossible unless there is some device by which
the subjects associate themselves with their rulers, as was the case in
Crete. For Onesicritus the Indian subjects of Musicanus had found
a solution. They enjoyed a kind of commonwealth without the necessity of chattel slavery but with a docile serf class which identified
itself as part of the community.

What particular institutions inspired Onesicritus' description is
more difficult to define. One thing is certain. He had little time for
observation. As Alexander's head steersman he will have participated
in the general reception which Musicanus arranged for his conqueror, and stayed in Alexander's entourage while Craterus fortified
the citadel to serve as a regional garrison point. That will have entailed a stay of weeks rather than days, but afterwards Onesicritus
will have moved on with the fleet. He never returned and certainly
did not witness the punitive expedition which crushed an ill-judged
revolt and ended in the mass crucifixion of Musicanus and his

[75] Hdt. 6. 137. 3; Polyb. 12. 6. 7 = Timaeus, *FGrH* 566 F 11b; Athen. 6. 264 D =
Timaeus F11a. Cf. F. W. Walbank, *A Historical Commentary on Polybius* ii (Oxford
1967) 337–8, observing that Timaeus distinguishes bought chattel slaves from serf
populations. Timaeus is explicit that in Locris the young did menial service for the old
(Athen. 6. 264 D).

[76] Athen. 6. 263 F = Sosicrates, *FGrH* 461 F 4; Hesych. s.v. ἀφημιῶται. 'All the
evidence goes to show that the *aphamiotai* were the serfs of the Cretan countryside...who were considered part of the *klaroi*, the family estates' (R. F. Willetts,
Aristocratic Society in Ancient Crete (London 1955) 47).

[77] Arist. *Pol.* 2. 1264ᵃ20–22 (cf. 1269ᵃ39–40, commenting on the absence of serf
uprisings in Crete).

Brahman advisers.[78] He experienced the Utopia before it was turned to hell, and his observations were based on a brief, privileged stay, which became rose-tinted in retrospect. There is no reason to believe that Onesicritus ignored or discounted the fate of Musicanus and his people. The most admirable government may be liable to error, and in preferring autonomy to the regime of Alexander Musicanus blundered fatally. The punishment which ensued was therefore fully justified.[79] In the same way the Conquistadors admired aspects of Mexican civilization, while entertaining no qualms about its destruction.[80]

We may assume that chattel slavery was not much in evidence at Musicanus' court. We may even believe that in Musicanus' palace some non-polluting domestic functions were carried out by the younger high-caste men. The term *parivestr*, denoting a younger man who assists an elder, is attested in Ancient India, and the relationship may well have been common in Musicanus' princedom.[81] If so, Onesicritus will have seen or recalled it as an example of primitive virtue. Similarly with the serfs. Alexander and his staff may well have had a favourable impression of the *śūdras* on the land and interpreted their condition as identical to that of the serf classes in Greece—only these quasi-helots accepted their status and there was no internal tension. Onesicritus, then, observed the inferior position of the *śūdras* but apparently had no conception of the theory of caste which determined their inferiority. Instead he adduced a Greek model and represented the land of Musicanus as unique. What we have is an impressionistic description based on an idyllic, short-term visit, written up several years later with retrospective nostalgia. There is fact beneath Onesicritus' description, but it is informed by Greek theory and deployed to present a model of an ideal communistic society.[82]

---

[78] Arr. 6. 17. 1–2. See below, p. 96.

[79] For the general philosophy see below, Ch. 5.

[80] Bernal Díaz writes of Montezuma with a warm sympathy which borders on admiration, and refers back to the wonders of Tenochtitlan with nostalgic regret: 'all is overthrown and lost, nothing left standing' (p. 270 (Maudslay), p. 215 (Cohen)). However, there is no suggestion that he considered the overthrowing as anything other than justifiable, and indeed commendable.

[81] The evidence is cited by W. Rau, *Staat und Gesellschaft im Alten Indien nach den Brāhmana-Texten* 48.

[82] A similar idea underlies Hecataeus of Abdera's description of the regime of the Egyptian Pharaohs: their servants were not chattel slaves, but sons of the most distinguished of the priesthood (Diod. 1. 70. 2 = *FGrH* 264 F 25).

Onesicritus claimed that the absence of slavery was a peculiarity of the land of Musicanus,[83] which he depicted as utopian and necessarily atypical. Megasthenes, however, went further and made the blunt assertion that no Indian employed slaves. All three derivatives (Arrian, Strabo, and Diodorus) are in agreement, and Arrian in particular is categorical: 'all Indians are free, and no Indian is a slave.'[84] That is entirely wrong, and the misstatement is all the more curious in that Megasthenes was referring to the totality of Indian society, not to a single eccentric principality. What is more, Megasthenes traversed the entire subcontinent as far as Pātaliputra and saw more communities than Alexander's staff. If, then, he chose to deny the phenomenon of slavery, it would seem that he did not acknowledge Indian slaves as slaves ($\delta o \hat{v} \lambda o \iota$) in the Greek sense. He will have seen slaves in domestic and agrarian service, but did not view them as a separate class, unfree in the Greek sense. Rather they were so integrated into their society that they were not identifiable as a discrete element. Why that should have been his impression is a matter for conjecture. Possibly there was no hierarchical designation of slaves. They could come from any caste, and slave and free, particularly at the level of the field labourer, were often hard to differentiate. Nor was it true that a slave could be forced to do any work. In some cases slaves were dispensed from the menial and polluting tasks of handling corpses and excrement. That was the function of the casteless *candalas*, the untouchables proper,[85] who were technically free, in the sense that they were not owned, but were far below most domestic slaves in status. Caste was the overriding consideration, which determined what a person *did* in society. Slavery was less fundamental, and one's caste status was not destroyed by the loss of freedom. What is more, there was a prejudice against enslaving Āryans,[86] not dissimilar to the prejudice in the Greek world against enslaving Hellenes. An Indian might be born into slavery or sink into slavery through debt, but it was not accept-

---

[83] Strabo 15. 1. 54 (710) = *FGrH* 134 F 25: 'Onesicritus declares that this [sc. the absence of slavery] is peculiar to the Indians in the land of Musicanus' (cf. Brown (above, n. 72) 156 n. 41).

[84] Arr. *Ind.* 10. 8–9 = *FGrH* 715 F 16; cf. Strabo 15. 1. 54; Diod. 2. 39. 5.

[85] *Arthaśāstra* 3. 13. 9 (exemptions: 'employing a slave to carry the dead or to sweep ordure, urine, or the leavings of food...shall cause the forfeiture of the value paid for him or her'). On the *candalas* see Sharma (above, n. 70) 125–7.

[86] *Arthaśāstra* 3. 13. 7. At 3. 13. 4 the text is categorical: 'never shall an Ārya be subjected to slavery.'

able to force him into a servile status. All this *could* have come together in Megasthenes' mind and suggested the conclusion that there were no slaves in India, no single class which performed the functions of slaves in the Greek world. However, Megasthenes, like Onesicritus, was prone to idealize. He may not have seen Indian society as Utopian, as Musicanus' realm was for Onesicritus, but he certainly viewed it from the perspective of Greek theory, and the absence of slavery was the consequence of the hierarchical division of Indian society. All classes had their specific functions, and there was no place for a subordinate pool of slaves. It was the type of community envisaged in the first, primitive blueprint of Plato's *Republic*,[87] supported by an agricultural abundance which ruled out the necessity for chattel servitude.

The philosophical model emerges clearly from Megasthenes' famous sevenfold description of Indian society.[88] This is not an account of the caste system as such, and indeed it is debatable whether Megasthenes had any concept of caste. What he describes is the principle of exclusiveness which underlies and perpetuates caste, but he relates the exclusiveness to *occupation*. No person who professes one calling is permitted to practise another, or even use techniques borrowed from elsewhere.[89] This might almost be Plato prescribing for his own ideal community. In Plato the specialization is absolute. The premiss that no person may be master of several trades is developed into a prohibition. No one may practise any profession unless schooled to it from childhood, and the myth of the metals is specifically concocted to keep the classes separate.[90] The salvation of the city depends upon the rigid enforcement of specialization, and the very definition of justice is some form of 'this principle of sticking to one's own job'.[91] Indian society, as described by Megasthenes, looks at first sight like Plato in practice, with

---

[87] Plat. *Rep.* 2. 369b–372d.

[88] Arr. *Ind.* 11. 1–12. 9; Strabo 15. 1. 39–49 (703–7) = *FGrH* 715 F 19; Diod. 2. 40. 1–41. 5 = *FGrH* 715 F 4. The most helpful contributions to this much-debated passage are O. Stein, *Megasthenes und Kautilya* 119–232; B. Breloer, *ZDMG* 88 (1934) 130–63; Zambrini, *ASNP*[3] 15 (1985) 806–23; R. Thapar, *The Mauryas Revisited* 33–60.

[89] Arr. *Ind.* 12. 8; Strabo 15. 1. 49 (707); Diod. 2. 41. 5.

[90] The principle of specialization is omnipresent. See particularly *Rep.* 2. 374b–d for the exlusiveness of each profession, and for the myth of the metals *Rep.* 3. 414b–415c.

[91] *Rep.* 4. 433a–b. The analogy between Plato and Megasthenes is noted by Zambrini, *ASNP*[3] 15 (1985) 803–14.

warriors, farmers, and tradesmen rigidly separated. However, there is a fundamental distinction. Plato's state notoriously insisted upon a community of wives and children, so that one's position was determined not by birth but one's natural talents. Megasthenes' India preserved its specialization by strict endogamy. One could not marry outside one's clan, and (according to Arrian) that entailed remaining within one's specialization: a farmer could not marry into craftsman status, and vice versa.[92] This covers more than simply marriage within one's professional group. All three versions of Megasthenes refer to the clan ($\gamma \acute{\epsilon} vo\varsigma$), not the wider subdivision of profession ($\mu \acute{\epsilon} \varrho o\varsigma$), and it would seem that Megasthenes envisaged a society in which the professions were monopolized by extended family groups. Since marriage was confined to the extended family, it followed that professional specialization was perpetuated. The Platonic principle operated in a social context alien to the philosophy of Callipolis; there was nothing to prevent unworthy parents procreating, and the system could produce cowardly warriors or cack-handed craftsmen. Endogamy might perpetuate specialization, but it was no guarantee of excellence.

We have identified an instructive contradiction. Megasthenes was predisposed to recognize the principle of specialization, which he explained by Greek philosophical models. However, he was also aware of Indian marital exclusiveness and reported the phenomenon, subsuming it to the overriding principle of separation of occupation. It is difficult to be more specific. One might suspect that Megasthenes was aware of the great kinship groups (*gotras*) which underlay the basic division of caste and were manifested in elaborate

---

[92] Arr. *Ind.* 12. 8: 'it is not lawful to marry from another clan, for instance from the craftsmen to the farmers or vice versa, nor is it lawful for the same man to profess two trades.' Strabo and Diodorus essentially agree, except that they give no examples; they merely note the prohibition of exogamy and the practice of more than one trade. The illustration may well be Arrian's, and it helps to obscure the issue. Other sources make a clear distinction between the clan ($\gamma \acute{\epsilon} vo\varsigma$) and the professional grouping ($\mu \acute{\epsilon} \varrho o\varsigma$). Arrian uses the same word ($\gamma \acute{\epsilon} vo\varsigma$) for both. In a work which consciously evokes Herodotus in style and dialect he is naturally influenced by Herodotus' description of the exclusive sevenfold social grouping of Egypt (Hdt. 2. 164. 1) and borrows Herodotus' terminology ($\gamma \acute{\epsilon} vo\varsigma$) for the professional group. The literary borrowing is somewhat forced, and Arrian uses the same term for the wider and narrower group. The clan is envisaged as a subgroup of the professions; hence the principle of endogamy necessarily results in the exclusiveness of each of the larger groups.

patronymics.[93] As far as we can tell, intermarriage was not proscribed, and unions even between members of disparate castes could occur, but endogamy was sufficiently common to be mistakenly identified as a binding rule. Megasthenes might well have been aware of parallels with Greek clans such as the Bacchiads, where endogamy was the regular practice but in exceptional circumstances outsiders were admitted. He realized the basic fact that Indian society was hierarchically exclusive and tended to intermarriage, but failed to identify the basic condition of caste. Instead he fixed upon features such as clan and profession which had counterparts in the world he knew. What was typically Indian was overlooked or ignored.

The same is true of the distinction of profession. Megasthenes identified philosophers, farmers, herdsmen, tradesmen, warriors, spies, and senior officials. By and large this is a credible division. In some cases there were near enough Greek parallels. Megasthenes, it would seem, was aware of the two great councils of Indian monarchs, the exclusive Council of Ministers (*parisad*, meaning 'those who sit with the king') and the wider assembly of officials (*rāja-sabhā*), which is said to have numbered 500 in the time of Chandragupta's successor, Bindusāra.[94] These institutions were easily represented in Greek terms, and there were obvious counterparts in the Hellenistic courts. It came naturally to see these great councils as the recruiting ground of the high officers of state, and it was equally natural to give Greek equivalences for their functions. Other features of Indian life were sufficiently bizarre to attract the observer—the non-military rural populace which would proceed calmly with its work on the land, secure from injury even when caught in a battle,[95] and the ubiquitous informers, so numerous as to be defined as a class in their own right.[96] Megasthenes even singled out the role of prostitutes in

---

[93] Cf. Agrawala 92 (examples of exogamy cited at 86). For example of marriages between castes see Sharma (above, n. 70) 118–19.

[94] Cf. Agrawala 399–400, 403–4; G. M. Bongard-Levin, *Studies in Ancient India and Central Asia* (Calcutta 1971) 109–22. The Indian terms are said to correspond to the division 'advisers (σύμβουλοι) and councillors (σύνεδροι) of the king' (Strabo 15. 1. 49 (707); Diod. 2. 41. 4: 'the class which deliberates and participates with those who administer public affairs'; Arr. *Ind.* 12. 6: 'those who deliberate on public affairs along with the king'). It is by no means certain that Megasthenes distinguished two separate bodies of royal advisers. Strabo may simply be pleonastic, and be misrepresenting a description of a single pool of advisers who sat with the king and shared his counsel.

[95] Arr. *Ind.* 11. 10; cf. Strabo 15. 1. 40 (704), Diod. 2. 40. 4.

[96] Arr. *Ind.* 12. 5; Strabo 15. 1. 48 (707); Diod. 2. 41. 3. On this group see in

disclosing the confidences of their clients, a role which is attested at length in the *Arthaśāstra*. This was intriguing in its own right, and possibly evoked reminiscences of the downfall of Alexander's marshal, Philotas, which was materially assisted by the disclosures of his mistress, Antigone.[97]

Megasthenes reported what was intrinsically colourful and would appeal to his Greek readership. He also presented it in a framework which made sense to an educated Greek. The terminology of the sections (μέϱη) of the state is borrowed from contemporary theory, such as Aristotle's critique of the Milesian town planner, Hippodamus, who had visualized an ideal city 10,000 strong and divided into three sections: craftsmen, farmers, and the defence force.[98] In Megasthenes' India these sections are augmented to seven, the number of classes in Herodotean Egypt, and there are internal checks to prevent the predominance of the military, which Aristotle had identified as the fatal flaw in Hippodamus' system.[99] Megasthenes was not simply creating a theoretical model, and his sevenfold division does not seem to be based on Herodotus. Rather he arranged the data he observed in categories which were meaningful to his readers. Indian exclusiveness is explained in terms of specialization of occupation and expounded in terminology which evoked current Greek political thought. The hierarchy of caste with the inferior *śūdras* and the casteless untouchables was ignored. Neither Megasthenes nor any other Greek writer on India addressed the phenomenon. Indian society is consistently defined in Greek terms.

Alexander himself had obvious difficulties coming to terms with Indian society, and the peculiar status of the Brahmans was par-

---

particular Stein (above, n. 88) 169–75. Aśoka later referred to his 'reporters' (*pativedakas*) in his sixth Rock Edict (Thapar (above, n. 70) 252–3), insisting that they had immediate access to his person. Megasthenes' group of 'overseers' appears to correspond to the informers of the *Arthaśāstra*, and it comprises informants of every social level. It is, I think, a misapprehension when Thapar (above n. 88, 41) confines them to the senior administrators listed in Strabo 15. 1. 50. The other sources (Arr. *Ind.* 12. 7; Diod. 2. 41. 4) make it clear that these administrators are drawn from the élite seventh group of royal advisers. The sixth group of 'overseers' seems far more indiscriminate.

[97] *Arthaśāstra* 2. 25. 15, 27. 30; 5. 4. 27. Cf. Stein (above, n. 88) 145–6. For Antigone's role in the downfall of Philotas see Plut. *Al.* 48. 4–49. 1; *Mor.* 339d–f, with Heckel 26.

[98] Arist. *Pol.* 2: 1267^{b}22–69^{a}28, esp. 67^{b}30–7.

[99] Megasthenes' class of soldiers lives a life of institutionalized idleness, supported from public revenues at a high level of subsistence (Arr. *Ind.* 12. 4; Strabo 15. 1. 47 (707); Diod. 2. 41. 2). For Aristotle's critique see *Pol.* 2: 1268^{a}17–29.

ticularly vexatious for him. For some observers the Brahmans were equated with philosophical ascetics, such as the two whom Aristobulus met at Taxila. These men displayed strikingly different modes of behaviour. One followed Alexander for a short distance and returned home, refusing to have anything more to do with the Macedonian court. The other had no such scruples. He changed his dress and mode of life, and answered his critics with the assertion that he had completed his forty years of discipline.[100] That is apparently a reference to the first *aśrām*, the period of studentship and asceticism which preceded the Brahman's assumption of the duties of householder,[101] but it comes in a problematic context. Aristobulus' sage was a recognized teacher with a following of disciples, hardly a student (*brahmachārin*), and, since he had children, he had already discharged the functions of householder. The information is clearly garbled. Aristobulus perhaps misinterpreted some discourse on the various stages of Brahman discipline, and assumed that his unorthodox Brahman had fulfilled the prescribed period of asceticism.

For Aristobulus the Brahmans were philosophers, and they could differ radically in doctrine and practice. Nearchus, however, seems to have defined the Brahmans exclusively as the narrow circle of royal advisers: the rest of the 'sophists' were natural philosophers.[102] This resembles the distinction later made by Megasthenes, who separated Brahmans from other philosophers, but made it clear that the Brahmans were an extensive group which professed the entire range of philosophy, including metaphysics. For Nearchus they were confined to the royal counsellors. Both he and Aristobulus define the Brahmans by their calling, philosophers or counsellors. Neither seems to have grasped that the Brahmans formed a caste in their own right, the first of the *varnas*, and that Brahmans might be found

---

[100] Strabo 15. 1. 61 (714) = *FGrH* 139 F 41. Aristobulus did not name the Brahman sages, but it is clear that they must be distinguished from Calanus and Dandamis, whom Onescritus (Strabo 15. 1. 64 (715–16) = *FGrH* 134 F 34) and Megasthenes (Strabo 15. 1. 68 (718) = *FGrH* 715 F 34; cf. Arr. 7. 2. 2–4) portrayed as the most prominent philosophers in Taxila. The latter were obviously Brahmans, even though Strabo does not explicitly label them as such. For a general survey of the sources see now R. Stoneman, *JHS* 115 (1995) 99–114.

[101] See, conveniently, Agrawala 81–2, 280–1. In this respect Megasthenes was far more informed; he identified the period of studentship (of 37 years' duration) and recognized that the student afterwards returned to secular life (Strabo 15. 1. 59 (712) = *FGrH* 715 F 33; cf. Stoneman (above, n. 100) 105–6).

[102] Strabo 15. 1. 66 (716) = *FGrH* 133 F 23.

in a broad spectrum of occupations. They were scholars, philosophers, and priests, but also might serve as regular troops. The stress on occupation obscured appreciation of caste.

This misconception had serious consequences. At first Alexander showed a polite interest in Brahman philosophy and annexed Calanus to his court as an exotic species of sophist.[103] Whether he equated philosophers with Brahmans is uncertain. He was presumably aware of the name and its association with study, but its precise connotations are unlikely to have been clarified. During Alexander's first year in India no friction is recorded between the Brahmans and their Macedonian conquerors. That happy situation changed abruptly early in 325. One of the many horrific episodes in the Malli campaign was an attack on a 'city of the Brahmans', which offered fierce resistance. The results were predictable. The city was taken by storm and there followed a blood bath in which the defenders either died fighting or cremated themselves in their houses. Arrian notes specifically that there were few survivors.[104] We cannot know what Arrian's source meant when it referred to the city of the Brahmans. The whole population can hardly have consisted of Brahmans, but Brahmans may have been particularly numerous there and could even have contributed warriors to the army—the *Arthaśāstra* emphasizes the bravery of Brahman troops.[105] Because of their dominance the Brahmans may even have been equated with the populace at large. If we may extrapolate from Diodorus, that was the view of Cleitarchus, who apparently described the realm of Sambus in western Sind as populated by 'the nation (ἔθνος) of Brahmans', and the city of Harmatelia is defined as a Brahman city.[106] For Cleitarchus Brahman became an inclusive, quasi-national nomenclature.

For all his interest in Brahman philosophers Alexander made no exception for Brahmans when it came to punitive action. 'The city of the Brahmans' which resisted him in the Malli lands was treated with the ferocity he displayed to the other recalcitrant communities.

---

[103] Arr. 7. 2. 3 (Megasthenes, *FGrH* 715 F 34b); cf. Strabo 15. 1. 68 (717), 64 (715) = *FGrH* 134 F 17a. Plut. *Al.* 65.5 alleges that it was the local ruler, Taxiles, who persuaded Calanus to join Alexander. On the tradition surrounding Calanus see Berve ii. 187–8, no. 396; R. Stoneman, *CQ* 44 (1994) 505–6. I shall address the matter more fully in a forthcoming paper.   [104] Arr. 6. 7. 4–6. See below, Ch. 5.

[105] *Arthaśāstra* 9. 2. 21–3. They could, however, be overinclined to clemency.

[106] Diod. 17. 102. 7, 103. 1; cf. Curt. 9. 8. 13–15, explicitly citing Cleitarchus (*FGrH* 137 F 25). Cf. J. R. Hamilton, in *Greece and the E. Med.* 133–5; Hammond, *Three Historians* 66–7.

There was indiscriminate slaughter, and the Brahman defenders died *en masse*. That was a miscalculation. Alexander had witnessed the veneration shown to the Brahman ascetics at Taxila, but he can hardly have realized the privileged position of the entire caste of Brahmans. Even under the Draconian penal code of the Mauryas they were explicitly exempted from torture and capital punishment,[107] and their position was buttressed by penal laws against the lower castes: a *śūdra* striking a Brahman would lose the offending limb.[108] In that social context the slaughter among the Malli was profoundly shocking: even Brahmans were butchered indiscriminately by the invader. The effect was immediate. We have a new phenomenon attested in the Indian campaign—the revolt of communities after subjugation. Before the Malli campaign there had been resistance aplenty, but once the resistance was crushed, there was no secondary rebellion, except in the Swāt valley—and that occurred only when Alexander and his army were far removed.[109] However, in Lower Sind capitulation was grudging and rebellion immediate. Musicanus surrendered only when Alexander's armada appeared on his borders, and he revolted soon after the invaders left his realm, encouraged, we are told, by his Brahman advisers.[110] His neighbour, Sambus, the ruler of the mountain territory to the west, was also reluctant to surrender, in part because of the favourable treatment of his enemy, Musicanus.[111] Sambus fled in the face of invasion, and, although his family offered homage to the conqueror, the cities in his realm were slow to acquiesce. Arrian mentions one city which revolted and was captured by storm; and the vulgate tradition, derived from Cleitarchus, tells of a general massacre involving 'very many' cities and 80,000[112] deaths. In both cases the instigators and the most notable victims of the revolt are said to have been Brahmans. Alexander punished resistance with his usual

---

[107] Cf. *Arthaśāstra* 4. 8. 27–9 (a Brahman excluded from torture: at worst branded and exiled); 4. 11. 11–12 (even for high treason, where the normal penalty was death by torture, a Brahman was blinded(?)).

[108] *Arthaśāstra* 3. 19. 8; cf. Sharma (above, n. 70) 161–2. Defilement of the kitchen of a Brahman was punished by excision of the tongue (4. 11. 21).

[109] Arr. 5. 20. 7 (after the Hydaspes). Cf. Bosworth, *HCA* ii. 321–2.

[110] Arr. 6. 15. 6–7 (surrender); 6. 17. 1 (revolt).

[111] Arr. 6. 16. 3–4. The relationship between Musicanus and Sambus is reminiscent of that between the two Poruses in the Punjab (Arr. 5. 21. 2–3); the submission of the one guaranteed the enmity of the other.

[112] Arr. 6. 16. 5; Diod. 17. 102. 6–7; cf. Curt. 9. 8. 13–15.

repressive methods. We need not doubt that there was significant slaughter of Brahmans in Sambus' territories, and the Brahman advisers of Musicanus were treated in exemplary fashion. They were crucified alongside their lord in his capital.[113] In Indian eyes this was an abomination. It was greeted with horror and terror. The ruler of Patala, at the head of the Indus delta, offered unconditional submission well before Alexander reached his land, and he and his subjects then fled in the face of the invasion, leaving the capital and its hinterland deserted.[114] It took considerable diplomacy to tempt the natives back to their domiciles, and Alexander certainly did not win their hearts and minds.[115] Once he was safely away to the west, in Las Bela and the Makran, Nearchus found himself virtually under siege in his naval base, and was forced out to sea prematurely.[116] Southern Sind had become hostile territory in a matter of months.

Alexander's treatment of the Brahmans had been singularly unfortunate. The massacre in the Malli city created a resistance among the Brahmans generally, and the ensuing repression which saw systematic execution of Brahmans can only have caused abhorrence and rejection. We do not have the evidence to elucidate his policy or his understanding of Indian social conditions. It is clear, however, that he had at least one informant close at hand—the Brahman sage, Calanus, who remained at court and apparently in favour throughout the repression in the south. Even if he did not explain the intricacies of caste (a formidable task through interpreters), he could have emphasized the reverence of the person of the Brahmans and their privileged status. That in itself may have been sufficient for Alexander to order the exemplary executions of Musicanus' advisers. Nothing could show better the frightful consequences of rejecting his rule, and, as we have seen, the inhabitants of Patalene were appropriately intimidated. But the terror was only effective while Alexander and his army were in the vicinity. His satrap, Peithon, did not have the resources for systematic repres-

---

[113] Arr. 6. 17. 1–2; cf. Curt. 9. 8. 16.

[114] Arr. 6. 17. 2, 5–6; Curt. 9. 8. 28–9; cf. Berve ii. 265, no. 536.

[115] According to Curtius (9. 8. 29) he overran the countryside, commandeering vast quantities of livestock and grain. That somewhat undermined the guarantee to the inhabitants that they could work their land as before (Arr. 6. 17. 6). They would have to, for there was nothing left!

[116] Strabo 15. 2. 5 (721) = *FGrH* 133 F 1(a). See below, p. 177.

sion,[117] and the Indians' loathing and resentment soon overcame their fear.

It remains probable that the Macedonians never appreciated what it meant to be a Brahman. They identified them as 'sophists' and recognized a privileged group of royal advisers, who for Nearchus were the Brahmans proper. They also seem to have realized that there was a wider population of Brahmans and defined cities and countries as peculiarly theirs. What they never seem to have isolated was the caste system which guaranteed that there would be Brahmans everywhere, a privileged class within the community, providing ascetics, philosophers, counsellors, and householders. Certain facets were recorded and appreciated because they could relate to Greek experience—the profession of the sophist or the royal council, but the perspective was always Hellenocentric. That was inevitable. Alexander and his men were less than two years in the Indus valley, encountering a bewildering number of communities and a totally different social system. There was no time to reach an informed sociological synthesis, and for all their curiosity about the local conditions Alexander's men could only set the details in the framework they knew. Consequently misunderstandings abounded. At best relations between conquerors and conquered were awkward and fumbling. At worst, as with his treatment of the Brahmans, Alexander rode rough-shod over the deepest sensitivities of his new subjects. We can hardly wonder that the conquest was not lasting.

[117] Even before Alexander's death, it would seem, Peithon was transferred to Gandhāra and Porus' nominal realm was extended to the Southern Ocean. Cf. Bosworth, *Antichthon* 17 (1983) 37–46, esp. 42–5; Heckel 324–5.

4
The Creation of Belief

THE complex process of interaction with the conquered peoples produced more than information. It had a direct impact on Alexander's view of his kingship and personal divinity. It can, I think, be shown that his staff conveniently reinterpreted local legends and integrated them into Greek mythology. Conversely the native peoples supplied information which they thought would attract the interest and approval of their conquerors. The result was a growing conviction in Alexander's mind that he was following in the footsteps of Heracles and (still more) Dionysus. This conviction was nurtured by the circumstances of campaigning. What can hardly be over-stressed is the cultural isolation of Alexander and his staff, particularly in the period of the Sogdian and Indian campaigns. It was not merely that he was further from the Mediterranean than any western army had ever penetrated, not merely that he was surrounded by culturally alien peoples with whom he could communicate only through interpreters—in some instances relays of interpreters.[1] For long periods he was isolated from his own headquarters and the coterie of Greek intellectuals which had followed him to Central Asia. For weeks or even months his companions were his troops and immediate staff, and the range of perspectives available to him was limited. It would hardly be surprising if his thinking lacked balance and took directions which appear bizarre to modern minds.[2]

---

[1] For interpreters in India see above, Ch. 1, n. 20; Ch. 3, n. 24. Difficulties were comparable in Sogdiana, where we hear of at least one specialist interpreter, Pharnuches of Lycia (Arr. 4. 3. 7). Despite the similarities between the Iranian languages of Persis, Bactria, and Sogdiana (Strabo 15. 2. 8 (724)) the regional variations were sufficiently complex to require specialist linguists (cf. Bosworth, *HCA* ii. 24–5). On the functions and status of Alexander's interpreters see in general P. R. Franke, in *Zum Umgang mit fremden Sprachen in der griechisch-römischen Antike*, ed. C. W. Müller, K. Sier, and J. Werner 85–96.

[2] There is a tendency to focus on the various themes outside their historical context. Deification has been a prime instance. It is easy to concentrate upon the reported details of the banquet at Maracanda or the *proskynesis* debate and dismiss them individually as fictitious, based on supposedly late and unreliable sources (George

The events of 328 make an interesting study. For the year's campaigning Alexander left much of his court at the satrapal capital of Bactra together with some at least of the corps of pages.[3] The Sogdian revolt was still at its height, and the army was divided into a number of campaign groups. The main force Alexander himself led eastwards from Bactra to suppress pockets of resistance south of the Oxus.[4] Then he crossed the river to take the campaign deep into Sogdiana. His forces were already dispersed. Four of the phalanx commanders had been left to continue operations in Bactria, and Craterus seems to have had a regional command in the vicinity of the capital.[5] This was the outcome of the policy of containment which had been evolved the previous year. Even the army which crossed the Oxus did not operate as a whole. It was split into no less than five columns, which then took separate routes through eastern Sogdiana.[6] None of them can have been particularly large, Alexander's group included, and the staff around him would have been sorely depleted. The spring and summer saw a succession of arduous siege operations, notably the epic scaling of the 'Sogdian Rock',[7] conducted in harsh and unforgiving terrain where the summer temperatures regularly exceed 40°C. Occasionally the dispersed army groups came together, and there was an interlude of relaxation and inebriation. The most famous took place at Maracanda (Samarkand) during the late summer of 328.[8] First Alexander led a

---

Cawkwell's recent essay, 'The Deification of Alexander', in *Ventures into Greek History* 293–306, esp. 296–7, is a case in point). What seems to me more important is the consistency of the source tradition, which documents a developing process of assimilation to the divine. The ideological milieu encouraged the recognition of outstanding achievement by divine honours, and the continuing success of the expedition, often in the most hellish conditions, was an ever accumulating proof of the superhuman qualities of the leader.

[3] Arr. 4. 16. 6 (cf. Bosworth, *HCA* ii. 116).

[4] Arr. 4. 15. 7; Curt. 7. 10. 13–15; *Metz Epit.* 14. On the interpretation adopted here see Bosworth, *JHS* 101 (1981) 23–9; *HCA* ii. 108–10; *contra* P. Bernard, *JS* (1982) 129–32.

[5] Arr. 4. 16. 1 (phalanx commanders); 4. 17. 1, Curt. 8. 1. 6 (Craterus).

[6] Arr. 4. 16. 2–3; Curt. 8. 1. 1. The source tradition is complex and reconstruction difficult (cf. Bosworth, *HCA* ii. 112–14).

[7] Placed in summer 328 by the vulgate narrative (Curt. 7. 11. 1–9; *Metz Epit.* 15–18; Diod. 17 index κε), in winter 328/7 by Arrian 4. 18. 4—19. 4. The tradition is tangled (Bosworth, *HCA* ii. 124–7), but the exact chronology does not affect the interpretation of the campaign.

[8] The date is certain. Curtius (8. 1. 19–2. 12) places the episode in the context of the campaign, in the summer halt at Maracanda (so Diod. 17 index κζ). Arrian's extended account is explicitly divorced from its context in the campaign narrative (4.

royal hunt at the great Persian game sanctuary of Bazaira, and then hosted a symposium in the citadel of Maracanda. The entire staff participated. Under the liberating influence of Dionysus the tensions of war relaxed, and some deep-seated passions were released. In a celebrated altercation Cleitus the Black, the commander of the Companion cavalry, abused his king and was killed, impaled by a Macedonian pike (*sarisa*) at the height of the carousing.

The symposium at Maracanda was a rare occasion at which a majority of the officers were assembled. There was also a spicing of Greek intellectuals. The prototype sceptic, Anaxarchus of Abdera, was certainly present, as perhaps was Alexander's court historian, Callisthenes. In the atmosphere of the feast all the themes which had featured in camp-fire discussions[9] over the past months came together in what proved to be an explosive combination. The sources offer different perspectives on the banquet conversation, but there is a measure of agreement over the matters which detonated the quarrel. Its context was the prevailing gross flattery which had come to dominate Alexander's court, as it later did the court of Demetrius. The king's achievements were eulogized and compared favourably with those of his father, Philip, and even those of the gods. He had won the Battle of Chaeronea and saved his father's life;[10] and his career had been uninterrupted glory in sharp contrast to Philip and his own officers, who had come to grief the previous summer in the Zeravshan valley and more recently in the vicinity of Bactra.[11] Alexander was invincible and godlike, surrounded by men who were

---

8. 1, 14. 4), but he makes it clear that the symposium took place at a palace complex, whose description corresponds with the actual site at Maracanda (4. 8. 9 = Aristobulus, *FGrH* 139 F 23; cf. Curt. 7. 6. 10 with Bosworth, *HCA* ii. 23; Bernard, *CRAI* (1990) 368–9).

[9] Such discussions are not recorded, but they must have taken place. The sources record flattering apophthegms evoked by the circumstances of the campaign, notably Dioxippus' famous essay in flattery (below, p. 114) and the even grosser *mot* of Nicesias on the invincibility of the flies which sucked Alexander's blood (Athen. 6. 249 D–E). There is of course no record of the private comments of the troops, but they are likely to have been pungent. Compare Arrian's description of the impromptu meetings before the Hyphasis 'mutiny' (5. 25. 2).

[10] Curt. 8. 1. 24–5. The episode cannot be dated, but it is unlikely to be fictitious. Denigration of Philip is also attested by Arr. 4. 8. 6 and Justin 12. 6. 2 and presupposed in Plut. *Al.* 50. 11.

[11] Plut. *Al.* 50. 8 alleges that there were recitations of poems lampooning the generals defeated by the barbarians. The allusion may simply be to the defeat at the Zeravshan in mid-329, but news may also have broken of the less than glorious defence of Bactra against Spitamenes and his nomads (Curt. 8. 1. 3–6; Arr. 4. 16. 4–17. 1; cf. Bosworth, *HCA* ii. 114–15).

all too fallible and mortal. That was the burden of the flattery, and it probably resumed any number of comments made casually in the recent past. Cleitus acted from pent-up exasperation. His irritation at court flattery was well known,[12] and once his grievances overcame his prudence, weakened as it was by inebriation, they were articulated with a fluency which came from long mental rehearsal. The devastating quotation from Euripides' *Andromache*, in which Alexander's ancestor, Peleus, criticizes the pretensions of the generals of the Panhellenic war, is not likely to have been an improvisation.[13] Its sour indictment of the exploitation of the rank-and-file was apposite and ironical in a play which celebrated the lineage of Olympias and Alexander,[14] and it may have been widely quoted among disgruntled observers of the royal cult of personality. The same applies to Cleitus' reminder that he had saved Alexander's life at the Granicus. It was a sharp riposte to the king's adventurous claim that he had done the same for Philip, and at the same time it was a boast which (not surprisingly) Cleitus had often made in the past.[15] The criticism came almost as an automatic reflex in the overheated atmosphere of the symposium.

For our purposes the most important element of the flattery is the comparison between Alexander and the divine. It centred on the figures of Heracles and the Dioscuri, all of whom had divine and human paternity and achieved divinity through their exploits on earth. The status of Heracles as hero god was well established, and Xenophon had stated explicitly that the Dioscuri had been elevated to immortality because of their nobility of soul,[16] as had Heracles himself. That was the context of the discussion at the symposium.

---

[12] Arr. 4. 8. 4; Plut. *Al.* 51. 1.

[13] Plut. *Al.* 50. 8, citing Eur. *Andr.* 693. The content of the following lines is paraphrased by Curtius 8. 1. 29, and Arr. 4. 8. 5 summarizes the tenor of Cleitus' criticism. The quotation is placed at different stages in the quarrel by Plutarch and Curtius, who evidently draw upon different sources, and it was clearly a standard item in the tradition. See further Aymard, *Études d'histoire ancienne* 51–7; H. U. Instinsky, *Historia* 10 (1961) 251–5.

[14] Eur. *Andr.* 1243–52 has Thetis prophesy the future of the Molossian line of kings, an unbroken succession from Neoptolemus and Andromache. This celebration of Alexander's Aeacid lineage (cf. Arr. 4. 11. 6) was presumably known and quoted at court.   [15] Arr. 4. 8. 6; Plut. *Al.* 50. 11.

[16] Xen. *Symp.* 8. 29; Chrysippus (*SVF* ii. 300. 31–3, F 1009) placed the Dioscuri alongside Heracles and Dionysus in the category of mortals who achieved divinity through their benefactions (διὰ τὰς εἰς τὸν κοινὸν βίον εὐεργεσίας: cf. Diod. 1. 13. 5 = Hecataeus, *FGrH* 264 F 25). That is precisely the thinking of Alexander's flatterers at Maracanda and Bactra.

It was held after a formal sacrifice to the Dioscuri.[17] Now the Dioscuri are hardly prominent among the deities honoured by Alexander, and the sacrifice itself seems slightly inappropriate. Landlocked Sogdiana was hardly the place to honour deities whose main function was the preservation of mariners.[18] In view of this it would seem that the sacrifice was intended as a cue to the courtiers at the symposium. It introduced discussion of the parentage of the Dioscuri and their somewhat questionable activities on earth.[19] From the viewpoint of benefactions to humanity their record was not particularly impressive. Alexander's credentials as a god among men far outweighed theirs. He could in fact be favourably compared with Heracles, and there was an obvious conclusion to be drawn. The king should here and now be given the honours appropriate to a god.

The discussion of the Dioscuri is a theme unique to Arrian.[20] It was not taken from Aristobulus, who (so Arrian informs us) was

---

[17] Arr. 4. 8. 2; Plut. *Al.* 50. 7. For Arrian the sacrifice was a chance thought of Alexander's ('some reason or other had caused him to think of the sacrifice'), and there is nothing to suggest any prior concern with the Dioscuri. It is most probable that the sacrifice was inspired by a local cult of twin deities who resembled the Greek Dioscuri, much as the Iranian Verethragna recalled Heracles. At least the cult enjoyed a vogue in Bactria during the 2nd century BC, when the Dioscuri figure as the predominant type in the coinage of the great ruler Eucratides I (*c.*166–135; for the chronology see A. Hollis, *ZPE* 104 (1994) 277–8 with Pl. VI(g)). Excavations at the great oasis complex of Dilberdjin, 40 km. north-east of Balkh (Bactra), have revealed a temple of the Dioscuri, complete with frescoes of the deities, which was founded around 150 BC (I. Kruglikova, *CRAI* (1977) 407–27). The cult existed alongside the worship of Heracles, Athena (in the guise of Anahita), and even the Indian god Śiva. Given the general tendency to syncretism, it is only too likely that the Dioscuri had a native counterpart.

[18] That is the aspect most stressed in the literature: *hHom.* 33. 6–17; Theocr. 22. 8–22; Alcaeus F 109 (Page, OCT).

[19] The Dioscuri were an embarrassment to Theocritus, who could not condone their forced abduction of the daughters of Leucippe. As is pointed out, they acted in a most improper way for heroes (Theocr. 22. 154–5; cf. A. S. F. Gow, *Theocritus* (Cambridge 1950) ii. 383–4). The story was in vogue by the early 5th century, when it formed one of the subjects of Polygnotus' paintings (Paus. 1. 18. 1), and it was well adapted to Alexander's flatterers. His ostentatiously scrupulous treatment of Darius' womenfolk contrasted favourably with the brutal and cavalier behaviour of the Dioscuri. The alternative story retailed by Pindar (*Nem.* 10. 60–72) is scarcely more complimentary; there is no reference to abduction, but the quarrel with the Apharetidae arises from a rather sordid cattle theft.

[20] Arr. 4. 8. 2–3. According to Curtius (8. 5. 8) the Dioscuri were mentioned later at the symposium at Bactra, where they take second place to Alexander the *novum numen*. The theme may have been familiar in popular rhetoric. The second discourse *On Fortune* ascribed to Dio Chrysostom claims that Alexander 'despised the Dioscuri and abused Dionysus' (D.Chr. 64. 20)—a reference to the adverse comparisons of the flatterers at Maracanda and Bactra.

silent about the quarrel which preceded the killing.[21] However, there is nothing in Arrian's exposition which suggests that he was drawing on the late secondary tradition or that Ptolemy omitted the episode.[22] He worked up the story from at least two sources (other than the variant Aristobulus), and they could well be contemporaries of the event—Ptolemy, Chares, or even Nearchus. The other extant sources provide indirect corroboration. Plutarch confirms that the symposium was preceded by a sacrifice to the Dioscuri,[23] and he and Curtius agree that Cleitus criticized Alexander's claim to divine paternity: if he masqueraded as son of Zeus Ammon, it was an affront to Philip, a renunciation of sonship, and, seen in some lights, his human father's achievements surpassed his own.[24] That amounts to a direct contradiction of the message of the flatterers. Alexander was no god manifest, eclipsing all previous triumphs of god and man, but the mortal son of a greater father and the exploiter of the troops whose devotion had won him his victories. The negative of Cleitus' critique coheres with Arrian's account of the court flattery. What Alexander was claiming (and his courtiers were maintaining) was superhuman status. He was son of Zeus and a god in his own right, having proved himself by unique and superhuman achievements. Cleitus denied it all, and died for doing so.

The death of Cleitus marked an epoch. The murder was chilling evidence that Alexander saw himself as unique, and reacted violently to candid criticism from his intimates. Its sequel was, if anything, more ominous. There is general agreement that Alexander's first reaction to the killing was bitter chagrin and self-reproach. He had butchered the brother of his wet-nurse, the man who had notori-

---

[21] Arr. 4. 8. 9 = *FGrH* 139 F 29.

[22] Arrian gives no indication that the episode is a *logos*, included only for interest's sake. He begins with a frank admission that the narrative is chronologically displaced and continues in indirect statement, breaking dramatically into direct speech at 4. 8. 8. The mode of introduction in the first person ('it will be pertinent for me to relate') hardly implies that the ensuing narrative has some special status (Hammond, *Sources* 240). The closest parallel is the beginning of Nearchus' ocean voyage (*Ind.* 19. 9–20. 2), where Arrian excuses himself from recording the exploits of Alexander in India and states that his theme is Nearchus' voyage (ὁ δὲ λόγος τοῦ παράπλου μοι ἀφήγησις ἔστω); he then digests Nearchus' account in indirect speech before reverting to direct statement at *Ind.* 21. 1. The construction of the Cleitus episode is similar. Arrian apologizes for interrupting the temporal sequence, and continues with the narrative from his sources. For the intricacies of the analysis see Bosworth, *HCA* ii. 52, 60–1.

[23] Plut. *Al.* 50. 7, agreeing that the sacrifice preceded the banquet.

[24] Plut. *Al.* 50. 11; Curt. 8. 1. 42, cf. 30–7 with Arr. 4. 8. 6.

ously saved his life at the Granicus. Whether or not he was overtaken by drunken remorse at the scene of the crime must remain in doubt.[25] It is, however, certain that he buried himself in his tent in an agony of conscience, and remained there for perhaps three days.[26] On any consideration this was irrational behaviour. All members of the expedition, whatever their nationality or social status, had an interest in recalling the king to his normal emotional condition. The troops are said to have convened a meeting and condemned Cleitus retrospectively.[27] They would have denied him burial, had not Alexander specifically ordered it. The rank-and-file countenanced the murder and did what they could to legalize it. Their vote would have given the king some comfort and support, even if it had no standing in law.

Justification at a more abstract, moral level was provided by the philosopher Anaxarchus, who chose an ostentatiously sarcastic and provocative address.[28] In his remorse, so Anaxarchus maintained, the king had adopted the posture of a slave, contradicting his real status as master of the universe. Alexander himself was living law, the exemplification of the parable of Hesiod, who represented Dike (Justice) as the companion (πάρεδρος) of Zeus.[29] Everything which was done by Zeus was by definition just, and the same applied to temporal kings, who were the vicegerents of Zeus on earth. This was a breathtaking vindication of autocracy. Kings (or at least universal kings) were the representatives of Zeus and, like Zeus, enjoyed unrestricted power. Not only was their power absolute; they created the norms of morality, and what they did was *ipso facto* just. This is the ultimate extension of Thrasymachus' cynical premiss (in Book I of Plato's *Republic*) that justice is the right of the stronger. In itself

---

[25] Arr. 4. 9. 2 (a variant); Plut. *Al.* 51. 11, *Mor.* 449e; Curt. 8. 2. 4; Justin 12. 6. 8. On the tradition see Bosworth, *HCA* ii. 63–4.

[26] So Arr. 4. 9. 4 (majority tradition); Curt. 8. 2. 10; Justin 12. 6. 8. Plutarch (*Al.* 52. 2) has a night of weeping and a day of lamentation until Alexander loses his voice.

[27] Curt. 8. 2. 12; cf. E. Badian, *Studies in Greek and Roman History* 198; R. M. Errington, *Chiron* 8 (1978) 108; *History of Macedonia* 109. For the invocation of the wrath of Dionysus, which gave a religious vindication of the murder, see below p. 121.

[28] The episode receives similar and overlapping treatment from Arrian 4. 9. 7–8 and Plutarch (*Al.* 52. 3–7; cf. *Mor.* 781a–b). There is clearly a common source. The scene of consolation is attested in other traditions. Justin 12. 6. 17 agrees with Plutarch that Callisthenes played a role, but says nothing of Anaxarchus. That may be one of Justin's all too frequent errors of contraction.

[29] Hes. *Erg.* 255–60. For the literary development of the theme see M. L. West's commentary *ad loc.* with Bosworth *HCA* ii. 67.

the little sermon of Anaxarchus might be thought trivial, but it cleverly encapsulates a tradition of political thought and reinforces a line of argument which must have been familiar to Alexander.

Anaxarchus' arguments are prefigured in the political theory compiled by Aristotle. There was clearly some intellectual sympathy for the idea of absolute monarchy in which the king was the canon and the interpreter of law. The theory arose from the deficiencies of statute law. In democracies or aristocracies legislation can only cover the general case: the many exceptions cannot be accommodated except by waiving the letter of the law, or in some instances reversing it.[30] The necessary supervision can only occur when there is an intelligent, educated monarch to monitor and correct the generality of the existing laws. For Plato in the *Politicus* the best dispensation was when 'the royal individual with practical intellect' enjoyed ultimate authority over the laws, and the principle, Aristotle claims, had some vogue in contemporary thought. Some believed it more advantageous to be ruled by the best man than by the best laws.[31] The ideal monarch will therefore have a grasp of the general principle underlying the law but will also have sufficient intelligence and experience to recognize the proper exceptions to the universal rule. That was the ideal. Harsh reality surfaces in Hypereides' Funeral Oration, delivered in the year after Alexander's death. Human happiness depends upon the primacy of the voice of law, not the caprice of a despot and the calumnies of his flatterers.[32] For the advocates of insurgency against Macedon Alexander was wilful and arbitrary, an object lesson in the dangers of monarchy.

Aristotle's ideal ruler was of course the concept underlying the flattery at Alexander's court. The form of government which such an individual would uphold is termed absolute kingship ($\pi\alpha\mu\beta\alpha\sigma\iota\lambda\epsilon\acute{\iota}\alpha$).[33] Though rare, the word has a distinct pedigree. The lyric poets,

---

[30] The main discussion is at *Pol.* 3. 1286[a] 8–26. Aristotle refers to the problem of the generality of the law at *NE* 5. 1137[b]13–33, and describes the virtue of *epieikeia*, which modifies the strict provision of the law according to circumstances. Here he does not see absolute monarchy as a prerequisite; decrees of a democracy ($\psi\eta\phi\acute{\iota}\sigma\mu\alpha\tau\alpha$) can perform the necessary adjustments. However, in the *Politics* he makes it clear that there was a school of thought which considered absolute monarchy the only solution (*Pol.* 1286[a]10, 1287[b]21–2).

[31] Plat. *Polit.* 294a (cf. 295d–e, 300c). Cf. Arist. *Pol.* 3. 1287[b]19–22 for the question 'whether it is preferable for the best law to rule or the best man'.

[32] Hyper. 6 (*Epitaph.*). 25.

[33] Arist. *Pol.* 3. 1285[b]30–4, 1287[a]9–11 ('this is the regime under which the king rules all men according to his will'); 4. 1295[a]18.

Alcaeus and Stesichorus, used it to describe the absolute kingship of Zeus, and in his *Clouds* Aristophanes twice applies it satirically to the divinities who were replacing Zeus in the Brave New World of rationalist philosophy.[34] Although he does not say so directly, Aristotle envisages the absolute king as the earthly counterpart of Zeus. The situation, he stresses, only occurs when a single person eclipses all the rest in virtue (ἀρετή), so that his excellence outweighs the totality of the rest of the community.[35] The man of outstanding virtue is a particular concern of Aristotle. If an individual is endowed with surpassing excellence, then it becomes absurd for him to be subjected to the norms of the community, for he would be like a god among men.[36] Conversely, if it can be shown that an individual (or individuals) stands out from the rest as gods and heroes stand out from mortals, then it is better for him to rule without constraint.[37] Moral excellence now becomes the defining criterion of absolute monarchy. The king must be genuinely outstanding, with the mental power to judge when to override the generality of the laws and the moral courage to act without fear or favour. Because of his virtue laws cannot be sensibly applied to him, for he himself is law.[38] This concept of the ruler as the embodiment of law had some literary antecedents. Xenophon's Cyrus considered the good ruler to be 'seeing law' because of his power to give direction and dispense punishment, and endeavoured to present himself as a model to his subjects, 'bedecked with virtue to the highest degree'.[39] Similarly in a context not unlike that of Anaxarchus' admonition Queen Parysatis persuaded her son, Artaxerxes II, to marry one of his daughters, on the grounds that he was a law to the Persians and arbiter of what was morally right and wrong.[40]

---

[34] Alcaeus F 143 (Page, OCT); Stesich. *Suppl. Lyr. Gr.* S 14 = *POxy* xxxii. 2617; Ar. *Nub.* 357, 1150.

[35] Succinctly stated at *Pol.* 3. 1288ᵃ15–19, 27–9; cf. 7. 1332ᵇ15–25, where the relation of ruler to subjects in India, as described by Scylax (*FGrH* 709 F 5), is taken as the paradigm.

[36] Arist. *Pol.* 3. 1284ᵃ3–12. On this the remarks of Balsdon, *Historia* 1 (1950) 368–70, remain pertinent (see also P. A. Brunt, *Studies in Greek History and Thought* (Oxford 1993) 335–6). It can hardly be denied that Aristotle was describing an ideal situation, or that his perfect ruler is characterized only by analogy as a god among men (so 1332ᵇ17–18). However, it was open for Alexander's courtiers to argue that the ideal conditions had been realized in their king.   [37] *Pol.* 3. 1288ᵃ18–20, 27–30.

[38] Explicitly formulated at *Pol.* 3. 1284ᵃ13–14.

[39] Xen. *Cyrop.* 8. 1. 21–2; cf. J. J. Farber, *AJP* 100 (1979) 504–5.

[40] Plut. *Artox.* 23. 5, adduced by W. L. Newman in his excellent commentary: *The Politics of Aristotle* iii (Oxford 1902) 243.

It is easy to see how Aristotle's theory could be given a negative direction. For him the ideal monarch was a theoretical construct. The man of surpassing excellence would be damnably hard to find,[41] and there was the problem of heredity—one could not guarantee that excellence would pass from father to son.[42] But in the language of flattery Alexander was unique. He had eclipsed all previous kings of Macedon, and by Aristotle's criterion he had shown himself the equal and superior of gods and heroes. He could legitimately be thought to be beyond the loose conventions of Macedonian custom, and in the unique circumstances of world conquest he could create precedents which would have lasting force. He now demonstrably occupied the position on earth which Zeus held on Olympus, and he might be considered equally free of constraint. Admittedly in the political philosophy of the Hellenistic world a king was expected to reinforce the norms of law by his own behaviour,[43] and it was paradoxical, to say the least, if the royal paradigm of virtue resorted to murder to discourage opposition. However, it could be argued that Alexander's divine filiation and superhuman achievements were quite self-evident, and to deny them was to strike at the very fabric of his monarchy. Malicious or not, Cleitus' intervention was treasonable and his death justifiable. That, at all events, was the crude message of the rank-and-file when they passed posthumous condemnation upon Cleitus, and Anaxarchus supplied vindication at a higher philosophical level. In both cases the message was the same. Alexander could create his own norms and violate prevailing custom at his choice. He was the man of surpassing excellence. A god among men and vicegerent of Zeus upon earth, he could redefine morality and legislate as he pleased. The effect was immediate. Alexander ceased to agonize over the murder and plunged into campaigning with gusto. The remorse he felt for Cleitus' death was not enduring, and to some extent he replayed the drama in 324 when he killed Oxathres, the delinquent son of the satrap of Susa, striking him down with a *sarisa* (perhaps again snatched from one of the

---

[41] Arist. *Pol.* 3. 1286[b]8–9 (men of excellence a rarity in the past).

[42] Arist. *Pol.* 3. 1286[b]24–8, adding the realistic comment that to pass over one's sons is an act of superhuman virtue. As Newman noted (iii. 289), it was an act achieved by Aristotle's friend, Antipater, who preferred Polyperchon to his own son, Cassander (Diod. 18. 48. 4; Plut. *Phoc.* 31. 1)—with ironically disastrous results.

[43] Instructive fragments are collected by E. R. Goodenough, *YCS* I (1928) 59–60 (Archytas); 65–7, 72–3 (Diotogenes); 76–7 (Ecphantus).

guards).[44] This was an act of summary justice, not unlike the killing of Alexander the Lyncestian, who was speared by his audience in the middle of his pathetic, fumbling attempt at a defence.[45] The result of the trial (if indeed Oxathres was formally arraigned) was taken for granted, and the king acted simultaneously as judge and executioner.

The events of summer 328 form a somewhat sinister concatenation. An arduous and unpleasant campaign had culminated in a grand symposium, at which the continuous outrageous flattery of Alexander's courtiers provoked a direct challenge. The challenge was immediately repressed, and the repression was justified on quasi-legal and quasi-philosophical grounds. It was a pattern to be repeated with ominous rapidity. The autumn and winter of 328/7 saw the army again divided for difficult and decisive action. In Maracanda itself Alexander's marshal, Coenus, dealt with a nomadic invasion with such exemplary strategy that he allegedly killed over 800 of the enemy for the loss of thirty-seven of his own troops. He broke the back of the resistance in the north-west, and the insurgent leaders, Spitamenes and Dataphernes, were deserted by their own allies.[46] In some ways Coenus eclipsed Alexander himself, who was first occupied in protracted siege operations at the great rock fortress of Sisimithres, operations which demanded elaborate and fatiguing construction work,[47] and then suffered considerable hardship and some casualties after he left his winter quarters prematurely.[48] Finally, after months of fatigue and exposure, king, staff, and army entered the Bactrian capital for a period of recreation, and it would not be surprising if the court propaganda of Alexander the superman was wearing thin among the men upon whose efforts his godhead rested.

---

[44] Plut. *Al.* 68. 7. Arr. 7. 4. 1 agrees that Oxathres was killed, but has nothing on the circumstances. The fact that Plutarch's report is colourful does not invalidate it (Berve ii. 291, no. 585; Badian, *CQ* 8 (1958) 148; Hammond, *Sources* 127–8; *contra* Tarn ii. 299; Hamilton, *Plut. Al.* 191).

[45] Curt. 7. 1. 9; Diod. 17. 80. 2.

[46] Arr. 4. 17. 4–7; Curt. 8. 3. 1–16; *Metz Epit.* 20–3.

[47] For sources and interpretation see Bosworth, *HCA* ii. 126–7, 234–9. The siege was preceded by an attack on the oasis area of Xenippa, which saw unusually high casualties (Curt. 8. 2. 14–18; *Metz Epit.* 19). On the filling of the ravine, a most difficult and unpleasant fatigue, which was the main feature of the siege of Sisimithres' citadel, see Arr. 4. 21. 3–6; Curt. 8. 2. 23–4.

[48] Curt. 8. 4. 1–20; *Metz Epit.* 24–9; Diod. 17 index κθ—one of the many instances of hardship not mentioned by Arrian (Strasburger, *Studien* i. 465; Bosworth, *HCA* ii. 139).

Naturally enough a symposium is attested at Bactra.[49] But this was no ordinary symposium. It was carefully orchestrated to lead to a specific result, the acknowledgement of Alexander's divine status and absolute monarchy. The issue was the introduction of Persian court ceremonial, in particular the act of *proskynesis*, the form of obeisance which involved the blowing of a symbolic kiss from a standing or a kneeling position.[50] For the Persians it was an age-old act of respect to a hierarchical superior, but for Greeks (and presumably Macedonians also) it was associated primarily with the worship of gods. *Proskynesis* at the Persian court had been familiar to Greek visitors for almost two centuries. It was accepted that the Persian king was a mortal and the act—for Persians—did not imply worship. However, it was a matter of acute embarrassment for Greek visitors when they were forced to conform to Persian court protocol.[51] According to Xenophon one of the inducements which the Spartan king offered the Persian satrap Pharnabazus was the freedom from performing *proskynesis*.[52] It was an act of intolerable servility with the overwhelming implication—for a Greek—that the person honoured was of divine status.[53] That emerges clearly from all the sources which recount the symposium at Bactra. For Arrian and Curtius, who give similar but independent stories, the court flatterers resumed the theme expounded at Maracanda. They again assimilated Alexander to the traditional divine benefactors of mankind, and argued that it was appropriate for the Macedonians to

---

[49] Full description in Arr. 4. 10. 5–12. 2; Curt. 8. 5. 8–6. 1; briefer references in Plut. *Al.* 54. 3; Justin 12. 7. 1–3. The most powerful defence of the tradition against its numerous modern sceptics is that of Badian, *Edson Studies* 28–32, 48–54; see also Bosworth, *HCA* ii. 77–87.

[50] A brief discussion of the problems is given by Bosworth, *HCA* ii. 68–70. For a full statement of evidence see J. Horst, *Proskynein* (Gütersloh 1932), esp. 44–51, and for the vexed question whether (for Greeks) the act involved prostration see P. von Straten, *BABesch* 49 (1974) 159–89.

[51] Note the deliberate evasion practised by Ismenias as late as 367 (Plut. *Artox.* 22. 8). Earlier ambassadors, notably the Spartans, Sperchias and Bulis, had refused to offer *proskynesis* to a mortal (Hdt. 7. 136. 1).

[52] Xen. *Hell.* 4. 1. 35. Compare Xenophon's proud boast to the Ten Thousand: 'you offer *proskynesis* to no man as master but to the gods alone' (*Anab.* 3. 2. 13).

[53] Cf. Xen. *Ages.* 1. 34: in 395 Agesilaus' victory at Sardes reversed the roles of Greek and barbarian—the Greeks who had formerly been forced to do *proskynesis* were now honoured by their oppressors, and the barbarians *who claimed for themselves the honours due to the gods* were not able even to look the Greeks in the face. Whatever the situation in fact, the philosophy underlying Xenophon's rhetoric is crystal clear: in demanding *proskynesis* from Greeks the Persians were arrogating the honours of the gods (cf. Isocr. 4. 151; Plut. *Them.* 27. 4).

worship him as a god, far more so than the Theban Dionysus or the Argive Heracles.[54] Once again it was the magnitude of Alexander's achievements which justified the apotheosis, and the Persian ceremonial was represented as proper recognition of his godhead. For the king's subjects there were two unpalatable consequences. In the first place *proskynesis* was the quintessential act of homage to the Persian king.[55] Its performance was recognition of the absolute power of the monarch. Greeks and Macedonians alike would acknowledge themselves to be what they had derided generations of Persians for being—slaves of a despot.[56] But the innovation went even further. *Proskynesis*, when offered by Greeks to a Macedonian ruler, would inevitably be construed as worship.

The protagonists of the new cult were Cleon of Syracuse and the court poet, Agis of Argos, and they certainly had substantial backing from the court intelligentsia, from Anaxarchus in particular.[57] Alexander tactfully absented himself from the conversation,[58] intending to return when all was agreed and receive the mass obeisance of the symposiasts. He cannot have been unaware of the resistance to his new initiative, and he had ensured that the most

---

[54] Arr. 4. 10. 6–7; Curt. 8. 5. 8–12 (cf. Justin 12. 7. 1–3).

[55] That was stressed long ago by Balsdon, *Historia* 1 (1950) 376–7, who claimed that Alexander *had* to impose *proskynesis* on all his subjects, Greeks and orientals alike, if he were to maintain credibility in the east (so, most recently, Cawkwell (above, n. 2) 296). However, if *proskynesis* was a political imperative without significant religious implications, two fatal questions arise: why did Alexander wait so long to introduce it, and why did he back down in the face of opposition? He had adopted elements of Persian court dress and ceremonial in late 330 (Bosworth, *JHS* 100 (1980) 5–8), but shrank from imposing *proskynesis*, even in the stressful period of insurgency instigated by Bessus in the eastern satrapies. It was only when the Sogdian revolt was suppressed and peace restored that he made his attempt to introduce the act, and after the experiment was dropped there is no evidence that the subject peoples disputed his credentials as king.

[56] In Plutarch's version of the quarrel with Cleitus (*Al.* 51. 2) the presence of Persian chamberlains is portrayed as a sign of despotism. How much more sinister was *proskynesis*, which had been represented as the typical act of homage to an eastern autocrat.

[57] Cleon (Berve ii. no. 487) is mentioned only by Curt. 8. 5. 8, who gives him the leading role assigned to Anaxarchus by Arr. 4. 9. 6. The latter with his well-known antipathy to Callisthenes is the more likely to have been foisted upon the debate. Cleon is too obscure to be an invention (Bosworth, *HCA* ii. 72), and he did most probably lead the argument for deification. Anaxarchus may have taken a supporting role comparable to that of Agis (Curt. 8. 5. 8, 21; Arr. 4. 9. 9; cf. Plut. *Mor.* 60b–c for his brand of flattery, an apophthegm which Philodemus ascribes to Anaxarchus himself (72 A 7 Diels/Kranz)).

[58] Curt. 8. 5. 9–10, 21; Arr. 4. 12. 2 with Bosworth, *HCA* ii. 86.

influential defender of Macedonian tradition, Craterus, was away from court during the period of the symposium.[59] The reluctance of the silent majority he thought would be easily overridden. Unfortunately the silent majority found a highly articulate spokesman in the court historian, Callisthenes. What motivated him we shall never know. There may have been some personal rancour at having lost favour to Anaxarchus, but there is no reason to dispute what is stated in the sources and embodied in the speeches placed in his mouth by Arrian and Curtius. In both versions Callisthenes states bluntly that a mortal may not receive divine honours.[60] The gulf between god and man remains absolute, however outstanding one's achievements may be. Alexander must be content as a mortal king of surpassing excellence. He cannot usurp the prerogatives of the gods.[61] This was no drunken outburst. It was a reasoned attack on the very concept of deification of a living man. Callisthenes had been willing enough to depict Alexander as the son of Zeus/Ammon and panegyrize his victories.[62] But divine sonship did not imply divinity, and victory, however brilliant and crushing, did not elevate a man beyond his mortality. Callisthenes' views, expressed with all the skills of a trained rhetorician, were so obviously endorsed by the mass of the Macedonian symposiasts that Alexander sent word to drop all talk of *proskynesis*, at least as far as it concerned Macedonians.[63] He returned to the feast in high dudgeon, and accepted *proskynesis* from

[59] Craterus had been dispatched to deal with the remaining unrest in Pareitacene (Arr. 4. 22. 1; Curt. 8. 5. 2; cf. Heckel 120–1). He received his commission before Alexander moved to Bactra, and was still in the field at the time of the Pages' Conspiracy (Plut. *Al.* 55. 6). For Craterus' opposition to oriental tendencies at court see Plut. *Eum.* 6. 3 with Bosworth, *JHS* 100 (1980) 7.

[60] For analysis and bibliography see Bosworth, *From Arrian to Alexander* 115–23; *HCA* ii. 77–86.

[61] This is the emphatic theme of Callisthenes' speech in Arrian (4. 11. 2–5), beginning with the emphatic assertion: 'there is a sharp division (διακεκρίσθαι) between honours paid to mortals and those to gods.' This echoes, perhaps deliberately, the sublime opening of Pindar's *Sixth Nemean*. Curtius' version (8. 5. 14–20) is set in the rhetorical pattern of the early Empire. What is stressed is not the impossibility of divine honours for mortals but the necessity to wait until the honorand was decently dead ('intervallo opus est ut credatur deus').

[62] For Callisthenes' work see particularly Pearson, *LHA* 33–8; Pédech, *Historiens compagnons* 51–65; L. Prandi, *Callistene*. On his description of the Pamphylian sea offering symbolic *proskynesis* to its new lord (*FGrH* 124 F 31) see Bosworth, *JHS* 110 (1990) 8–9.

[63] So Arr. 4. 12. 1 ('he sent word instructing the Macedonians to pay no further attention to *proskynesis*'); Curt. 8. 5. 21 (barbarians alone permitted to prostrate themselves); Justin 12. 6. 3.

his Persian guests. Their deference was profound; for Macedonians or Greeks it was kow-towing in its most grovelling form. However, thanks to Callisthenes' intervention, the sight of Persian chins low and posteriors high provoked ribald laughter from one of the Companions.[64] It was furiously checked by Alexander, but the damage was done. The demonstration had turned to farce, and *proskynesis* would not, at least for the moment, be reconstituted as a solemn act of homage and worship. Ten years were to elapse, and with them Alexander's death (or translation), before Eumenes and his Macedonian officers offered *proskynesis* at the throne of the deceased king. Now that Alexander had joined the gods, they worshipped him as a god.[65]

In 327 Callisthenes deliberately thwarted Alexander, and he paid for it. Implicated in the Pages' Conspiracy (but never convicted), he was tortured and crucified,[66] a frightful demonstration of the consequences of opposition. The context of his downfall is particularly interesting, a plot by the youngest of the Macedonian élite to remove their king. The details of the plot are obscure and difficult.[67] We shall never know, for instance, whether it was Alexander's unexpected all-night drinking which saved his life. The allegation was certainly made when the plot was revealed, and Aristobulus later exploited it, claiming that the gods themselves had sent him back to drink.[68] But the atrocity of the conspiracy was intensified by its supposed hair's-breadth failure, and the immediate threat to the king's life justified the savagery of the repression. The broader issues also remain an enigma. Our sources stress the motive of personal revenge, Hermolaus' outrage at the corporal punishment inflicted on

[64] Arr. 4. 12. 2; Curt. 8. 5. 22–6. 1. The culprit is variously termed Leonnatus or Polyperchon (Bosworth, *HCA* ii. 86–7; Heckel 96–8, 190–1). Polyperchon's mission to Bubacene (Curt. 8. 5. 2) does not rule him out. He may have returned by the time of the symposium. At least the letter reporting the Pages' Conspiracy, which was sent to Craterus and his lieutenants (Plut. *Al.* 55. 6), did not include Polyperchon among the addressees, and he may have been no longer in the field.

[65] Diod. 18. 61. 1 ('they offered *proskynesis* to Alexander as to a god'; cf. 3); Polyaen. 4. 8. 2; Nepos *Eum.* 7. 2; Plut. *Eum.* 13. 8.

[66] Arr. 4. 14. 3 = Ptolemy, *FGrH* 138 F 17; cf. Curt. 8. 8. 21; Plut. *Al.* 55. 9. For later imaginative embroideries on his fate see the passages compiled by Jacoby, *FGrH* 124 T 18). There is a variant tradition, ascribed to Chares and Aristobulus, that Callisthenes died from disease in custody (*FGrH* 125 F 15, 139 F 33). This is clearly tainted by apologetic (cf. Badian, *Edson Studies* 50–1, *contra* L. Prandi, *Callistene* 32–3. Pédech, *Historiens compagnons* 18, combines the two versions).

[67] For sources and discussion see Bosworth, *HCA* ii. 90–101.

[68] Arr. 4. 13. 5–6 = *FGrH* 139 F 30; Curt. 8. 6. 15–19.

him at Alexander's orders. But, however compelling the personal injury may have been for Hermolaus himself, it is insufficient to explain the involvement of at least half a dozen other conspirators. Some, like Hermolaus' lover, Sostratus, had personal reasons for antipathy against Alexander,[69] but there must have been some collective motive, or motives. The closest the sources come to an answer is in the vulgate tradition of Hermolaus' defence at his trial, when he supposedly arraigned the king's arrogance. Alexander's killing of Philotas, Parmenion, and Cleitus, his excessive drinking, his adoption of Median court dress, and his attempted introduction of *proskynesis*, all received adverse comment. Some of this must be pure embroidery, but there could be a substratum of truth.[70] It is quite possible that the dissident pages were deeply disenchanted with recent developments at court. Several of them were relatively new arrivals, having left Macedonia in Amyntas' great convoy of reinforcements, which joined Alexander as he advanced into Persis in winter 331/0. The autocracy of the court may well have been an unpleasant shock. If so, the shock was accentuated when Alexander returned from the Sogdian rebellion in spring 327.[71] Many, if not all, of the pages had taken no direct part in the campaigning, and had been billeted at Bactra during the eventful months of 328.[72] They witnessed the experiment with *proskynesis* without having experienced the banquet at Maracanda which laid the groundwork for deification or the numerous camp-fire discussions when Alexander was assimilated to the gods. It would not be surprising if they responded with outrage both to the act of *proskynesis* and its implications, and considered regicide their only option.

---

[69] This is alleged by Curtius (8. 6. 8); Arrian (4. 13. 3) only mentions Sostratus' erotic sympathy and makes him a second Aristogeiton.

[70] Reported by Arrian 4. 14. 2 with a cautious disclaimer ('there have been some who gave the following account'). The themes he outlines are elaborated in an extended speech which Curtius places in the mouth of Hermolaus (8. 7. 8–15, rebutted by Alexander at 8. 8. 1–19) and were obviously a part of the vulgate.

[71] Diod. 17. 65. 1; Curt. 5. 1. 42; cf. Bosworth, *HCA* ii. 92. If (which seems most unlikely) Hammond, *Historia* 39 (1990) 265–8, is correct in arguing that new drafts of Pages came out from Macedon every year after 331, there would be a pool of newcomers absolutely green to developments at court. One of the conspirators, Antipater, son of the ex-satrap Asclepiodorus, could well have come up to Bactra with his father, arriving in winter 329/8 (Arr. 4. 7. 2, 13. 4).

[72] Arr. 4. 16. 6. There is no record (*pace* Curt. 8. 6. 4) of pages actually present in battle with the King. Philip, brother of Lysimachus, who died from exhaustion in Sogdiana (Curt. 8. 2. 35–9) was clearly in his early maturity ('tum primum adultus'), a member of the hypaspist *agema* rather than the pages (Berve ii. no. 774; Heckel 288).

Under those circumstances Alexander's horrific response is understandable. This was no drunken effusion, to be checked by drunken violence. It was secret opposition, and did not baulk at assassination. The king's reaction was to inflict exemplary punishment: torture and execution for the culprits,[73] and even worse treatment for Callisthenes, who had openly attacked the institution of *proskynesis* and had cordial relations with some at least of the conspirators. Whether or not he was directly involved (as the court historians, Ptolemy and Aristobulus alleged),[74] he had given a moral example which encouraged the conspirators to take more drastic action, and he could be regarded as the ultimate instigator of the plot. His punishment, as Ptolemy and the majority of sources recorded it, was extreme, visited on the most stubborn recalcitrants, such as the treacherous Musicanus in Sind. It was an object lesson not to resist innovations dear to Alexander's heart.

Proskynesis was shelved, but the flattery which spawned it continued in vogue. Some months after the experiment at Bactra Alexander was wounded at the siege of Massaga in the valley of the Lower Swat. It was a superficial flesh wound in the lower leg, but caused disproportionate pain.[75] On this occasion Alexander's complaints about the very human pain of the wound were answered by a highly flattering comparison with Aphrodite's wrist wound at the hands of Diomedes; the blood which flowed was 'ichor such as pours from the immortal gods'.[76] Alexander was not made of mortal stuff, and even the most evident proof of his human condition could be enlisted as a mark of divinity. This episode was a favourite in the rhetorical tradition, and there are several later metamorphoses in which

---

[73] Arr. 4. 13. 7, 14. 3; Curt. 8. 8. 20; Plut. *Al.* 55. 6.

[74] Arr. 4. 14. 1 = *FGrH* 138 F 16, 139 F 31. Despite the consensus of the primary sources Arrian is unconvinced of Callisthenes' guilt, claiming that his opposition predisposed Alexander to believe that he was involved (4. 12. 7; cf. Plut. *Al.* 55. 1; Curt. 8. 6. 1, 24–5; Justin 12. 7. 2).

[75] Arr. 4. 26. 4; Curt. 8. 10. 28–9; *Metz Epit.* 40; cf. Plut. *Mor.* 341b.

[76] The complaint about the wound is attested in Curtius (8. 10. 29), and it is the perfect foil for Dioxippus' comparison of the blood with ichor (Athen. 6. 251 A = *FGrH* 139 F 47). For rhetorical elaborations of the theme, which make Alexander the author of the quotation, see Plut. *Mor.* 180e, 341b; *Al.* 28. 2; [D.Chr.] 64. 21 (Diog.L. 9. 60 attributes it to Anaxarchus, Sen. *Suas.* 1. 5 to Callisthenes). The obvious point that Dioxippus is hardly likely to have been invented as the author of the apophthegm (in view of the circumstances of his death) is well made by T. S. Brown, in *Greece & the E. Med.* 86–7 and Badian, in *Edson Studies* 64. For the Homeric quotation (*Il.* 5. 339–40) and its relevance see Bosworth, *HCA* ii. 173–4.

Alexander uses the quotation ironically to confute his flatterers. However, the earliest assignable reference, ascribed to Aristobulus, interprets it as sheer adulation, comparable to the comment of the egregious Nicesias that even the gods feel pain.[77] What is more, Aristobulus named the flatterer as Dioxippus. Now, there can be no doubt of Dioxippus' identity. He was the Athenian pancratiast, reputedly the strongest man of his day, who won an uncontested victory at Olympia[78] and so distinguished his family that the alleged adulterer of his sister was prosecuted at Athens by impeachment (εἰσαγγελία).[79] Dioxippus had joined Alexander's court some time before 327. Perhaps he came to compete at the famous games held at Tyre in 331,[80] and remained as a regular competitor and court favourite. He was a courtier of the highest social standing, not an impoverished adventurer, as Alexander's flatterers are often taken to be, rather a counterpart of men like Oxythemis at the court of Demetrius Poliorcetes, a confidant of the king and a master of the carefully turned compliment.[81] For Dioxippus Alexander was god manifest, and even the pain of his wound could be taken as corroboration of his godhead.

It is worth taking Dioxippus' career further, for it provides us with a perfect illustration of the perils of the symposium. The backcloth for the episode is the great celebration which Alexander staged to commemorate the surrender of the Oxydracae in 325.[82] This marked

---

[77] Athen. 6. 251 C. Here Alexander does give a disillusioned answer to the flattery, which may be the inspiration for Plutarch's inversion of Dioxippus' *mot*. For Nicesias' other apophthegm see Athen. 6. 249D–E; Berve ii. no. 564.

[78] Pliny, *NH* 35. 139. For the picturesque witticism of Diogenes on the occasion of his return see Diog. L. 6. 43, 61; Plut. *Mor.* 521 B; Ael. *VH* 12. 58.

[79] For the evidence see M. H. Hansen, *Eisangelia* (Odense University Classical Studies 6: 1975) 106–7, no. 119. Lycophron was defended by Hypereides, and Lycurgus spoke in support of the indictment, drawing a parallel between Dioxippus' sister and the sister of Harmodius (Lyc. F 6–7 (Conomis)) and claiming that Lycophron was in effect creating a counterculture of immorality to undermine the existing laws (F 2). On the speech in general see N. C. Conomis, *Klio* 39 (1961) 128–36. Predictably Hypereides 2 (*Lyc.*). 12–13 maintains that the prosecution is an outrageous abuse of the *eisangelia* procedure.

[80] Arr. 3. 6. 1; Moretti, *ISE* no. 113; Plut. *Al.* 29. 1–6. This was the occasion for which the actor Athenodorus broke his contract to appear at the Athenian Dionysia (Plut. *Al.* 29. 5), and it would naturally have attracted Dioxippus along with many others.

[81] On the career of Oxythemis see conveniently Billows 404–8, no. 86. For his heroization at Athens see below, p. 129.

[82] Curt. 9. 7. 14–15; cf. Arr. 6. 14. 1–3. Diod. 17. 100. 1 mentions only entertainment in celebration of Alexander's recovery, but it comes at exactly the same point as it does in Curtius, and we need not doubt that the Oxydracan envoys were present.

the end of the Malli campaign, which was exceptional for its carnage and the physical hardships endured by the Macedonians under Alexander's command, and the dangerous wound which Alexander sustained had thrown the entire army into a temporary panic. Not surprisingly the banquet released tensions, this time between Greeks and Macedonians. Dioxippus found himself the butt of animosity, reviled for taking his ease while the fighting men took the brunt of the campaigning.[83] His privileged status evoked jealousy, and the exchange of words culminated in a challenge. A certain Corrhagus, newly transferred from the ranks to Companion status,[84] formally proposed a duel, and in the heat of the symposium the king gave it his blessing.[85] That was a mistake. On the appointed day the two met before the entire army, which was in a state of high excitement, polarized on ethnic grounds, Corrhagus resplendent in full armour and weaponry and Dioxippus dressed as Heracles and armed solely with a club.[86] In a classic *aristeia* Dioxippus' athletic skills proved superior. His overweighted opponent was humiliated, and only Alexander's intervention prevented the *coup de grâce*.[87] But it was a bitter victory. According to Curtius Alexander was mortified by its effect on Macedonian propaganda.[88] Indian spectators had witnessed one of the supposedly invincible Macedonian élite disarmed and incapacitated by an unarmed man and with effortless ease. One may add that it was tactless to masquerade as Heracles before a Heraclid who had made it so much his business to emulate the hero.[89]

[83] Curt. 9. 7. 16. This is an addition to Diodorus' laconic description of the quarrel, but it is hardly an elaboration by Curtius himself (so Berve ii. no. 284—'ausgeschmückt'). The gibes against athletes, particularly their addiction to food, are familiar, reminiscent of Euripides' diatribe against athletes (Eur. F 282 Nauck), which the symposiasts may have known and quoted.

[84] That is my interpretation of Diod. 17. 100. 2 (ἐν τοῖς ἑταίροις παραληφθείς 'admitted among the Companions'; cf. Diod. 1. 18. 5; 16. 73. 2).

[85] Diod. 17. 100. 2–3; Curt. 9. 7. 17–18.

[86] Diod. 17. 100. 5–6; Curt. 9. 7. 19–20; Ael. *VH* 10. 22.

[87] Diod. 17. 101. 1; Curt. 9. 7. 22. Aelian (*loc. cit.*) erroneously states that Dioxippus killed his adversary.

[88] Curt. 9. 7. 23: 'tristis spectaculi eventus non Macedonibus modo sed etiam Alexandro fuit, maxime quia barbari adfuerant: quippe celebratam Macedonum fortitudinem ad ludibrium recidisse verebatur.'

[89] According to Ephippus (*FGrH* 126 F 5 = Athen. 12. 537F) Alexander himself often assumed the club and lion-skin of Heracles, and during his reign the features of Heracles on his coinage came to bear a striking resemblance to his own (see below, Ch. 6, n. 6). Dioxippus' physique would have been more in keeping with the traditional image of Heracles.

Dioxippus had behaved hubristically, and like Callisthenes he paid for it. Within a matter of days he was falsely accused of theft, and committed suicide in chagrin. The charge was calumny, and openly admitted as such—once Dioxippus was dead! The Athenian pancratiast was not attacking policy, but he had done indirect damage. Placed on his mettle, he had responded devastatingly to taunts of cowardice, so devastatingly that he threatened to undermine the myth of Macedonian invincibility. That could not be forgiven, and Dioxippus was removed.[90] There was an ominous parallel in the death of Coenus only a matter of days after he represented the grievances of the troops at the Hyphasis and thwarted Alexander's plans of further conquest.[91] His death may have been fortuitous, but it was uncomfortably close to his great offence, and the lesson will have been clear. Opposition in any form was dangerous, and the symposium, in which tongues were loosened and speech flowed freely, was a particularly perilous institution. For all its negative colouring there is some element of truth in Ephippus' picture of Alexander's court in his last years with its prevailing atmosphere of terrified silence. Macedonian *parrhesia*, at least as far as Alexander was concerned, was a thing of the past. Criticism and dissent gradually disappeared. After the traumatic events of 328 and 327 there were few who had the prestige or courage to contest the departures from traditional mores. Coenus' death, accidental or not, was a warning to the most powerful, and Craterus, who had prestige and popularity, and is alleged to have defended Macedonian tradition, was gradually marginalized.[92] After 329 he spent relatively little time in the king's immediate entourage, and in 324 he was despatched westwards to repatriate the veterans of Opis. In that climate nobody had an interest in tempering the king's fervid aspirations to divinity with the cold water of rationalism. Quite the reverse. Alexander's staff excelled in discovering traces of the passage of Heracles and

[90] Curt. 9. 7. 24 makes the connection explicitly ('hinc ad criminationem invidorum adopertae sunt regis aures'), and Diod. 17. 101. 3 agrees that the king was gradually alienated, implying that the process took longer than the few days in Curtius' account.

[91] Arr. 6. 2. 1; cf. Curt. 9. 3. 20 (a pointed gibe by Alexander). For differing interpretations of his death see Green 416; Heckel 63–4; and for discussion of his role at the Hyphasis see Bosworth, *HCA* ii. 351–5.

[92] For his absence from the symposium at Bactra see above, n. 59. His career after 329 is well covered by Heckel 118–25. Apart from the stay in Parapamisadae in summer 327 and the campaign on the Hydaspes in 326 there are few occasions in the latter part of the reign when Alexander and Craterus can be shown to have been together.

Dionysus, and found local stories of the failures of earlier conquerors. Alexander was always competing, always proving himself the equal or superior of the gods, demonstrating beyond cavil (in his own eyes) that he was a superman, beyond any constraint of law or custom, and had achieved divinity through his benefactions.

The process began during the passage of the Hindu Kush, which Alexander's men believed to be an extension of the Caucasus range and relatively close to the Caspian Sea. There the local inhabitants pointed out a cave which was immediately identified as the place where Prometheus was tormented by the eagle until his release by Heracles—there was even an eagle's roost and traces of chains to add verisimilitude.[93] We can only conjecture what lay behind this strange fabrication. The natives presumably had their legends of the exploits of Verethragna, the Iranian hero who was equated with Heracles in the Seleucid period. What is more, the name Parapamisus, used of the Hindu Kush, could be translated 'beyond the flight of the eagle'.[94] A mountain range which was equated with the Caucasus, connected with the Iranian Heracles, and suggested the discomfiture of an eagle was a very convenient home for the Prometheus legend, and it was easy to believe that Heracles had been physically present there. The view was strengthened by the local legends around Mt. Aornus (Pir-sar), the mountain fastness overlooking the Indus which Alexander captured in 327/6. It had resisted attack even from a deity, and the deity was irresistibly identified as Heracles.[95] Alexander's success could be balanced against an exceptional failure by the founder of his dynasty.

For the great Alexandrian scholar, Eratosthenes, the evidence of Heracles in the east was sheer chicanery, deliberate and conscious fabrication.[96] That was to oversimplify the issue. The local myths

[93] Diod. 17. 83. 1; Curt. 7. 3. 22 (cf. Philostr. *VA* 2. 3). On the tradition and its interpretation see Bosworth, *HCA* ii. 213–17.

[94] From the Iranian *Uparisena*; cf. Herzfeld, *The Persian Empire* 336; Vogelsang, *The Rise and Organisation of the Achaemenid Empire* 51–2.

[95] Arr. 4. 28. 2; Diod. 17. 85. 2; Curt. 8. 11. 2; Justin 12. 7. 12–13; *Metz Epit.* 46–7. The story is consistent in the vulgate, but, as Arrian's account clearly shows, it was also embedded in at least one of his primary sources. It was certainly not confined to the vulgate.

[96] Explicit in Strabo 15. 1. 9 (688): 'that these stories are fabrications of the flatterers of Alexander is obvious' and Arr. 5. 3. 1: '(Eratosthenes) says that everything which was ascribed to the divine by the Macedonians was so attributed for the favour of Alexander and to add solemnity' (see also *Ind.* 5. 8–13). On Eratosthenes' views on myth see the commentary in *HCA* ii. 213–19.

were real enough. There *was* a cave in the Hindu Kush, and there *were* legends that Aornus was impregnable, even for a divinity. The equation with the Greek deity may have been suggested by Alexander's interpreters, and his staff were ready to develop the idea. The process is well illustrated by the conceits of two Thessalian writers, Medeius of Larisa and Cyrsilus of Pharsalus, both officers of Alexander.[97] For them the Armenians were descendants of the Thessalian Armenus, who had left his home city to sail with the Argonauts to Colchis. The etymology was supported by analogies between Thessalian and Armenian dress and horsemanship, and it was thought probable that the Armenian river Araxes was named after the Thessalian Peneius, whose original name was also Araxes. Once the basic premiss was accepted, supporting evidence could easily be found. If Heracles was thought to have penetrated to the far east, then the brand mark of his club might well have persisted among the Indian Sibi,[98] just as the Armenians wore long chitons after the example of their Thessalian eponym. Medeius and Cyrsilus were using myth to glorify their national origins, and they were clearly following the precedent of their king. If Alexander could follow his ancestors into India, they might find evidence of Thessalian penetration in the far north.[99] For Alexander himself there was considerable inducement to believe the myths which were created for him. It was some comfort to be following in the footsteps of his ancestor, and the possiblity of outdoing him was intoxicating.[100] For Arrian Heracles' failure at Aornus was a gross improbability and suggested falsification, but for Alexander it was a challenge which could not be evaded. The impossible must be proved a reality.

Even more than Heracles, Dionysus proved an inspirational example. That is at first sight paradoxical, for Dionysus did not

[97] Strabo 11. 14. 12–13 (530–1) = *FGrH* 129 F 1 (cf. 11. 4. 8 (503) with Pearson, *LHA* 68–70; Robert, *OMS* v. 529–31). The story is also found (in brief) in Justin (42. 2. 10, 3. 5–6), and might have been included as a digression on Alexander's stay in Hyrcania (Justin 42. 3. 7).   [98] Arr. 5. 3. 4; *Ind.* 5. 12; Strabo 15. 1. 8 (688).

[99] When Medeius and Cyrsilus developed their foundation myth is unknown. Medeius, however, was a lieutenant of Perdiccas in 321 (Arr. *Succ.* F 24. 6), and probably fought with him in Cappadocia in 322. At that time a Macedonian force was active in Armenia under Neoptolemus (Plut. *Eum.* 4. 1, 5. 1–2), and details of Armenian geography and *mores* would have been more familiar.

[100] Arr. 4. 28. 4. The motivation is already explicit at the siege of Gaza (late 332): 'the engineers expressed the opinion that it was impossible to take the city by force because of the height of the mound, but in Alexander's eyes the greater the impossibility, the more the necessity to capture it' (Arr. 2. 26. 3).

originally belong in the Argead genealogy. For the speakers at the *proskynesis* symposium he was a Theban deity, of much less relevance to Macedonians than Alexander himself,[101] and before the time of Alexander, apart from a famous and controversial line in the *Bacchae* of Euripides, there was no literary reference to any exploits of the god in the far east.[102] That was a discovery made by Alexander's staff. In their pursuit of Saca nomads north of the Syr-Darya the Macedonians had passed a number of trees wreathed in ivy, which they took to be the sign of the god's presence.[103] The ivy was particularly remarkable. Its absence had been noted in Asia east of the Levantine coast,[104] and its sudden appearance in the north of Sogdiana clearly stimulated speculation. The Syr-Darya was thought to be an eastern tributary of the European Tanais (Don), the traditional boundary between Europe and Asia. The territory to the north was accordingly considered to be Europe, its Saca inhabitants European Scyths.[105] If the pursuit had taken Alexander back into Europe, then ivy might be expected to have appeared. However, there was a celebrated line from the *Bacchae*, a play which Alexander knew well and quoted with devastating effect. In it Dionysus refers to his visiting 'the forts of Bactria and the wintry terrain of the Medes'.[106] Now, Theophrastus refers to ivy in the north of Media, where it is found to this day, and he presumably based his report on information from Alexander's expedition. The ivy, it might be thought, marked the passage of the god and confirmed the somewhat impressionistic itinerary of Euripides.

[101] Arr. 4. 10. 6; cf. Bosworth, *HCA* ii. 78–9.

[102] Cf. A. Dihle, in G. Pollet (ed.), *India and the Ancient World* 52–3, *contra* Goukowsky ii. 11–13. The absence of attestation is not simply a quirk of transmission, for Eratosthenes was apparently able only to quote the Prologue of the *Bacchae* as evidence for Dionysus in the east (Strabo 15. 1. 7 (687)).

[103] Curt. 7. 9. 15; cf. *Metz Epit.* 12. The episode does not occur in Arrian, who is principally concerned with Alexander's gastric seizure (4. 4. 9–10).

[104] See particularly Theophr. *HP* 4. 4. 1 with S. Amigues's commentary in the recent Budé edition.

[105] Cf. Arr. 4. 1. 1, 15. 1; Curt. 7. 6. 12, 8. 1. 7. For the supposed proximity of Chorasmia to Colchis and the Amazonian heartland see Arr. 4. 15. 4 with Bosworth, *HCA* ii. 105–7.

[106] Eur. *Bacch.* 15–16: Βάκτριά τε τείχη τήν τε δύσχιμον χθόνα | Μήδων ἐπελθών. For Albrecht Dihle and several others these lines are interpolated (cf. Dihle, *Der Prolog der 'Bacchen'* 11–27). That theory has been hotly disputed (M. F. Ferrini, *AFLM* 18 (1985) 117–43), and, even if we allow interpolation, the lines were in the texts of the play known to Eratosthenes (above, n. 102) and were in all probability familiar to Alexander.

Ivy was discovered in Sogdiana late in the summer of 329, when the Macedonians alleged that they had passed the limits of Dionysus. The god returned in sensational fashion in 328, when Alexander's murder of Cleitus was interpreted by his seers as divine punishment for the neglect of a sacrifice.[107] The sacrifice was duly performed, much to the relief of the king, who preferred to see himself as the victim of divine revenge rather than an irascible, drunken despot.[108] Dionysus had now come to the fore, and he was invoked as a precedent in the *proskynesis* debate. He was a deity, but a deity whose achievements could be eclipsed by Alexander. In some respects this is a classic example of doublethink, the capacity to believe two contradictory propositions simultaneously. When it suited him, Alexander could see himself as the tool of an overmastering divinity, but on other occasions the god could be represented as an equal or even inferior. The two modes of thought were not necessarily irreconcilable. One thinks, for instance, of the Conquistadors in Mexico, who could simultaneously condemn human sacrifice and use the fat from a dead Indian to dress their wounds[109] —and would later offer their own holocausts in preservation of their faith. Under the shock of the killing of Cleitus Alexander confronted his human frailty, and welcomed the Euripidean concept of the vengeful, irresistible god. Later, as the procession of victories continued and Sogdian resistance ended, he could resume the role of the superman, challenging and surpassing the achievements of the gods.

Dionysus had bulked large in the conversations at court during the spring of 327. That is the only explanation of the curious sequel at the Indian town of 'Nysa' in the highlands of Nuristan east of the River Kunar. Here, when the inhabitants surrendered after a brief, half-hearted resistance, they threw themselves upon the conqueror's

[107] Arr. 4. 8. 1–2, 9. 5; Curt. 8. 2. 6. Curtius states that the neglect of the sacrifice was only noticed after the event, and Arrian (9. 5) implies the same. If the sacrifice actually was an annual event (as both sources state), it was an insignificant affair, easily overlooked. The whole institution may be *post eventum* fabrication.

[108] So Arr. 4. 9. 5 ('it was not displeasing to have the catastrophe ascribed to divine wrath rather than his own moral failure').

[109] The two episodes are narrated in startling proximity and (of course) without comment in the classic work of Bernal Díaz, p. 141 (Cohen), p. 179 (Maudslay) (Cortés denouncing sacrifice): 'we vassals of our lord the King who had sent us to these parts to put an end to human sacrifices and the eating of human flesh'; p. 143 (Cohen), p. 187 Maudslay: 'we dressed our wounds from the flesh of a stout Indian whom we had killed and cut open.' On this 'cultural blockage' see S. Greenblatt, *Marvelous Possessions* 136–9.

mercy, and alleged that they were the descendants of Bacchantes who had followed in the god's train to India and were settled in a city foundation which was in all respects comparable to Alexander's own.[110] In later years Eratosthenes was to excoriate the story as Macedonian invention, 'fabrications of the flatterers of Alexander';[111] but the sources themselves state unequivocally that the natives themselves claimed descent from Dionysus' companions. They were also able to point out the growths of ivy on nearby Mt. Meros as proofs of the god's presence. The proofs were particularly welcome to Alexander because, as Arrian states, he felt that the troops would not resist further hardship because of their emulation of Dionysus' deeds.[112] The army was encouraged to find traces of the god's passage, and Alexander himself was presented with a flattering list of achievements which he had equalled. The inhabitants of Nysa were obviously well briefed about the beliefs of the invaders, and rectified the error of their resistance by a clever appeal to Alexander's vanity. They were adroit enough to manufacture a connection with Dionysus, and knew enough to provide convincing proof (in the form of ivy) of their claims.

What should be stressed at this point is the close connection between the Cophen valley (the old satrapy of Gandhara) and the satrapies of Parapamisadae and Bactria. While the Sogdian revolt was still in full swing Alexander had been approached by the prince of Taxila, who offered submission and agreed to be his ally if there were resistance in India.[113] This was hardly a unique overture, and it may have taken place relatively early. In 328, when the revolt still had a year to run, Alexander represented it as his firm intention to invade India.[114] By the summer of 327 he had established contacts with a

---

[110] Arr. 5. 1. 1, 5–7; *Ind.* 1. 4–6, 5. 9. For the rest of the abundant source tradition see Bosworth, *HCA* ii. 198–9, 203–7.

[111] So Strabo 15. 1. 9 (688) in a full digest of Eratosthenes' criticisms. Arrian (5. 3. 1–4; Ind. 5. 8–12) is briefer and confirms the outline of the argument.

[112] Arr. 5. 2. 1. The text (if correctly emended) mentions Alexander's own desire to outstrip the god, and adds that his men would also emulate their divine forerunner.

[113] Diod. 17. 86. 4; cf. Curt. 8. 12. 5; *Metz Epit.* 49. Some details in the story have been doubted (Berve ii. 370, no. 739), but there can be no doubt that contact was made during the Sogdian revolt. Arrian (4. 22. 6) confirms that Taxiles was among the dynasts summoned to meet Alexander at the borders of Parapamisadae (summer 327), and he had already offered token submission.

[114] Arr. 4. 15. 6 (the invasion of India is the final stage of world conquest). It should be noted that Alexander had Indian informants on his staff, men such as Sisicottus, who had served Bessus until his capture in 329 and transferred his allegiance to

substantial number of Indian dynasts, whom he ordered to meet him on the frontier as he marched south from Parapamisadae. They duly arrived, hailing Alexander as the third son of Zeus to have visited their lands; Dionysus and Heracles they knew by hearsay, but the king was manifest before them.[115] The echo of the themes of the great symposia is too exact to be fortuitous. Indian visitors to Bactria and Parapamisadae had listened to the conversations at court, and informed themselves with great discretion. They were aware of the Greek penchant for religious syncretism, conscious of the desirability of equivalents within their own pantheon, and they produced a tradition of the presence of Greek deities, notably Dionysus and Heracles, whom the king was known to emulate. Here we have evidence of the birth of a myth. There was real, if exiguous, literary support for extending Dionysus' wanderings eastward to Bactria, and the discovery of ivy in 329 had given material proof. Now the Indians were taking his exploits even further east and supplying evidence to back their claim. That evidence ensured the favour of the conqueror and (in the case of Nysa) a lenient settlement which overlooked their initial resistance. In the southern Punjab the Oxydracae were to try the same tactics, claiming that they had been autonomous since the time of Dionysus and providing further evidence of the god's presence—the cultivation of the vine and the Bacchic dress of their rulers.[116] These, as Eratosthenes sourly noted, were common to all the Indian peoples of the area, and the Oxydracae had no monopoly.[117] However, the claim suited them in their precarious situation. The 1,000 warriors they sent as hostages were promptly returned, and they avoided the dreadful repression visited upon the neighbouring Malli who had lost a sizable portion of their population.[118]

Alexander (Arr. 4. 30. 4). Such men acted as advisers and interpreters, and could brief any of their fellow nationals on the customs and interests of the invaders.

[115] Curt. 8. 10. 1; *Metz Epit.* 34. Arrian (4. 22. 6) merely gives the fact of the meeting. The comparison with Dionysus and Heracles *may* be an elaboration of the vulgate (cf. Goukowsky ii. 35); and Curtius' comment on the physical presence of Alexander ('ipsum coram adesse cernique') is reminiscent of the Athenian hymn to Demetrius (Duris, *FGrH* 76 F 13 = Athen. 6. 253 E). However, it is not impossible that the Indian princes related Alexander to their own pantheon, and acknowledged his divine sonship, as Arr. 6. 14. 2 claims the Oxydracae did.

[116] Arr. 6. 14. 2; *Ind.* 5. 9; cf. Strabo 15. 1. 8 (687–8), 33 (701). Curt. 9. 7. 12–13 describes the embassy in terms similar to Arrian's, but has nothing about the Dionysiac origins of the Oxydracae.

[117] Strabo 15. 1. 8 (688); cf. Arr. *Ind.* 5. 9, 7. 9.

[118] Arr. 6. 14. 3; cf. Curt. 9. 7. 16 (garbled). As for the Malli, Arrian twice inserts

What cannot be ignored is the contribution made by Alexander's interpreters. They were close to his person, and, as bilinguals, would be acquainted with Greek modes of thought. Of all people they would be most aware of the obsession with Dionysus and the need to find precedents for conquest. As they interviewed the native speakers, it was inevitable that they transformed their responses into terms which would make the most acceptable sense to their employers. What Mithropastes did with the legend of Erythras,[119] they probably did with the Dionysiac conquest. There is an instructive parallel from the history of the Spanish invasion of Mexico. In his dealings with the inland peoples Cortés made use of two interpreters. The first, Gerónimo de Aguilar, was a Spaniard, shipwrecked off Yucutan, who had learned the Mayan dialect of the coast.[120] His intermediary was a remarkable Indian woman, whom the Spaniards named Doña Marina.[121] She was included in a batch of captives given to Cortés early in the campaign, and became the indispensable companion of the Conquistador. She was the consort of several of Cortés' lieutenants, and eventually bore a son to Cortés himself. From birth a speaker of Nahuatl (the Aztec language), she learned Mayan in captivity, and, as a dispossessed person, she threw in her lot with the invaders from the beginning. Díaz writes with considerable warmth of her services: 'without Doña Marina we could not have understood the language of New Spain and Mexico.'[122]

The Indian interpreter was on the most intimate terms with Cortés and his entourage; and she quickly assimilated herself to the new culture, embracing Christianity from the outset. She was privy to her employer's ambitions, and could phrase the information she received in terms acceptable to him. Whatever she translated into Mayan would then be given a distinctively Castilian shape by Aguilar. It comes as no surprise to find that the Mexican emperor,

---

the chilling note that their ambassadors represented 'the surviving population' (6. 14. 1, 3).

[119] See above, pp. 66–9.

[120] On the history of Aguilar see Hernán Cortés, *Letters from Mexico* 17–19; Díaz pp. 63–6 (Cohen), pp. 93–5 (Maudslay).

[121] The biography of Doña Marina is briefly sketched by Anthony Pagden, in Hernán Cortés, *Letters from Mexico* 464–5. See also the perceptive comments of Stephen Greenblatt, *Marvelous Possessions* 141–5.

[122] Díaz ch. 37, p. 87 (Cohen), p. 117 (Maudslay). For an impressive tribute to her courage and loyalty see Díaz p. 153 (Cohen), p. 200 (Maudslay): 'though she heard every day that the Indians were going to kill us and eat our flesh with chilli...yet she betrayed no weakness but a courage greater than that of a woman'.

Montezuma, is given almost a Christian perspective when his addresses to Cortés are recorded. He disposes of the allegation that he was a god to his people with a dramatic appeal: 'see that I am flesh and blood like you and all other men, and I am mortal and substantial.'[123] This phrasing occurs in other reports of the interview, and must represent what was actually translated. The Catholic Aguilar gave Montezuma's statement a colouring which recalled the scriptures. Furthermore, Montezuma's astounding and incredible allegation that the Spaniards were the descendants of the founder of his own culture must be the result of conscious deformation. Marina and Aguilar together gave Cortés the perfect justification for his Mexican adventure.[124] Here there was collusion between interpreters and employer, collusion which we may expect to have been paralleled in the entourage of Alexander. All the inducements were to provide evidence for the passage of Dionysus, and each and every deity could be transmogrified into a local manifestation of the Hellenic god.

Thanks to the compliance of the native peoples, interpreters and informants alike, a new myth was born. It was to be fully expounded by Megasthenes in the years immediately following Alexander's death. Dionysus, the great civilizer, had invaded the Indian lands, converted the inhabitants from their state of barbarism, and bestowed the gifts of agriculture and urban living, complete with the rule of law and the art of war.[125] Indian civilization was the gift of Dionysus, as was Indian kingship. The first king, Spatembas, was a follower of the god, and his progeny comprised the first dynasty of kings.[126] Megasthenes also mentioned Heracles, but made him a native Indian quite distinct from his western counterpart, although comparable in his dress and exploits.[127] The effect was to elevate and justify Alexander's conquest, which was represented as unique. The only precedent of an alien invader was that of Dionysus himself, and it was highly significant. Once Dionysus had been included in the Argead lineage, as probably happened in Alexander's last years,[128] he

---

[123] This is the version of Cortés (*Letters from Mexico* 86), substantially confirmed by Gómara (pp. 141–2: 'touch my body, then, which is of flesh and bone') and Díaz (p. 223 (Cohen), pp. 287–8 (Maudslay)). On the background see J. H. Elliott, *Transactions of the Royal Historical Society*[5] 17 (1967) 41–58, esp. 51–3.

[124] See below, pp. 162–3.

[125] Arr. *Ind.* 7. 2–9 = *FGrH* 715 F 12; Diod. 2. 38. 2–6 = *FGrH* 715 F 4.

[126] Arr. *Ind.* 8. 1–3; 9. 9; Diod. 2. 38. 7 (garbled).

[127] Arr. *Ind.* 8. 4–6 (cf. 5. 13) = *FGrH* 715 F 13; Diod. 2. 39. 1 = *FGrH* 715 F 4.

[128] The connection of Dionysus with the Argead line may already have been

could be viewed as the direct descendant of the god, taking what was rightfully his. What is more, the India conquered by Dionysus was a land of primitives, unschooled in military technique, whereas Alexander had to subjugate peoples who owed their warlike traditions to Dionysus. The task of conquest was incomparably harder, and here, as elsewhere, Alexander surpassed his divine forebear.

Megasthenes was developing the propaganda of Alexander's court. That is evident in his list of conquerors who, he alleged, failed to invade India.[129] The canonical list (including Sesostris and Semiramis) contained some very remarkable additions, notably Nebuchadnezzar of Babylon and the seventh-century Ethiopian dynast, Taharka. Both are said to have penetrated as far as the Straits of Gibraltar, and Nebuchadnezzar, a king greater than Heracles, is credited with transplanting population from Spain to the Black Sea (hence the Iberi of the Caucasus).[130] All this is strongly reminiscent of Alexander's Last Plans: his project to conquer the entire coast of North Africa, his planned invasion of the Black Sea, and the memoranda which envisaged exchanges of population between Europe and Asia.[131] Here there were precedents from the past, examples to be emulated. One reflects on the local legends of Cyrus' and Semiramis' failures in the Gedrosian desert, which according to Nearchus inspired Alexander to prove himself superior to them.[132] As for the west the examples of Nebuchadnezzar and Taharka showed his plans of conquest to be feasible and at the same time provided a yardstick of success. What legends were exploited and transformed to produce these remarkable parallels lies beyond conjecture, but it is clear that Alexander's staff had become proficient in the manufac-

suggested in Attic drama, which has at least one dark hint about the origins of Deianeira (Eur. *Cycl.* 38–40). The stemma was fully fledged in the Ptolemaic period (Satyrus, *FGrH* 631 F 1; *POxy* 2465, col. ii. 2–11), and there was every reason for its evolution at Alexander's court.

[129] Strabo 15. 1. 6 (686–7) = *FGrH* 715 F 11; cf. Arr. *Ind.* 5. 4–7, 9. 10–11; Diod. 2. 38. 1, 39. 4. Megasthenes underlined the novelty of his exposition ('he bids us have no faith in the ancient stories about the Indians', Strabo *loc. cit.*), and was clearly aware of the paradox.

[130] This was also noted in later literature, notably by Josephus (*c. Ap.* 1. 144; *AJ* 10. 227) and Abydenus (*FGrH* 685 F 6. 11), who had an interest in Nebuchadnezzar and mentioned the aberrant version of Megasthenes (*FGrH* 715 F 1).

[131] Diod. 18. 4. 4. On the invasion plans for the Black Sea see Arr. 4. 15. 6; 5. 27. 7; 7. 1. 3. The literature on the Last Plans is immense. For a recent survey see Bosworth, *From Arrian to Alexander* 185–211.

[132] Arr. 6. 24. 2–3; Strabo 15. 1. 5 (686), 2. 5 (722) = *FGrH* 133 F 3. See below, pp. 182–3.

ture of myth. Megasthenes used and developed their efforts. In his work we see the end result of a complex development. Alexander's advisers became adept at processing local information, extracting stories which could be equated with Greek tradition. On the other hand the native informants had studied their invaders and could produce material which their questioners were predisposed to exploit. The process acquired its own momentum, and a fully blown mythology of conquest emerged.

One interesting and informative episode took place in the south of the Punjab shortly after the campaign against the Malli. In the stretch of river just before the Acesines merged with the Indus (see Fig. 9) he was received by a tribe which the sources term Sambastae (or Sabarcae).[133] They hailed him as Dionysus, an identification which had been encouraged since the beginning of the river journey, and offered him 'heroic honours'.[134] That is a paradox. The hero cult was primarily a cult of the dead, and differed radically from the honours paid to the gods. City founders were given heroic honours, but only after their death. That tradition persisted into the Hellenistic age. Cineas, the founder of Aï Khanum, was interred in a specially constructed *herôon* at the heart of the city, and Aratus, the creator of the Achaean League, was also given heroic honours after his death.[135] For a living man the hero cult was a contradiction in terms, and the only attestation before Alexander is the heroic honours supposedly offered to Dion at Syracuse.[136] The evidence for the latter is suspect. There is no other direct testimony, and Diodorus

---

[133] Diod. 17. 102. 1–4; Curt. 9. 8. 4–6. The Abistani mentioned by Arr. 6. 15. 1 cannot be, as is usually assumed (cf. A. E. Anspach, *De Alexandri Magni expeditione Indica* 112–13, n. 356; Goukowsky ii. 44), identical with the Sambastae. They were subjugated by Perdiccas (ἐν παρόδῳ), and Alexander and his fleet did not impact upon their territory. It is better to assume two peoples with vaguely similar names, rather than two totally discrepant accounts of the same transaction.

[134] Curt. 9. 8. 5 (identification with Dionysus); Diod. 17. 102. 4 (heroic honours). The two versions are clearly complementary and set in the same context (cf. Hammond, *Three Historians* 155). The common source clearly mentioned both aspects of Alexander's reception: the identification with Dionysus/Śiva, which helped overcome resistance (cf. Diod. 17. 102. 3), and the honours which were offered in his presence (Curtius breaks off with the embassy of surrender).

[135] On Cineas see above all Robert, *CRAI* (1968) 431–8 = *OMS* v. 525–32. For the inscription identifying the *herôon* and *temenos* see *Fouilles d'Aï Khanoum* i. 211–37. On Aratus' heroic honours see Polyb. 8. 12. 8; Plut. *Arat.* 53; Paus. 2. 9. 4.

[136] Diod. 16. 20. 6; Plut. *Dion* 46. 1 mentions acclamations of Dion as saviour and god (σωτῆρα καὶ θεόν), but reports nothing of heroic honours. The tradition has been discussed sympathetically by C. Habicht, *Gottmenschentum und griechische Städte*[2] 8–10, 244–5, more sceptically by Badian, *Edson Studies* 42–3.

may well be garbled, confusing a vote for *ultimate* honours as a second founder (after Dion's death)[137] with immediate recognition of heroic status. However, in Alexander's case it is clear enough that the Indians performed some sort of ceremony before him which was reminiscent of the Greek hero cult.

The ceremony presumably included some type of fire sacrifice, such as was practised in India from Vedic to modern times.[138] Megasthenes was to describe some of its characteristics, the absence of the garlands, libations, and incense which were appropriate for the Greek gods and the slaughter of the sacrificial animal by suffocation.[139] Some aspects of the ritual were strongly suggestive of the Greek hero cult. Immediately after death the throat was cut and the blood (together with entrails and excrement) was poured into a trench at the extremity of the grounds of sacrifice. The rest of the beast was cooked in the fire and eventually consumed in totality, any remnant scattered to the four quarters of the heavens. This ceremony, strange and exotic to Greek observers, was far more reminiscent of the blood offerings and holocaust of the hero cult than the standard sacrificial ritual for the gods, in which the victim was struck down with an axe and its entrails, bones, and fat were the sole oblation to the divinity honoured.[140] The fire sacrifice might well have been seen as a heroic rite, and Alexander, perhaps encouraged by his interpreters, concluded that it was offered to him.

It may be sheer coincidence that heroic honours surface at Alexander's court when his friend and favourite, Hephaestion, died,

---

[137] This would be comparable to the heroic honours for Hieron at Aetna. They were actually performed posthumously (Diod. 11. 66. 4), but the cult was prefigured in his lifetime, when he was termed 'founder' (cf. Pind. *Pyth.* 1. 31; F 105 Snell/Maehler). Dion may similarly have had provision in his lifetime for his future posthumous cult, as indeed may Diocles in the previous century (Diod. 13. 35. 2).

[138] J. Schwab, *Das altindische Thieropfer* (Erlangen 1886), esp. 106–12, remains the classic compilation of evidence. On the re-enactment staged in Kerala (without the sacrificial animal) in April 1975 one may consult the massive 2-volume work by F. Staal, *Agni. The Vedic Ritual of the Fire Altar* (Berkeley 1983): i. 48–9 deals with the method of sacrifice. See also C. Z. Minkowski, *Priesthood in Ancient India* (Vienna 1991) 50–5.

[139] Strabo 15. 1. 54 (710) = *FGrH* 715 F 32. The prescription for killing (by suffocation or strangulation) is given in the *Srauta Sūtra* (*Kātyāyana* 6. 5. 17 = H. C. Ramage, *Kātyāyana Srauta Sūtra* (Poona 1977): 'They hold the animal's mouth tight and control its breath, so that it breaths its last without making any noise.').

[140] 'Offrande qui ne coûte beaucoup plus qu'un simple *benedicite*': M. Delcourt, *Légendes et cultes de héros en Grèce*—a succinct description of the two sacrificial rituals. See also Ph.-E. Legrand, in DS iv. 970–2 and, for exceptions to the rule, A. D. Nock, *Essays on Religion and the Ancient World* 590–2.

late in 324.[141] After all Hephaestion had founded cities at Alexander's behest in Sogdiana and the Punjab,[142] and might reasonably have been awarded the traditional heroization of a city founder. However, Hephaestion's cult was not localized in the cities he had established. It was aggressively promoted throughout the Mediterranean world,[143] sanctioned by the oracle at Siwah, and represented as compulsory by the hostile Hypereides.[144] The hero cult was clearly important to Alexander, and after his death it was extended to the living courtiers of Demetrius Poliorcetes, who received heroic honours at Athens.[145] By the end of the fourth century heroization of a living man was no longer a paradox, and it could be argued that the Indian honours for Alexander set a precedent. The Sambastae had honoured him in native style as the avatar of some local god deemed to be the equivalent of Dionysus, and Alexander interpreted the honours as heroic. If he himself could be recognized and fêted as a living hero, it opened the way for others to receive heroic honours while he stood above them as god manifest. The two tiers of honour for Demetrius and his courtiers may well have been prefigured in the thinking of Alexander himself.

What had happened to Alexander during his years in the east was no metamorphosis. It was a reinforcement of existing ideas and attitudes. Autocracy had always been a characteristic of Macedonian kingship. In their relations with the Greek cities of the south Philip and Alexander had operated with prudential moderation, creating a superficially traditional system of control, in which the Macedonian king acted as the executive leader (*hegemon*) and pursued policy endorsed by a representative council (*synedrion*) of autonomous allies. However, as the Thebans could testify, the mask of moderation might slip under the stress of a political crisis. The city's very existence was terminated by an *ad hoc* meeting of allies who hap-

---

[141] Arr. 7. 23. 5–8 (cf. 14. 7); Plut. *Al.* 72. 3. The vulgate tradition (Diod. 17. 115. 6; Justin 12. 12. 12; cf. Lucian *Calumn.* 17) incorrectly speaks of full deification, perhaps confusing Alexander's original request (Arr. 7. 14. 7) with what was actually conceded.

[142] Arr. 4. 16. 3; 5. 29. 3; 6. 21. 5. Cf. Bosworth, *HCA* ii. 113–14, 358.

[143] Particularly in Alexandria, where Cleomenes constructed *heroa* on the mainland and on the island of Pharos (Arr. 7. 23. 7).

[144] Hyper. 6 (*Epit.*). 21. On reading and interpretation see Cawkwell (above, n. 2) 297–300, who interprets the compulsion as the moral constraint of the oracle rather than the political constraint of the Macedonians. That I find singularly hard to accept.

[145] Demochares, *FGrH* 75 F 1 = Athen. 6. 253 A. Cf. C. Habicht, *Gottmenschentum und griechische Städte*[2] 55–8, 255–6.

pened to be present at the siege,[146] and, if the council had any involvement, it was only to give its retrospective blessing. Similarly some precedent for Alexander's claims to superhuman status may be found in Philip's actions before his assassination in 336. Even if he did not claim divine status outright, he certainly associated himself closely with the Olympians,[147] and his son may well have been predisposed to see himself as divine. If so, he was confirmed in his belief as the campaign progressed. The visit to Siwah justified his belief that he had divine parentage, and his courtiers reiterated the message that his achievements more than equalled the most exemplary sons of Zeus, whose benefactions to humanity had given them divinity. At the same time his staff was constructing a triumphal progress in the far east for Heracles and Dionysus, a progress which Alexander was constantly matching. The evidence accumulated that his conquests were unique and the uncontestable proof of his divinity. As a god himself and the counterpart of Zeus on earth there were no constraints upon him, and the hallmark of his regime became the categorical imperative.

The events in the east provide the explanation and justification for most of the episodes after Alexander's return to the west, particularly those which modern scholars have been reluctant to accept because of their outrageous exuberance. The empire-wide command to disband mercenary armies was a global answer to the problems of satrapal subordination and came easily from the counterpart of Zeus on earth. Similarly the repatriation of Greek exiles could be viewed as a universal benefaction which should not be shackled by the vested interests which happened to be enshrined in the Corinthian League.[148] The king had achieved divinity through his magnanimity and he continued to dispense his inexorable gifts[149] unconcerned by the fine print of current treaties. At a more trivial level the mentality is well illustrated by the command to Phocion to take control of one

---

[146] Arr. 1. 9. 9; Justin 11. 3. 8. Diodorus (17. 14. 1) implies that the *synedrion* was convened, but see Bosworth, *HCA* i. 89–90; B. Gullath, *Untersuchungen zur Geschichte Boiotiens* 84.

[147] On the evidence see the conflicting views of E. A. Fredricksmeyer, *TAPA* 109 (1979) 39–61, and in *Macedonian Heritage* 94–8; G. T. Griffith, in Hammond and Griffith, *History of Macedonia* ii. 682–4; Badian, in *Edson Studies* 39–42, 67–71.

[148] Diod. 18. 8. 4 purports to cite the words of the edict, which disclaim responsibility for the exiles and proclaim the restitution as a benefaction. On the implications of the decree see Bosworth, *Conquest and Empire* 220–8.

[149] This is the formulation of Fritz Schachermeyr ('Wohltun ohne Pardon'); cf. his *Al.²* 602, expanded in *Entretiens Hardt* 22 (1976) 68–79.

of four cities of Asia (Greek and non-Greek are grouped together; it made no difference).[150] Refusal, it is added, would incur the king's anger. The benefaction was paramount. Its recipient could not decline the offer, and at stake were the political life and revenues of entire civic entities. They were at the disposal of the royal benefactor.

Alexander's actions stemmed from his belief in his godhead. That is the reverse of the famous theory, enunciated by Eduard Meyer[151] and often reformulated, which interprets Alexander's divinity as a conscious political creation. In Meyer's view his world monarchy was intended to guarantee individual liberties and the autonomy of small communities. That ideal condition would only be realized under an enlightened regime, controlled by a despot who would override abuses of autonomy by individuals or communities. However, such an overriding position was a contradiction of Greek concepts of autonomy, and could only be tolerated if the regime was based on law rather than caprice, 'if the King is more than a man, if he is elevated to a God.' Meyer's Alexander *was* Aristotle's superman. The word had become flesh. Accordingly Alexander propagated his divinity to ensure that his political benefactions would be accepted by his subjects. In particular the Exiles' Decree, which subverted the Corinthian League for the greater good of its members, could only be implemented if the Greek cities became part of the monarchy. That was achieved by their recognition of Alexander as a god; 'what he ordered was thereafter law for them, not because he was King but because he was God.'[152]

---

[150] Plut. *Phoc.* 18. 7–8; Ael. *VH* 1. 25. The tradition has recently been defended against the sceptical arguments of Tarn, *Al.* ii. 222–7, by T. Corsten, *Historia* 43 (1994) 112–18. Plutarch gives the four cities as Cius, Gergithus, Mylasa, and Elaea; Aelian substitutes Lycian Patara for Gergithus.

[151] The essay, 'Alexander der Grosse und die absolute Monarchie', had an interesting genesis, written around 1902, to appear first in (incompetent) translation in an American magazine (cf. E. Badian, in *Eduard Meyer. Leben und Leistung eines Universalhistorikers*, ed. W. M. Calder and A. Demandt, 8–28, 33–8). Its German version appears in Meyer's *Kleine Schriften* (2nd edn.: Halle 1924) i. 267–314. The key passage is at i. 293–4: 'die moderne absolute Monarchie kann nur dann ein Reichstaat sein, in dem, wie in der athenischen Demokratie, nicht die Willkür sondern das Gesetz herrscht, wenn der König mehr ist als ein Mensch, wenn er zum Gott erhoben ist.'

[152] *Kleine Schriften* i. 313–14. The formulation was sharpened and trivialized by Tarn, *Al.* i. 113: 'The Covenant bound Alexander of Macedon; it would not bind Alexander the god; the way therefore to exercise authority in the cities was to become a god' (cf. ii. 370–3). An interesting variant was excogitated by K. M. T. Atkinson, *Athenaeum* 51 (1973) 310–35, esp. 332–4, who has Alexander promote his cult in order to make his opponents liable to charges of perjury.

For Meyer even Alexander's apotheosis had a rational basis. The king needed to cancel existing compacts in the general interest of humanity. He could only do so if there was some supreme, unchallengeable sanction, and that sanction was the ruler's divinity. The cult was therefore designed as a tool of universal monarchy. This was an attractive theory under the Hohenzollerns, and Meyer duly included it in a wartime speech of 1918, commemorating the birthday of the Kaiser.[153] But Meyer wisely refused to address the central premiss of his thesis. That Alexander's actions as god could not be challenged he presumably thought self-evident. Yet the Greek cities were demonstrably reluctant to accept the benefaction, did so only under constraint, and rebelled against it the moment their new god was translated to the heavens. In crude terms Meyer had it exactly the wrong way around. Alexander did not become god in order to enact the Exiles' Decree; he enacted it because he was convinced of his divinity. He had the temporal power to impose whatever he decreed, and, as living law, the counterpart of Zeus, he could and would cancel any dispositions brokered by his mortal father. His power and his achievements made him a god among men, and he considered it proper for his divinity to be adequately recognized. On his suggestion the cities of the Greek mainland, including Athens and Sparta, enacted cult honours for him, and according to Aristobulus he considered it appropriate for him to become the third god of the Arabs alongside Uranus and Dionysus. Yet again his conviction was reinforced, as cults were showered upon him and Greek embassies approached him crowned with wreaths as though they were consulting a god. Whether or not that was an act of worship remains controversial, but the similarities to sacral embassies were surely deliberate and intended to suggest that the person they approached was divine. The process begun in Sogdiana had reached its logical conclusion. There was now no need for *proskynesis* to symbolize the king's claim to divinity. It was universally and openly recognized.

---

[153] The speech, entitled 'Vorläufer des Weltkriegs im Altertum', was delivered on 24 Jan. 1918. The passage at issue appears in Meyer's *Kleine Schriften* ii. 529.

5
The Justification of Terror

EARLY in 325 Alexander embarked on one of the most savage campaigns of repression recorded in our sources. It was directed against the Malli (Malavas), an independent people of the southern Punjab. Comparatively short (little more than a week) in duration, it was horrendously violent in execution, and the Malli suffered enormously. After the campaign Arrian refers to them as a remnant, 'those of the Malli who survived',[1] and from the narrative it is clear that whole communities came close to extermination. The ferocity of the fighting has always raised eyebrows. For the humanitarian Tarn the campaign was 'unique in its dreadful record of mere slaughter',[2] and he had an explanation ready for the aberration: the culprits were the Macedonian troops, who were reluctant to fight and responded by giving no quarter. This raises interesting and important questions. How unique was the Malli campaign? To what extent were the troops unwilling? Why was it necessary to fight in the first place? Tarn's observations have the merit of focusing precisely on the issue of repression. Much of Arrian's narrative in Books 4–6 is a veritable chronicle of slaughter, punctuated by siege narratives and the mass killing which was the depressing concomitant of capture by storm. It must necessarily have had an effect upon the army, but whether it produced a reluctance to fight is highly debatable. Alexander's own response also deserves examination. Why did he launch such an atrocious and apparently unnecessary campaign, and why did he harry the civilian population with such uncompromising ruthlessness?

Arrian introduces the Malli just before his dramatic description of the rapids at the confluence of the Hydaspes and Acesines, and outlines Alexander's reasons for attacking them. They were the most

---

[1] Arr. 6. 14. 1, 3 (τῶν Μαλλῶν τοῖς ἔτι σωζομένοις).

[2] Tarn, *Al.* i. 103, a verdict repeated verbatim (and without acknowledgement) by A. K. Narain, *G&R* 12 (1965) 160.

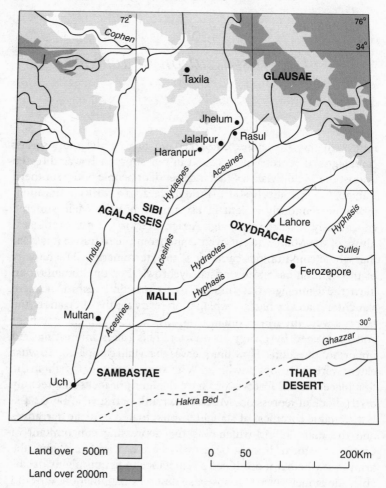

Fig. 9. An approximation of the configuration of the Punjab in antiquity
(the river courses are wholly conjectural)

populous and warlike people of the area, and were reported to be
bent on resistance; they had evacuated their women and children,
placing them in the most securely defended cities, and were ready to
take the field against Alexander (Arr. 6. 4. 3). Other sources suggest
that they had formed a defensive alliance with their northern neigh-

bours, the Oxydracae,[3] but negotiations for a unified command had foundered.[4] However, there was certainly the prospect of general resistance in the Rechna Doab (the land enclosed between the rivers Chenab and Ravi), and it was in Alexander's interest to attack while the two peoples were at odds. There was also military kudos to be gained by an invasion, as the Malli and Oxydracae had a reputation for bravery. Porus, who had unsuccessfully attempted to subjugate the autonomous peoples of the region,[5] might well have given an inflated impression of their military potential. Everything encouraged Alexander to organize a pre-emptive strike. The Malli were to be crushed before they could form a common front with the Oxydracae, and, given their reputation, their defeat would deter others from similar resistance.

Alexander, as we have seen,[6] was meticulously informed about the topography of the area he intended to attack, and he was able to impinge on Malli territory where he was least expected. It was also a point of refugee concentration, one of the cities chosen to support evacuees from the heartland, and it is hard not to see the attack as the first act in a campaign of calculated terror. The Malli had intended to save their women and children by relocating them in safe havens at the extremity of their territory. So Alexander struck there first. From his base at the confluence (of the Jhelum and Chenab) he struck out eastwards across the desert with a relatively small force: the indispensable nucleus of hypaspists, Agrianians, and archers, a single phalanx battalion, the Iranian horse archers, and half the Companion cavalry (Arr. 6. 6. 1). In all this attack group can hardly have numbered more than 12,000, but it comprised the most

[3] The Oxydracae (Kśudrakas) were associated with the Malli (Malavas) in Indian epic, which occasionally refers to them as a composite entity, the *Kśudrakamalava* (see, conveniently, O. Stein, *RE* xviii. 2024, 2030). That may help explain why the rhetorical tradition persistently and incorrectly locates Alexander's campaign among the Oxydracae, not the Malli (cf. Arr. 6. 11. 3 with Bosworth, *From Arrian to Alexander* 76–7).

[4] Diod. 17. 98. 1–2. Curt. 9. 4. 24–6 has a confused story that the Oxydracan army took the field; it attempted battle at the foot of a mountain (hard to find in the Punjab plain), but dispersed before the encounter. This seems an erratic conflation of Diodorus' story of the abortive alliance and Arrian's tradition of a dawn attack (cf. Curt. 9. 4. 25) on the Malli territory.

[5] Arr. 5. 22. 2. The Malli and Oxydracae are mentioned as paradigms of military valour, like the Cathaei who were attacked by Porus. Arrian does not explicitly state that they suffered in Porus' invasion (cf. Bosworth, *HCA* ii. 328), but they were close enough to the Cathaei to be threatened. Porus, at any rate, had every inducement to encourage Alexander to subjugate them.   [6] Above, Ch. 3 with n. 29.

experienced, battle-hardened troops in Alexander's army. This contingent with Alexander pushed directly across the band of desert which lay between the Chenab and Ravi river systems.[7] Two other groups under Hephaestion and Ptolemy were to follow the line of the Chenab eight days apart. Their function was to intercept any refugees who tried to escape to the rear of Alexander's attack.[8] If the fugitives sought sanctuary to the west, in the direction of the Chenab, then they were in a lethal trap, between two columns of Macedonian troops. To the east the Ravi was a significant, though (at low water) not insuperable obstacle. The entire Rechna Doab in effect became a killing ground, and the campaign was designed to maximize the slaughter.

The execution more than lived up to expectations. Alexander's attack force crossed the desert by night, quickly enough to forestall any rumour of its coming, and at dawn it entered the territory of a sizeable Malli city which had been selected as a reception point for refugees. They had never expected that Alexander would come from the desert, and Arrian drives the message home: 'The majority of the Malli were outside the city and unarmed. The reason why (as was now clear) Alexander had brought his men by this route was that it *was* difficult, and consequently it did not appear credible even to the enemy that he would take it. So he fell upon them totally by surprise, and killed the majority of them, who did not even offer resistance, seeing that they were unarmed' (Arr. 6. 6. 3). This was a premeditated massacre of a population which was largely defenceless. The Macedonians were not, as Tarn would have it, reacting spontaneously; they were pursuing a policy of terror devised by their leaders.

[7] The exact route cannot be traced, since the river system of the Punjab has changed since antiquity, and both the Chenab and the Ravi will have flowed considerably to the east of their present course. One may assume that the distance between them corresponded *roughly* to the present width of the Rechna Doab; it is approximately 80 km. from the confluence of the Jhelum and Chenab to the nearest point on the Ravi. That coheres pretty well with Arrian's figure of 500 stades (Arr. 6. 6. 2), or 100 km., but, given the highly unpleasant conditions in the desert and the fact that most of the marching took place overnight, in unfamiliar terrain, it is hard to credit that such a distance was covered in a single day and night. The distance may be exaggerated, or (more probably) the time required for the transit minimized.

[8] Arr. 6. 5. 6–7; cf. Tarn, *Al.* ii. 27; Heckel 81. Another interpretation (Berve ii. 172, 332; J. Seibert, *Die Eroberung des Perserreiches* 163–4) has Hephaestion precede Alexander into Malli territory and Ptolemy follow: in other words they did not follow the course of the Chenab. That violates the clear sense of the text, and one is hard put to explain why neither column is mentioned during the actual fighting in Malli territory.

Alexander, moreover, did everything in his power to preserve the advantage of surprise. Perdiccas was sent ahead to seal off a neighbouring city, which had received some of the survivors from the countryside, and he had explicit instructions to prevent news of the invasion spreading. It was too late. The inhabitants had already fled in panic, and all Perdiccas could do was harry the stragglers, until the bulk of the fugitives reached the riverain marshes (Arr. 6. 6. 6). The news now spread among the Malli communities, and it precipitated a general evacuation of the west bank of the Hydraotes (Ravi).

In the meantime Alexander had captured the first city. The defenders who had managed to acquire arms deserted the walls and took refuge in the citadel. That gave some respite, but after an interval (a few hours at most) it was taken by storm, with Alexander himself pressing on the attack; and all the defenders, some 2,000 according to Arrian, were killed. Arrian underlines the intensity of the fighting and the relentless ruthlessness of the attackers,[9] and the theme recurs constantly in his description of the campaign. The Macedonians are chillingly competent in the art of killing, and Alexander is represented as practically frenzied, abandoned to the excitement of combat. Accordingly the campaign began with a massacre, and the momentum rarely slackened.

Alexander had been able to capture some of the civilian population, and his native guides in any case will have informed him of the geography of the area. As he rested his troops after the capture of the citadel, he learned of the evacuation, and once again moved in the most devastating manner. Once again he marched overnight, and at dawn he reached one of the main crossing points of the Hydraotes. When he arrived, the river was still blocked by refugees. Arrian gives a sober account of what happened next: Alexander attacked, killed a great number of refugees at the ford, and crossed the river to overhaul the vanguard of the evacuation. 'Many he killed, some he took alive, the majority fled into a fortified stronghold' (Arr. 6. 7. 2). The stronghold itself soon fell to Peithon, who took it by direct assault, and enslaved the refugees there, 'those at least who had not died in the attack' (Arr. 6. 7. 3). Once more Arrian's qualification is eloquent. Alexander himself had pressed rapidly onwards to the 'city

---

[9] Arr. 6. 6. 5: 'for a time they resisted, seeing that the position was elevated and difficult to attack; but when the Macedonians pressed the assault vigorously from all quarters and Alexander himself appeared at the various points of the action the citadel was taken by storm.'

of the Brahmans',[10] which he had learned was another refugee
centre, and he arrived before the population could be evacuated.
Siege operations began immediately. Mining made short work of the
mud-brick wall, and the Macedonian catapults stripped away the
defenders to their ultimate refuge in the citadel. Some of the
Macedonians followed so closely that they were trapped inside the
fortifications, and twenty-five of them were killed (Arr. 6. 7. 4). Their
comrades continued the siege of the citadel, undermined a tower,
and badly damaged a curtain wall. At this point Alexander himself
appeared on the wall at the head of the assault, and galvanized his
men into following him. The citadel was promptly captured; and the
Indians fired their houses, and for the most part perished in the
conflagration. Arrian again counts the toll: 5,000 enemy dead, a
mere handful taken alive because of the vigour of the defence.

One slightly discordant detail stands out in this episode. It is not
so much that Alexander appears at the head of the final attack; what
is significant is that the rest of the Macedonians 'were ashamed'
(αἰσχυνθέντες) by his initiative. That gives the impression of reluctance, the unwillingness for combat identified by Tarn. However,
these reluctant troops were eager enough to be trapped in the citadel
alongside the Indian fugitives, and their morale seems to have been
reasonably high. But one should look again at their programme over
the last few days: a forced march across some 80 km. of desert,
lasting at least a day and a night; massacre at the first Malli city,
followed by a sharp action to storm its citadel; a few hours' rest and
another night march to the Hydraotes ford; another massacre at the
crossing and again a forced march, with intermittent killing, to the
Brahman city; mining works at the outer walls, and finally the attack
on the Brahman citadel. The exertions had been prodigious and
practically unrelenting; and by the time they reached the Brahman
city the Macedonians must have been bone weary. If the attack was
flagging, it was through sheer fatigue. It took the immediate danger
to Alexander's person (and the collateral danger for themselves if he
died)[11] for them to expend their last reserves of energy in capturing
the citadel. Their reward was rest—for an entire day. The momentum of the invasion necessarily slackened, but there were limits to

---

[10] On the status of the city and the impact of Alexander's operations there see
above, pp. 94–7.
[11] Vividly depicted (from Nearchus) by Arr. 6. 12. 1–2. See above, pp. 55–9.

human endurance. During the rest day most of the neighbouring cities were deserted by their inhabitants, who took refuge in the desert east of the Hydraotes, and, rather than pursue them further, Alexander rested his troops for another day (Arr. 6. 8. 1–2).

The campaign then resumed in full force. Peithon and Demetrius were sent along the Hydraotes, clearing the woods of fugitives. They had specific instructions, which they scrupulously obeyed, to kill any Malli they encountered, 'except those who voluntarily surrendered their persons' (Arr. 6. 8. 1–2). Immediate, unconditional capitulation was the only escape, and one wonders how often the Macedonians allowed it. Arrian at least reports many killings but no surrenders. By this stage the Malli had been reduced to demoralized panic. They abandoned their capital without resistance, and its population was evacuated away from the invading forces, to the west bank of the Hydraotes (Arr. 6. 8. 4). An attempt to hold the banks against Alexander became a pathetic fiasco. As they saw the Macedonian cavalry approach, its advance enshrouded by the dust of the dry season,[12] the Malli warriors assumed that Alexander's entire army was with him, and withdrew from the bank. Once Alexander was midstream, and the dust subsided, they realized their mistake and turned back. But even then they did not engage directly. Alexander's small advance group of cavalry was able to hold the crossing point, making threatening forays against the mass of Malli defenders until the infantry finally appeared on the scene (Arr. 6. 8. 6–7). Then, in language which recalls the flight of Darius at Gaugamela,[13] Arrian describes the final pursuit. The Malli turned tail, and headed for the nearest city in the vicinity (usually referred to as 'the Malli town'). There was the mandatory slaughter of stragglers, after that the immediate investment of the city by infantry and cavalry. Arrian (6. 8. 8) adds that the attack was deferred until the following day because of the army's fatigue.

The siege that ensued followed the pattern of the earlier engage-

[12] This detail is not in Arrian, but it is a necessary condition of the action. It explains why the Malli only realized that the cavalry were detached from the rest of the army when Alexander was midstream (Arr. 6. 8. 6). The dust raised by the cavalry must have been a significant factor; the Indian conditions enhanced Sir John Fuller's appreciation of Gaugamela (J. F. C. Fuller, *The Generalship of Alexander the Great* 172 n. 2: 'Anyone who has witnessed a cavalry charge in the dry weather, over an Indian maidan will be able to picture what the dust at Arbela was like').

[13] Arr. 6. 8. 7: ἀμοῦ σφισι πάντων τῶν δεινῶν προσκειμένων. Cf. 3. 14. 3: πάντα ὁμοῦ τὰ δεινὰ...ἐφαίνετο. It is a unique match of terminology in Arrian, and must be deliberate.

ments—the Malli immediately abandoned the walls and retreated into the citadel (Arr. 6. 9. 1). At this point the sources stress that the assault flagged, and there is some agreement that there was a delay in bringing up the siege apparatus.[14] Alexander, as ever, headed the attack, and was able to break through a postern in the outer wall. The second assault group under Perdiccas was forced to scale the walls, and did so for the most part without ladders.[15] As a result the attack on the citadel faltered, and Alexander, chafing at the delay, stormed up a ladder himself. As his troops followed *en masse*, the ladder broke under their collective weight, and the king was virtually isolated on the ramparts. The celebrated wound ensued.[16] What concerns us here is the Macedonian reluctance to attack the citadel. There was certainly a delay at the foot of the walls, and clearly a shortage of scaling ladders. The few that were brought to the scene collapsed under the weight of numbers, and Arrian carefully explains why so few were available, ascribing the failure to lack of judgement in Perdiccas' command.[17] The delay was therefore rational. The troops were waiting for more ladders before taking the offensive— and we may well believe that after the rigours of the campaign they *were* unwilling to proceed before they could mount the attack in full force. That was unacceptable to Alexander, who pressed on in an uncontrollable fury. It was the military counterpart to his killing of Cleitus. The troops were not refusing action. They were exercising a proper caution, but their leader was beyond control.

The capture of the citadel was inevitable. Alexander's self-imperilment simply accelerated it, and gave it a particular hideousness. The massacre was general, and no quarter was given, even to

---

[14] Diod. 17. 98. 5 (τῶν Μακεδόνων διατριβόντων); Curt. 9. 4. 30 ('cunctantibusque ceteris'); Plut. *Al.* 63. 3.

[15] Arr. 6. 9. 2. The stress on Perdiccas' leadership is evident and calculated. Arrian allows for genuine misunderstanding: the troops thought that the defence had collapsed, and were unwilling to burden themselves with unnecessary apparatus. None the less, it *was* a miscalculation, and it imperilled Alexander and the entire army. It hardly reflected credit on Perdiccas' leadership, and the bias is what we should expect from his enemy, Ptolemy (cf. Pédech, *Historiens compagnons* 306; Heckel 141–2).

[16] Arr. 6. 9. 3–10. 1. Cf. Diod. 17. 98. 5–6; Curt. 9. 4. 30–3; Just. 12. 9. 5–12; *Metz Epit.* 76–7; Plut. *Al.* 63. 3–7.

[17] Arr. 6. 9. 2–3. The wording is extremely circumspect. Alexander suspected the troops of deliberate shirking (βλακεύειν αὐτῷ ἐδόκουν), and taken in isolation, this would seem to be corroboration of Tarn's hypothesis that the troops were unwilling to fight. However, the context in Arrian makes it clear that Alexander was mistaken. The shortage of siege ladders was due to a misunderstanding, ultimately to a failure in command.

women and children.[18] Enslavement was not an option. The siege brought the campaign to an end. There might have been a flicker of resistance at the rumour of Alexander's death, but it was quickly scotched by his demonstration that he was alive and well.[19] The surviving Malli sent an embassy of surrender, as did the neighbouring Oxydracae,[20] who had watched the campaign with appalled fascination, effectively deterred from assisting their old comrades-in-arms. A week of savage fighting had resulted in total victory, total demoralization of the Malli; and it would probably be an understatement to describe the carnage as decimation.

There are various lessons to be drawn. The overwhelming military superiority of the invaders is nowhere more evident than in the description of this campaign. The bows and spears of the Malli seem to have been ineffectual against the thrusting pikes and missile weapons of the Macedonians. It was far more than superior weaponry.[21] What was decisive was the superior skill imparted by a decade of more or less continuous warfare. The scene in Arrian where Alexander with his handful of cavalry at the ford holds at bay some 50,000 armed Malli epitomizes the campaign.[22] The numbers are certainly exaggerated, but the general picture rings true. Alexander was able to intimidate a vastly greater force by sheer technical mastery and the mystique of his reputation. As so often, the episode is reminiscent of the Conquistadors in Mexico. Díaz records a comparable incident in the Tlaxcalan campaign of September 1519. Cortés and his little army were attacked by a force of Indians which Díaz estimates at 50,000 (Cortés had given the amusingly precise figure of 149,000).[23] The armament of the two

---

[18] Arr. 6. 11. 1; Curt. 9. 5. 19–20; Diod. 17. 99. 4; *Metz Epit.* 77.

[19] Curt. 9. 6. 1. See above, p. 56.

[20] Arr. 6. 14. 1–2; cf. Strabo 15. 1. 8 (687–8). See below, p. 123.

[21] Nearchus gave a careful description of Indian bows and broadswords (Strabo 15. 1. 66 (717) = *FGrH* 133 F 23), and stressed the penetrative power of the Indian archery (Arr. *Ind.* 16. 7: 'nothing withstands an arrow shot by an Indian archer, neither shield nor breastplate, however strong its make'). It is clear that the Indian weaponry was technologically adequate (cf. Arr. 5. 18. 5, with Bosworth, *HCA* ii. 306–7), but the soldiers had neither the experience nor the discipline to counter the massed tactics of the Macedonian phalanx.

[22] Arr. 6. 8. 6–7. The scene is not dissimilar from the fighting at the crossing of the Granicus (cf. Arr. 1. 14. 6–15. 3, with Bosworth, *HCA* i. 120–2), but unlike the Persians, who attack in force, the Indians hold back.

[23] Díaz pp. 148–50 (Cohen), pp. 193–7 (Maudslay). He describes the situation thus: 'We were four hundred, many of whom were sick and wounded, and we stood

sides was of disproportionate quality, but within their stone-age context the Indians had formidable weapons: clubs set with razor-sharp obsidian, which were able to decapitate a horse,[24] javelins, and fire-hardened arrows. For Díaz it was the Spanish expertise with sword and crossbow which carried the day ('only by a miracle of sword play were we able to drive them back and save our lives'). In addition the Indians were so tightly packed 'that every shot wrought havoc'. There were also clear signs of demoralization, as the Indians in some cases refused battle. Both Malli and Tlaxcalans faced invaders immeasurably more skilful in the basic techniques of combat, and in both cases the result was wholly disproportionate slaughter.

The Malli campaign is a clear example of conquest through terror. Its object was to kill as many of the Malli as was physically possible and deter resistance elsewhere. However, it was no unique display of terrorism. Arrian admittedly dwells upon the campaign, as did Ptolemy, his primary source for the episode.[25] However, there was a dramatic reason for the abundance of detail. Both authors were interested in the circumstances of Alexander's wound, and sketched in the background. Other campaigns with less dramatic consequences are passed over more baldly, but their horrors may well have been comparable. Something similar had happened shortly before Alexander's invasion of the Malli lands. Arrian writes very laconically of Alexander's activities on the lower Hydaspes: some peoples surrendered voluntarily, but others turned to arms and were subjugated.[26] In place of this deliberately generalized description the vulgate tradition supplies two specific names. The Sibi, who boasted descent from Heracles, surrendered voluntarily, but the Agalasseis, who were under arms, Alexander attacked. He defeated them in the

---

in the middle of a plain six miles long, and perhaps as broad, swarming with Indian warriors.' Cortés p. 60 deals with the battle in a few sentences, suggesting that the 149,000 Indians were repelled without trouble in 4 hours' fighting (rhetorically embellished by Gómara p. 104).

[24] Recorded by Díaz p. 145 (Cohen), p. 189 (Maudslay) as well as Francisco de Aguilar pp. 139–40 (de Fuentes), who emphasizes that the warriors 'were very well armed in their fashion'.

[25] It is a universal assumption that Arr. 6. 6. 1–10. 4 is an elaboration of Ptolemy, who is cited by name for a detail of the narrative (6. 10. 1–2; see above, pp. 62–4). For the attribution see Strasburger 45; Kornemann 81–4; Hammond, *Sources* 268–9.

[26] Arr. 6. 4. 2. The qualification ('those who now (ἤδη) turned to arms he subjugated') suggests that this was the first serious fighting of the river journey. For a similar expression see Arr. 5. 21. 6.

field with heavy slaughter, and enslaved the survivors who had taken refuge in nearby towns (reminiscent of the instructions to Peithon at the Hydraotes). Other refugees had concentrated in a major city, which Alexander besieged and captured, losing a significant number of Macedonians in savage street-fighting. In the end the Agalasseis themselves set fire to their houses, just like the defenders of the city of the Brahmans, and the 3,000 surviving warriors surrendered the acropolis voluntarily.[27] Here the pattern is exactly that of the Malli campaign. Taking arms against the invasion provokes the most savage intervention, and refugee concentrations are systematically harried. The only escape from death or enslavement is unconditional surrender. Arrian has glossed over the episode in a few general words, but elsewhere he reports the surrender of the Sibi, which he reserved for the discussion of Heracles in his monograph on India.[28] He may have felt that it would reduce the impact of his description of the Malli campaign if he prefaced it by a very similar episode. The brevity of his report does not justify rejecting the facts recorded by Diodorus and Curtius.

The river voyage of 326/5 entailed some singularly vicious fighting, but there was nothing atypical in its circumstances. When Alexander first entered the Indian lands, late in 327, he had operated in a very similar fashion. There were reports that the Aspasii of the Alingar valley had evacuated the countryside and taken refuge in mountain strongholds and fortified cities.[29] The king's response was to lay siege to the first city he encountered. The resistance, as in the Malli communities, was hopeless. The outer wall was in poor repair and indefensible, and the defenders fled from the inner citadel once the Macedonian siege ladders and catapults came into play. No prisoners were taken. Arrian suggests that the massacre was a spontaneous reprisal for the superficial shoulder wound Alexander suffered during

---

[27] Diod. 17. 96. 2–5; Curt. 9. 4. 1–8; Justin 12. 9. 2. There is some dispute about the location of this campaign, which has been identified with the strike against the neighbours of the Malli, recorded by Arr. 6. 5. 4 (A. E. Anspach, *De Alexandri Magni expeditione Indica* 96–7; J. Seibert, *Die Eroberung des Perserreiches* 162–3). But that comes after the passage of the rapids at the confluence of the Hydaspes and Acesines, whereas in the vulgate the campaign against the Agalasseis antedates the fleet's arrival at the confluence. The Sibi and Agalasseis most probably lay to the south-west of the Hydaspes, just before its confluence with the Acesines. But wherever the campaign is sited, it bears a close resemblance to the war against the Malli.

[28] Arr. *Ind.* 5. 12; cf. *Anab.* 5. 3. 4; Strabo 15. 1. 8 (688). The direct source is certainly Eratosthenes. Cf. Bosworth, *HCA* ii. 213–19.

[29] Arr. 4. 23. 2. For the location of the campaign see Bosworth, *HCA* ii. 155–7.

the siege, but, according to the vulgate tradition, it was a direct command, issued before the siege began.[30] That is quite plausible, and Curtius describes it in so many words as terrorism ('ut... terrorem incuteret'). It was no isolated act. Craterus was left in the Alingar valley with explicit instructions to destroy all cities which were not surrendered voluntarily, while Alexander moved on to the next river system, where the same strategy of pursuing and harrying refugees took effect.[31] By the time he had completed his campaign in Swat and captured the stronghold of Aornus, the population was reduced to panic. As Alexander went south through the territory of Dyrta (modern Buner), he found city and country alike devoid of inhabitants, and it took some effort to capture a handful of informants to brief him about local conditions, in particular the location of the royal elephant herd.[32] The region was indubitably pacified, but it was literally desert. In the same way, when the fleet entered the delta area of the Indus in summer 325, it found an empty land. The ruler of Patala had offered submission, but found it prudent to disappear with the majority of his subjects before Alexander arrived in person. It required a proclamation of immunity for persons and property before any could be tempted to return.[33]

What we have observed is a conscious policy of repression. Throughout the campaigns in India, from his entry point in the Cophen valley to his exit west of Karachi, he demanded instant, unconditional surrender. The price of resistance, or even intended resistance, was invasion, destruction of urban centres, and harassment of refugees. The frightfulness could be terminated by capitulation, but opposition of any sort brought destruction. To some degree this was foreshadowed in Sogdiana, after the great revolt of summer 329. On that occasion Alexander could be represented as the injured party. There had been a general revolt against him, and his garrison troops had been slaughtered by the insurgents.[34] The savagery of his

[30] Arr. 4. 23. 5; cf. Curt. 8. 10. 5 ('praecipit ne cui parceretur').

[31] Arr. 4. 23. 5–24.2. For Ptolemy's account of the operations see above, pp. 41–8.

[32] Arr. 4. 30. 5–7. For a minor skirmish in the area see Curtius 8. 12. 1–2 with Bosworth, *HCA* ii. 194.

[33] Arr. 6. 17. 5–6; Curt. 9. 8. 28–30. Curtius mentions that a great quantity of booty was taken and has nothing on the return of the natives (see above, Ch. 3, n. 112). One may well question how numerous or confident these returnees were. The scene in Arrian is reminiscent of Cortés' story (p. 74) that after the massacre of Cholula (below, p. 161) the non-combatants returned to the city 'all unafraid, as though nothing had happened'.

[34] Arr. 4. 1. 4–5; Curt. 7. 6. 13–15; *Metz Epit.* 9.

response is here understandable. Five cities were allegedly captured in two days, their male inhabitants killed at Alexander's express command and the women and children enslaved.[35] Similarly after his troops were ambushed in the Zeravshan valley, he ravaged the land, and killed any inhabitants he found in the strongholds, simply on suspicion that they had collaborated with Spitamenes and his nomads.[36] This was Draconian, but understandable behaviour, and it was paralleled in India when rulers who had surrendered to Alexander retracted their submission. Musicanus, who revolted after belated submission, was crucified along with his Brahman advisers, and his cities were either destroyed (their inhabitants enslaved) or turned into garrison centres.[37] However, rebellion after submission was a very different thing from refusal to admit an invader, and in practice there was little difference in Alexander's treatment of the two categories. One could hardly argue that the Malli suffered less than the people of Musicanus.

By most criteria Alexander's behaviour was shocking. It was at first sight unprovoked aggression. His initial invasion of Persia had been sanctified by the pretexts of religion and revenge. Xerxes' sacrilege against Greek temples, a century and a half in the past, needed to be punished, and punished it was by the destruction of Persepolis and the transfer of the empire to Alexander.[38] On a lesser scale the subjugation of independent peoples could be justified as self-defence, or reprisal for injuries received. Xenophon's Cyrus felt it appropriate to punish the Pisidian depredations upon his territory

---

[35] Arr. 4. 2. 4 (attributing the massacre to a specific order of Alexander: οὕτως ἐξ Ἀλεξάνδρου προστεταγμένον). See also Curt. 7. 6. 11, who records a prearranged signal 'ut puberes interficerentur'.

[36] Arr. 4. 6. 5: 'they *were reported* to have joined in the attack on the Macedonians'. The authors of the reports are not named. They were hardly authoritative, for Spitamenes and his men had disappeared into the desert, and the locals would not incriminate themselves. Alexander's informants were presumably the bewildered survivors of the defeat (Arr. 6. 6. 2; Curt. 7. 7. 39), who would have had litttle idea of the identity of all their attackers. However, their allegations were sufficient to justify a massacre which according to the vulgate tradition achieved epic proportions (Diod. 17 index χγ; Curt. 7. 9. 23: 'urique agros et interfici puberes iussit').

[37] Arr. 6. 17. 1–2; Curt. 9. 8. 16. See above, Ch. 3.

[38] Diod. 16. 89. 2. For the fulfilment of the propaganda of revenge see Arr. 3. 18. 12; Strabo 15. 3. 6 (730); Plut. *Al.* 37. 7, 56. 1; *Anth. Pal.* 6. 344; and (an extreme case) Curt. 7. 5. 28–30—the massacre of a defenceless populace was justified on the grounds of revenge (H. W. Parke, *JHS* 105 (1985) 62–5; Bosworth, *Conquest and Empire* 108–9; on the revenge motive in general see H. Bellen, *Chiron* 4 (1974) 43–67).

by wholesale expulsion;[39] and Alexander acted similarly with the mountain peoples of the Zagros. The Uxii south of Susa had attempted to hold him to ransom, as they had successive Persian kings, and Alexander responded by reducing them to tributary status—for the time of his passage.[40] Similarly the Cossaeans, who lived between Media and Babylonia, had been notorious for their inroads on the settled agricultural communities, and are character-ized as brigands by the Greek sources.[41] Their aggression, or alleged aggression, justified invasion. Accordingly Alexander attacked them during the winter of 324/3, and the brief reports of the campaign are reminiscent of his attack on the Malli. He invaded at the season when the defenders were least expecting him, ravaged the land, killed a great number of the enemy, and took captive a good deal more, whom he released in exchange for the general surrender of the people.[42] The taking of prisoners as hostages is a novelty here, but Cossaean territory was far more inaccessible than the flat Malli lands, and refugees could not be slaughtered so readily. The geo-graphy of the campaign meant that the defenders enjoyed more humane treatment. But the humanity was relative. Plutarch can represent the episode as mass slaughter, a blood offering at the tomb of Hephaestion, and the campaign is described as a royal hunt, with human quarry.[43] That is rhetorical exaggeration, but there can be little doubt that the invasion was costly in Cossaean lives. However, for the historians of Alexander the killing had ample justification. Alexander was civilizing the Cossaeans, making honest agricultural-ists and city-dwellers out of shiftless nomads,[44] and the campaign was a reprisal for their earlier brigandage.

[39] Xen. *Anab.* 1. 1. 11–2. 1; cf. 1. 9. 14; Diod. 14. 19. 6.

[40] Arr. 3. 17. 1–6. On the complexities of the source tradition see Bosworth, *HCA* i. 321–3; P. Briant, *Rois, tributs, et paysans* 161–73; Badian, in *CHIran* 441–2.

[41] This is explicit in Nearchus' description of the Zagros peoples, (*FGrH* 133 F 1 (g))—summarized by Arrian (*Ind.* 40. 6–8) and Strabo (11. 13. 6 (524)). See also Arr. 7. 15. 2; Diod. 17. 111. 4, and, for the general reputation of the mountaineers, P. Briant, *État et pasteurs* 64–81.

[42] So, most fully, Diod. 17. 111. 5–6. See also Arr. 7. 15. 3; Polyaen. 4. 3. 31.

[43] Plut. *Al.* 73. 4. Polyaen 4. 3. 31 also records that the campaign was said to have been consolation for the death of Hephaestion.

[44] So Nearchus (Arr. *Ind.* 40. 8). The city foundations are also attested by Diod. 17. 111. 5. If they were ever established, they had a short life. The Cossaeans had reverted to their old habits by the summer of 318, when Antigonus refused their demand for passage money and came close to disaster as a result (Diod. 19. 19. 3–8; cf. Horn-blower, *Hieronymus* 217–18; Billows 92–3).

With the Malli and the other independent peoples of southern India there was no such justification. There is no suggestion of aggression, actual or contemplated, against Alexander, merely the intention to resist if attacked. Now, in Greek eyes the Malli were barbarians, and it might be thought that Greek conventions of warfare did not properly apply to them. That is not the case. Both before and after Alexander there is evidence that an attack upon an innocent population was considered unjustifiable. There is a good example in the Nabataean campaign fought by Antigonus and Demetrius in 312/11 BC. It is recorded at some length by Diodorus, who drew directly upon Hieronymus of Cardia, an eyewitness of the events whom Antigonus placed in charge of the abortive enterprise to collect bitumen from the Dead Sea.[45] For Hieronymus the invasion was totally unprovoked. The Nabataean Arabs were in the way, 'a hindrance to (Antigonus') affairs', and their cattle made tempting booty (Diod. 19. 94. 1). In other words the campaign was to remove an independent people which might have allied itself with Ptolemaic Egypt, and at the same time to make a handsome profit. The Antigonid general, Athenaeus, made a surprise attack on Petra, and made off with a satisfying haul of incense and silver bullion to the tune of 500 talents. He was ambushed on his return, losing all his troops, and the Nabataeans made a formal diplomatic complaint to Antigonus. The dynast denied responsibility, and alleged that his general had contravened his orders (Diod. 19. 96. 1–2). Hieronymus, however, emphasized that Antigonus was acting in bad faith; he sent out a second expedition under his son, Demetrius, 'to punish the Arabs in whatever way he could'.[46] This second force was hardly more successful than the first. The Nabataeans protected their herds, and defended their central stronghold. They also sent a message to Demetrius, which Hieronymus repeated verbatim. It accused the Antigonids of unprovoked aggression, and stressed that the Nabataeans had done no harm and indeed had chosen a way of life

[45] Diod. 19. 96. 1–100. 3. Hieronymus' activities are recorded at 19. 100. 1–2 (=*FGrH* 154 T 6; cf. Hornblower, *Hieronymus* 12–13, 47–9, 144–50). On the Nabataean operations in general see J. Seibert, *Das Zeitalter der Diadochen* 122; G. W. Bowersock, *Roman Arabia* 12–16; Billows 129–31.

[46] Diod. 19. 96. 4. Plut. *Demetr.* 7.1 gives a brief outline of the campaign, suggesting that Demetrius made off with a large booty, including 700 camels (contrary to Diod. 19. 97. 2, 6, who suggests that the 'booty' was in fact a gift from the Nabataeans after Demetrius came to terms).

which could do no harm.[47] Much to his father's displeasure, Demetrius implicitly recognized the justice of the Nabataean complaints,
and concluded a formal treaty of friendship.[48] If nothing else, it
protected him during his retreat. However, his reaction, like Antigonus' earlier disclaimer of responsibility, indicates that there was
some embarrassment over unprovoked aggression, even when it was
directed against an undeveloped, barbarian people.

The narrative of Hieronymus echoes some famous passages of
Herodotus, who records some memorable protests by barbarians.
The closest parallel to the Nabataean complaints is probably the
response of the Ethiopian king to the emissaries of Cambyses. It
accuses the Persian conqueror of injustice: 'if he were just, he would
not have set his heart on any land other than his own, nor would he
attempt to enslave men who have done him no injustice.'[49] In this
instance there is no *casus belli*, and no war can be justified unless
there is a prior injury. If there *is* some pre-existing delict, then
invasion is justified, even centuries after the offence. For that reason
the neighbours of the European Scyths refuse to give assistance
against Darius: 'You invaded the Persians' land without us, and
dominated the Persians for as long as God gave you mastery; and
they, elevated by that same God, are repaying you like for like. We
did those men no injury at that time, and we shall not now venture
to be the first at fault.'[50] For Herodotus the Scyths are in the wrong
because of their ancestors' attack upon the Median empire (which
included Persia), and the justification of Darius' expedition is
remarkably similar to Alexander's own pretext for the war of revenge
against Persia. Indeed Herodotus may have been one of the many
sources of inspiration for Philip and his advisers when they concocted their propaganda for the invasion. Alexander's famous letter
of justification to Darius III begins with a sentence that is almost
Herodotean: 'I crossed into Asia wishing to punish the Persians—

---

[47] Diod. 19. 97. 3–4. Note particularly 97. 4: 'For we, since we are in no way willing
to become slaves, have all taken refuge in a land that lacks all the things that are valued
among other peoples and have chosen to live a life in the desert and one altogether like
that of wild beasts, harming you not at all.'   [48] Diod. 19. 97. 6, 100. 1.

[49] Hdt. 3. 21. 2. On the historical background to this episode see A. R. Burn, *Persia
and the Greeks* 86–8.

[50] Hdt. 4. 119. 2–4; cf. 4. 1. 1–2, 4. 4. On the general theme see L. Pearson, *Popular
Ethics in Ancient Greece* (Stanford, Calif., 1962) 142, 168–9; S. Clavadetscher-
Thürlemann, *ΠΟΛΕΜΟΣ ΔΙΚΑΙΟΣ und Bellum Iustum* (Zurich 1985) 54–8.

and you began the conflict.'[51] It is hard to believe that Alexander himself was unaware of Herodotus and in particular Herodotus' story of Cyrus' attack upon the Massagetae. The Massagetic queen, Tomyris, accused him of aggression, and recommended that he stay within the limits of his kingdom (Hdt. 1. 206. 1–2). Cyrus notoriously failed to take in the lesson, and paid for it with his life. There could be no more instructive illustration of the dangers of unprovoked aggression, and it cannot have been far from Alexander's mind when he followed in Cyrus' footsteps to the land of the Massagetae.

The warning to Cyrus is reflected in the historical tradition of Alexander's reign, most remarkably in the episode, unique to Arrian, of the admonition of the Indian ascetics. They beat their feet on the ground as the king passed, and, when questioned about the meaning of the gesture, they represented it as an intimation of mortality. Alexander in fact occupied no more ground than he stood upon. He was a mortal like everybody else, 'except that you are ambitious and reckless, traversing such a vast span of land, so remote from your home, enduring troubles and inflicting them upon others'.[52] This is practically Tomyris' warning to Cyrus, and it depicts Alexander as a self-centred aggressor. Arrian's source is impossible to determine.[53] The episode is part of an extended homily on the dangers of glory for its own sake, and may be taken from some subsidiary source which had the right material for the sermon.[54] However, there is nothing to

---

[51] Arr. 2. 14. 4: τιμωρήσασθαι βουλόμενος Πέρσας...ὑπαρξάντων ὑμῶν. For the phraseology compare Hdt. 7. 9. 2: Ἕλληνας...ὑπάρξαντας ἀδικίης οὐ τιμωρησόμεθα (cf. 7. 11. 2–4, 9. 78. 2). The sentiment is exactly paralleled in Curtius 4. 1. 10–11, but the Herodotean colouring may be an elaboration by Arrian.

[52] Arr. 7. 1. 5–6. The restiveness here criticized is exactly what Tomyris reprehends in Cyrus: 'you will not be willing to take this advice but will do everything in the world other than stay at peace' (Hdt. 1. 206. 2). There is an earlier echo of Cyrus' downfall, when Callisthenes reminds Alexander of his chastening at the hands of the 'poor and autonomous Scyths' (Arr. 4. 11. 9). Cyrus' death was the classic example of the consequences of hubris.

[53] The story is recorded by Arrian alone. The substance of the ascetics' admonition recurs in a papyrus compilation of the early 2nd century AD (*Pap. Genev.* 271, published by V. Martin, *MH* 16 (1959) 77–115; see also G. C. Hansen, *Klio* 43–5 (1965) 351–80). The extant text begins with the statement that Alexander is a man like other men, possessing as much earth as anybody else (col. i. 1–2), and goes on to reprove him for the human cost of his ambitions (col. ii. 5–12). That is much the same sentiment as we find in Arr. 7. 1. 6, and Arrian's comment that Alexander was unable to follow the sages' advice is exactly paralleled in the papyrus (col. ii. 43–9 = Arr. 7. 2. 1–2). Elsewhere the papyrus demonstrably draws on Megasthenes, and the rest of the material shared with Arrian probably goes back to a first-generation source.

[54] That is the general assumption (cf. Kornemann 158; Hammond, *Sources* 282,

exclude Arrian's primary authorities, and he reverts from indirect to direct speech to state categorically that Alexander praised the speech and the speakers but in practice did the opposite of their recommendation (Arr. 7. 2. 1). That recalls Aristobulus, who had an interest in the Indian ascetics and expressed some reservations about Alexander's unqualified pursuit of conquest. In particular he discussed the pretext for attacking the Arabs of the Persian Gulf, dismissing the alleged reason for invasion, the failure to offer submission, and stating outright that Alexander was insatiable of conquest.[55] For all his apologetic tendency Aristobulus was uneasy with his king's imperial ambitions. The aggression was essentially unprovoked, and the alleged grievances were a sham or, at best, a pretext. In Aristobulus' eyes the Arabs were the innocent party. Once again the mode of thought is Herodotean, as is a little passage in Curtius, in which a Sacan chieftain from the lands north of the Syr-Darya reproaches Alexander for his ambition. 'If the gods had wished your stature to be commensurate with your greed, the world would not contain you... What business have you with us? We have never touched your country. May we not continue to live in our empty forests, ignorant of who you are and where you come from?' (Curt. 7. 8. 12–16). This comes in a highly rhetorical speech, which Curtius presents as an example of barbarian wisdom,[56] and it must be largely his own composition.[57] However, he claims to be faithfully following material in his sources, and it would be imprudent to dismiss it all as fiction.[58] Cleitarchus, like Aristobulus, may have considered criticism

missing the transition to direct speech), but the mere addition of 'they say' (λέγουσιν) hardly proves that Arrian is diverging from his primary authorities. For the principle at issue see Bosworth, *From Arrian to Alexander* 62–5; *HCA* ii. 7.

[55] Arr. 7. 19. 6: Strabo 16. 1. 11 (741) = *FGrH* 139 F 55–6. See the fuller discussion below, p. 153.

[56] Curt. 7. 8. 10–11. Dr E. Baynham draws my attention to a similar comment about the Median astrologer, Cobares (Bagodaras in Diod. 17. 83. 7), whose advice to Bessus is adduced as the type of *prudentia* to be expected of a barbarian (Curt. 7. 4. 13): both speeches contain earthy aphorisms and picturesque proverbs, which Curtius no doubt considers typical of alien wisdom.

[57] So Tarn *Al.* ii. 94, (and Hammond, *Three Historians* 143) on the grounds that the speech contains one of Curtius' best epigrams and shows off his knowledge of the literature of fables. Perhaps the embellishment *is* Curtius' own (one would hardly expect otherwise), but the gist of the speech may already have been in his source.

[58] Curt. 7. 8. 11: 'quae, utcumque sunt tradita, incorrupta perferemus'. Curtius' claim that he is faithful to the traditions is probably a borrowing from Herodotus (cf. Hdt. 2. 123. 1, 130. 2, 7. 152. 1–3), but even so there must surely be some substance to the claim. It would be totally perverse if the speech is an invention from first to last.

of Alexander's imperialism to be of some relevance. His Sacan envoy evokes the message of the Massagetic queen to Cyrus, and the episode takes place in exactly the same geographical setting as Herodotus' story, before the crossing of the Syr-Darya, the Araxes of Herodotus. What is more, it looks ahead to Hieronymus' account of the Nabataean campaign. The Nabataeans, like Curtius' Sacae, live in remote isolation, and have done no harm to any potential invader. It seems a coherent stream of thought, transmitted from Herodotus to the early Hellenistic period: invasion and conquest, even of a barbarian people, were unjustified, unless there was some prior grievance to avenge.

Alexander apparently knew and accepted the principle. He made a point of publicizing the virtuous barbarian peoples who voluntarily accepted his regime. The Ariaspians of the Helmand Valley, who were supposed to have given Cyrus providential assistance, were duly honoured by the new conqueror. Alexander gave them their 'freedom', expanded their territory—and placed them under the control of the governor of Gedrosia.[59] More pertinent still is the embassy from the independent Sacan people which begins Book 4 of Arrian. This tribe was domiciled in the salt desert (Kyzyl Kum) east of the Syr-Darya, and it was identified with the Abii of Homer, who (on one interpretation) lived in the far north, beyond the Thracians, and were 'the most just of mankind'.[60] From the time of Cyrus, so it was alleged, they had preserved their independence, thanks to a blend of poverty and moral rectitude. For Arrian their poverty preserved them from aggression, and Curtius states explicitly that they refrained from warfare unless provoked.[61] That is exactly the claim of Curtius' Sacan ambassador and Hieronymus' Nabataeans, and in this case it is turned to Alexander's advantage. The most virtuous people of the area, celebrated from Homeric times, voluntarily sought his friendship, and (if Curtius is correct) submitted to his rule. They *chose* him as their master, and he respected their

---

Curtius is emphatic. He puts his *fides* on the line and professes to transmit his material uncorrupted. It recalls Tacitus' proud boast of historical impartiality ('incorruptam fidem professis': *Hist.* 1.1).

[59] Arr. 3. 27. 4–5; Diod. 17. 81. 1–2; Curt. 7. 3. 3–4. See further, Bosworth, *HCA* i. 365–6.

[60] Arr. 4. 1. 1; Curt. 7. 6. 11. Arrian makes the connection with Homer (*Od.* 13. 6) explicit. On the literary background see Bosworth, *HCA* ii. 13–15.

[61] διὰ πενίαν τε καὶ δικαιότητα (Arr. 4. 1. 1); 'iustissimos barbarorum constabat: armis abstinebant nisi lacessiti' (Curt. 7. 6. 11).

autonomy.[62] The whole context of the episode suggests that Alexander endorsed the principle that harmless peoples should not be attacked without due cause. How, then, are we to explain the Indian campaigns, which read as sustained, unprovoked aggression?

The sources present us with an explanation—of a kind. According to Arrian the Malli had never sent any embassy to Alexander. That, at any rate, is later admitted by their allies, the Oxydracae: 'they declared that they had committed a venial error in not sending embassies long before' (Arr. 6. 14. 2). The fact that no submission was offered is taken as a *casus belli*. That is almost a leitmotiv in Arrian's narrative. Alexander insisted on the appearance of the local rulers in person. When Abisares, the monarch of the mountain Indians south of Kashmir, failed to present himself, he threatened invasion, and was only mollified by assurances (true, as it turned out) that Abisares was too ill to travel.[63] Similarly, in Sind the complaint against Musicanus was that he had never met Alexander to offer submission, nor had he sent ambassadors nor (an interesting addition) made any request of the invader. Musicanus quickly rectified his error, as the Oxydracae had done, by heading an embassy of capitulation, complete with royal gifts (including his entire elephant stable). Above all he admitted his error, 'which was the most efficacious way of gaining what one asked of Alexander'.[64] Somewhat later Alexander is described as set on attacking the Oreitae of Las Bela because they had made no friendly overtures; and their eastern neighbours, the Arabitae, were equally aloof, and fled into the desert rather than submit.[65] There is a standard pattern. Alexander insisted on a formal act of submission, performed in person by the local ruler or magistrate, and non-compliance was considered sufficient justification for war.

Perhaps the most informative commentary comes in Aristobulus' discussion of the motives for Alexander's planned invasion of Arabia. Aristobulus is quite candid in admitting that Alexander was attracted by the legendary (and unfounded) reputation of the area

---

[62] The same applied to the Indians of Nysa, who were given their liberty and autonomy—subject to the provision of a contingent of cavalry to his army (Arr. 5. 2. 2–4; cf. *Metz Epit.* 37–8; (Plut. *Al.* 58. 8–9) with Bosworth, *HCA* ii. 209–10).

[63] Arr. 5. 20. 6; Curt. 9. 1. 7–8; Diod. 17. 90. 4; *Metz Epit.* 65. Cf. Arr. 5. 29. 5; Curt. 10. 1. 20.

[64] Arr. 6. 15. 6 (see above, p. 95). The only consequence of the belated submission was a garrison in the capital (Arr. 6. 15. 7; Curt. 9. 8. 10).

[65] Arr. 6. 21. 3–4; cf. Diod. 17. 104. 4; Curt. 9. 10. 6.

for growing spices spontaneously, and adds that the king wished to be considered the third god of the Arabs.[66] Personal vanity and commercial exploitation were the real reasons for the attack. However, Alexander claimed that the Arabs had never sent an embassy or shown him any mark of honour. Both Arrian and Strabo agree that this was a pretext adopted for public display,[67] but the very fact that a pretext was required is significant.[68] Even in 323, in the last months of his life, Alexander was unwilling to embark on an 'unjustified' war against a remote people which could not conceivably have injured him. He required a *casus belli*, and the official ground for the war was the Arabs' failure to offer the appropriate homage. For Strabo the Arabs of the Persian Gulf were the only people in the world not to send an embassy.[69] This seems rhetorical exaggeration of Aristobulus' original statement, anticipating Strabo's next allegation, that Alexander wished to be ruler of all humanity. Arrian is more circumspect, claiming that the Arabs were the only people *in that part of the world*[70] not to have made overtures. The more cautious formulation is preferable; the Arabs were unique in the Near East in never having offered submission. The fact that their failure is singled out as justification for war practically proves that

[66] Arr. 7. 20. 1; Strabo 16. 1. 11 (741). Strabo's categorical statement (from Aristobulus) that Alexander wished to be the Arabs' third god is represented by Arrian as a *logos*. That reveals his personal doubt about the story (so rightly, P. Högemann, *Alexander der Große und Arabien* 130). It is a sign of desperation to conclude (with Cawkwell, in *Ventures into Greek History* 296–7) that Aristobulus himself gave the detail as a 'story', a supposed witticism of Alexander.

[67] Arr. 7. 19. 6: a *prophasis* (pretext). Strabo 16. 1. 11: the formal ground of complaint (*aitia*). On the distinction (or lack of it) between the two concepts see the classic essay of Lionel Pearson, in *Selected Papers of Lionel Pearson*, ed. D. Lateiner and S. Stephens, 95 ('It is worth remembering that *aitia*, in the sense of complaint, can be practically identical in meanig with *prophasis*'). We can only guess what was Aristobulus' terminology. The only pointer I can suggest is that Arrian invariably refers to a pretext as *prophasis*, whereas Strabo uses the two terms indifferently and is probably more likely to borrow the wording of his source.

[68] One should perhaps recall the observation of Thucydides' Cleon, that those who attack without justification (μὴ ξὺν προφάσει) are committed to annihilate the enemy, for fear of reprisals if he survives (Thuc. 3. 40. 6). On that principle the more unprovoked the assault, the worse its savagery.

[69] Strabo 16. 1. 11: μόνοι τῶν ἁπάντων...ὀρεγόμενον πάντων εἶναι κύριον. The antithesis is surely Strabo's own. P. Högemann, *Alexander der Große und Arabien* 128 claims that Strabo is closer to the original text, and in some cases he may be (see above, n. 67). However, one should expect that he was as prone to vary the text of Aristobulus as was Arrian (for other instances see Bosworth, *From Arrian to Alexander* 40–6). Neither author can be assumed to be a faithful representation of the original text.

[70] Arr. 7. 19.6: μόνοι τῶν ταύτῃ βαρβάρων.

Alexander felt that he was entitled to rule the Arabs, that they were *already* his vassals. That can only mean that he he was aware of the old Achaemenid claims to the area. Maka (Oman) is a standard entry in the lists of subject peoples recorded between the reigns of Darius I and Artaxerxes III,[71] and it occurs in immediate proximity to Arabia proper, the land of the Arabs of the Fertile Crescent. The Persians had never relinquished their pretensions to the tribute of the southern Arabs. Alexander will also have been aware of Herodotus' description of the area. According to Arrian, he shared Herodotus' mistaken belief that cassia grew in the marshes of Arabia,[72] and he will certainly have noted Herodotus' assertion that the Arabs offered 1,000 talents of frankincense annually to the Great King, and did so in addition to their tribute.[73] As the successor of Darius III and the occupant of the Achaemenid throne, Alexander considered that he had inherited sovereignty over the Arabs. By refusing, or omitting to approach him they were confirming their rebellion against legitimate authority, and the invasion with all its concomitant horrors was thereby justified.

The same principle was invoked in India. Under the Achaemenids there were three Indian satrapies: Gandhara, Thataguš (Sattagydia), and Hinduš. Their control of the Indus valley was probably short-lived in fact, but, as with Maka (Oman) they never relinquished their claims to sovereignty, and all three satrapies figure consistently in the friezes and lists of subject peoples.[74] Gandhara seems to have had closer ties than the rest, and, if not subject to Darius, the area was certainly allied and sympathetic. The fifteen elephants present at Gaugamela came from India west of the Indus,[75] almost certainly

---

[71] Cf. DB I 17, XPh 25, A?P 29 (the texts and translation may be found in R. G. Kent, *Old Persian* (New Haven, Conn. 1953)). See also the Persepolis Fortification Tablets which attest a satrap at Makkaš (the Elamite form of Māka): PF 679–80. On the Achaemenid presence in Oman see D. T. Potts, *The Arabian Gulf in Antiquity* 394–400; J.–F. Salles, in *Achaemenid History* 4. 114–15, 124–8.

[72] Arr. 7. 20. 2; cf. Hdt. 3. 110. On the actual provenance of cassia in China, see J. I. Miller, *The Spice Trade of the Roman Empire* (Oxford 1969) 42–7; L. Casson, *The Periplus Maris Erythraei* 122–4.

[73] Hdt. 3. 97. 5, where πάρεξ τοῦ φόρου can only mean 'over and above the tribute'.

[74] For convenient discussion of the Indian satrapies see D. Fleming, *JRAS* (1982), 102–12; H. D. Bivar, in *CAH* iv². 199–210. There are good illustrations of the friezes of throne-bearers, identical in sequence and composition between Darius I and Artaxerxes III, in Erich Schmidt, *Persepolis* iii (Chicago 1970) 108 ff.

[75] Arr. 3. 8. 6. For the expression 'India this side of the Indus' (ἐπὶ τάδε τοῦ Ἰνδοῦ) compare Arr. 3. 25. 8; 4. 22. 6, 28. 6 (explicitly defining Gandhara). For the elephants of the area see Arr. 4. 22. 6, 25. 5, 30. 5–8.

from the Cophen valley, Achaemenid Gandhara, where the local rulers kept elephant herds of modest size. Alexander, then, had some reason to believe that the Indus valley and Gandhara were his by right. Accordingly, long before he entered India itself, he sent to the local rajahs as far as the great city of Taxila, whose ruler had made overtures to him during the Sogdian revolt. When he reached the frontier, he was duly met by a whole bevy of petty rulers, ready with gifts appropriate to his royal status.[76] This was taken as submission; Alexander was receiving homage from the vassals he had inherited from the Persians. Those who had declined to send embassies were considered insubordinate, and fair game. Alexander accordingly burst upon the Aspasii, apparently without warning, and inaugurated the campaign with indiscriminate slaughter. He continued the tactics in the Swat valley, in the eastern Punjab, where he attacked the autonomous Cathaei,[77] and in the lower Indus. Resistance constituted rebellion, and rebels could expect the most extreme treatment.

There is an interesting detail, found only in Arrian. The local rulers of India tended to be independent dynasts, with no Indian overlord, and they are described as such by the other sources, which refer to them as minor kings. In Arrian, however, they are designated *hyparchs*, or 'under-rulers'.[78] Elsewhere the term is used to denote satraps, the regional governors employed by the Persians, and also the feudal barons who controlled large tracts of Bactria and Sogdiana.[79] However powerful and autocratic in their own domains, these dignitaries always had a superior, the Great King himself, who

---

[76] On this episode see above, p. 123.

[77] Arr. 5. 22. 1. Here the Cathaei are attacked because they contemplated resistance (like the Malli). After the destruction of Sangala the hard lesson was learned and the neighbouring cities surrendered before it was too late (Diod. 17. 91. 4; Curt. 9. 1. 20–3).

[78] Arr. 4. 22. 6, 8 with Bosworth, *HCA* ii. 147–9, 153. A good instance is Arrian's treatment of Taxiles, who is termed *hyparch* at 4. 22. 6; 5. 8. 2, 6, before and after his submission to Alexander. Other sources, including Hieronymus, referred to him as king as late as the conference at Triparadeisus (Diod. 18. 3. 2, 39. 6; cf. Arr. *Succ.* F 1. 36; Diod. 17. 86. 4–7; Strabo 15. 1. 28 (698); Plut. *Mor.* 181c). From the perspective of his subjects he *was* a king; for the Macedonians he ruled by the grace of Alexander and so was properly a *hyparch*. That is what Plut. *Al.* 60. 15 states explicitly of Porus: his role after the conquest was 'to rule over the land of which he was the king with the title of satrap'.

[79] On Arrian's use of *hyparch* to designate satraps see Bosworth, *CQ* 24 (1974) 55–8; and for the hyparchs of Bactria/Sogdiana see Arr. 4. 1. 5, 21. 1, 9 with P. Briant, *L'Asie Centrale* 82–6.

authorized their regimes and tolerated their local pretensions. It was perfectly justifiable to term them 'under-rulers'. The extension of the nomenclature to the Indian dynasts again implies that they had a natural superior. For Arrian's source, who is certainly Ptolemy,[80] the Indian rajahs, whatever the appearances, were not independent rulers. They were vassals of the Great King, and therefore of Alexander. He had a right to expect their capitulation, and they were duty bound to pay their respects to their new master. For Ptolemy, it would seem, the invasion of India was the re-establishment of the sovereignty lost during the Achaemenid period but always claimed as the right of the King of Kings.

The claims made for Alexander lived on after his death. Perdiccas' Cappadocian campaign of 322 is almost a carbon copy of Alexander's methods in India. It was launched against the dynast of northern Cappadocia, Ariarathes. Now, under Alexander Cappadocia had been disputed territory. Alexander himself only passed through its southern fringes when he occupied the Cilician Gates in the late summer of 333. He imposed a satrap, and levied tribute; but, according to Arrian, only part of the territory east of the river Halys was occupied.[81] Ariarathes clearly did not submit. That was explicitly stated by Hieronymus; 'he did not touch these peoples at all, but took another route against Darius, along the coastal district of Pamphylia and Cilicia'.[82] This passage is quoted by Appian, who is somewhat doubtful about it. However, he was not aware that there were two distinct satrapies in Cappadocia under Achaemenid rule.[83] Alexander only impinged upon the southern district, whereas Ariarathes ruled in the north, untouched by his invasion.[84] Subse-

---

[80] At 4. 24. 5 Arrian uses *hyparch* to refer to a local dignitary of the Aspasii, and does so in a context taken directly from Ptolemy (*FGrH* 138 F 18, see above, p. 45).

[81] Arr. 2. 4. 2: 'he took in all the land west of the river Halys and a good deal of that beyond the Halys as well.' Cf. Curt. 3. 4. 1.

[82] App. *Mithr*. 8. 25 = *FGrH* 154 F 3; cf. Diod. 18. 3. 1. On this see the discussion of Hornblower, *Hieronymus* 240–3. The actual itinerary of Alexander between Ancyra in Phrygia and the Cilician Gates is not known (cf. Bosworth, *HCA* i. 189), but time was pressing, and it is likely that he took the most direct route. In that case he only touched the south-west fringes of Cappadocia. He was certainly closer to Pamphylia and Cilicia than he was to the satrapy of Ariarathes.

[83] So Strabo 12. 1. 4 (534). Appian appears to believe that Alexander intervened in the north, because of his restoration of democracy at Amisus (*Mithr*. 8. 24) on the Black Sea coast. However, he did not need to visit the city in person: a written directive could have been all that was necessary for the change of constitution.

[84] Diod. 31. 19. 2–4 reproduces the genealogy of the later Cappadocian kings (including the great Datames), and refers to the territory throughout as a 'kingdom'.

quently Ariarathes was able to send contingents to Darius' army at Gaugamela.[85] There is no record that he was affected by the operations in Asia Minor, when Antigonus dealt with the Persian survivors of Issus, and at the time of Alexander's death he had turned his satrapy into a monarchy,[86] supported by a strong army of local and mercenary troops. Up to that point he had made no overture to Alexander, but as an ex-satrap of the Achaemenids he was considered a vassal of their successors. In the distribution of satrapies which followed Alexander's death his territory was combined with southern Cappadocia, and assigned to Perdiccas' adherent, Eumenes of Cardia.[87] Ariarathes was in effect deposed and replaced by the chosen representative of the new Great King.

In Macedonian eyes Ariarathes had withheld homage and recognition of the new regime, and was therefore in rebellion. His offence was compounded when he refused to accept the new dispensation; and Perdiccas, the grand vizier of the new Kings, brought the royal army to impose his fiat. A short, mismatched combat saw Ariarathes defeated and captured with the loss of a quarter of his grand army. He then suffered the fate of Musicanus, tortured and crucified alongside his court.[88] Ariarathes' 'kinsmen' (συγγενεῖς) were the counterparts of the courtiers of the Great King (whose institutions Ariarathes had aped).[89] As such they were considered his accomplices, and went the way of Musicanus' Brahman advisers. The situation is nicely captured by an antithesis in Appian (*Mithr.* 8. 25): Ariarathes was either in revolt or defending his regime against the Macedonians. It was a matter of perspective. For Ariarathes the war

---

[85] Arr. 3. 8. 5, 11. 7; Curt. 4. 12. 12. Cf. Bosworth, *HCA* i. 29. 1–2.

[86] Diod. 18. 16. 1 terms him 'dynast' and claims that he was aiming at kingship (βασιλείας ἀντιποιούμενος). Justin 13. 6. 1 calls him 'king' (*rex*), while Plut. *Eum.* 3. 4 claims that he 'enjoyed royal power.' (ἐβασίλευεν). It is likely enough that Ariarathes' ambitions evolved during the years of Alexander's absence in the east. By 324 there was widespread agitation in the central satrapies, with a pretender emerging in Media to claim the kingship (Arr. 6. 29. 3; cf. 6. 27. 3; Curt. 10. 1. 23) and a purported descendant of Cyrus usurping the satrapy of Persis (Arr. 6. 29. 2; Curt. 10. 1. 23). In remote Cappadocia Ariarathes may well have felt that he could safely indulge his regal pretensions.

[87] Plut. *Eum.* 3. 3; Diod. 18. 3. 1; Arr. *Succ.* F 1a. 5; Dexippus, *FGrH* 100 F. 8. 3; Justin 13. 4. 16.

[88] Diod. 18. 16. 2; Arr. *Succ.* F 1. 12; Plut. *Eum.* 3. 13; App. *Mithr.* 8. 25. Another tradition (Diod. 31. 19. 4) has it that Ariarathes fell in battle.

[89] Diod. 18. 16. 3. On the royal kinsmen of the Achaemenid court see Arr. 3. 11. 5; Diod. 17. 20. 2, 59. 2; the institution was adopted by Alexander (Arr. 7. 11. 6) and his Successors.

was in defence of the realm which he had made his own, but for Perdiccas it was suppression of long-lasting, contumacious rebellion.

The sequel is even more clear-cut. To the south of Ariarathes the city communities of Isaura and Laranda were the recipients of a savage punitive attack. Located in Lycaonia, they had never been willing subjects of Persia, and the Younger Cyrus treated their territory as hostile during his march inland.[90] Alexander himself had never touched their territory, but Antigonus had made a sortie there;[91] and, more fatefully, Alexander's satrap of Cilicia died in battle against them.[92] This man, Balacrus son of Nicanor, was no nonentity: a Bodyguard of Philip and Alexander, and husband of Antipater's eldest daughter, Phila.[93] His death needed avenging, as much as the wounds inflicted upon Alexander in India, and those responsible were depicted as rebels of the deepest dye. They had traditionally resisted royal authority (like the peoples of the Zagros), and had killed a distinguished Macedonian who was attempting to reduce them to subjection. There could be no compromise. Even before the invasion Isaura and Laranda were earmarked for destruction.[94] Laranda accordingly was taken by storm, its male population butchered, the rest enslaved, while at Isaura the defenders committed mass suicide, perishing in the conflagration of their city.[95] Perdiccas was behaving exactly as Alexander had at the height of the Sogdian rebellion. All the inhabitants were regarded as culpable, and mass slaughter was justified. In the case of Ariarathes there had been no armed resistance before Perdiccas' invasion, no Macedonian

---

[90] Xen. *Anab.* 1. 2. 19; 3. 2. 23.

[91] Curt. 4. 5. 13. For the background to this campaign see A. R. Burn, *JHS* 72 (1952) 81–4; P. Briant, *Antigone le Borgne* 53–74; Billows 43–5.

[92] Diod. 18. 22. 1. The date of his death is controversial. It is usually placed late in Alexander's reign (eg. Berve ii. no. 200; Heckel 260–1), but there is no reason to reject an earlier dating, in the aftermath of Antigonus' operations in Lycaonia. That would simplify the problems of Menes' appointment in the Levant (Arr. 3. 16. 9; cf. Bosworth, *HCA* i. 319; ii. 41–3).

[93] Arr. 2. 12. 2 (Bodyguard). The marriage to Phila is only attested by the novelist, Antonius Diogenes (Phot. *Bibl.* cod. 166, 111ᵇ2–3), but the detail is circumstantial and should be accepted (cf. Heckel, *ZPE* 70 (1987) 161–2; Badian, *ZPE* 72 (1988) 116). The liaison helps explain the prominence of Balacrus' son, Nicanor, in the period after Antipater's death (Bosworth, *CQ* 44 (1994) 57–65).

[94] So Diod. 18. 22. 1: 'they decided upon the destruction (ἔκριναν ἀναστάτους ποιῆσαι) of two cities.'

[95] Diod. 18. 22. 2–6. He notes explicitly (22. 4) that they realized that their fate was inexorable (ἀπαραίτητον).

setback to be redressed. It was only the self-proclaimed 'king' and his court who were tainted with rebellion. The rest could be given quarter, and survive as tributary subjects of their new overlords.

One should not exaggerate the Macedonians' respect for legality. Quite plainly Alexander would have invaded India whether or not there had been Achaemenid sovereignty there in the past. Equally Perdiccas would have attacked Ariarathes, irrespective of his previous status as satrap of the Great King. However, there was a feeling that aggression needed justification, and the resumption of sovereignty was an acceptable pretext. It may have been no more than the salving of conscience, but it is significant that consciences needed salving. We may not be far from the mentality of the Spartans during the Archidamian War, who felt that the reverses they suffered were the consequence of their refusal to accept the Athenian offer of arbitration before hostilities began.[96] It was important to appear the aggrieved party, even when the other side was non-Greek. Once again there are significant parallels in the Spanish conquest of the Americas, where the aggressors enacted elaborate charades to convince themselves that the natives had voluntarily accepted vassalage. In the very beginning Columbus had unfurled the royal standard, taken possession of the Indies by proclamation—and there was no opposition ('y no me fué contradicho').[97] The natives were given the opportunity—in theory—to speak now or forever hold their peace. By their silence they were deemed to be acquiescent in the act of annexation, and any resistance could be redefined as rebellion.

As usual, Cortés supplies us with the most dramatic parallel. After his alliance with the people of Tlaxcala he prepared to move on to the territory allied with Montezuma. Warned by his newly found Tlaxcalan friends that their neighbours were untrustworthy and had the firm intention of killing him, Cortés sent ahead to the city of Cholula, demanding that its chiefs appear before him. As the Tlaxcalans again foretold, the chiefs refused to come, protesting that they were ill, and sent proxies (the precedent of Alexander and

[96] Thuc. 7. 18. 2–3, emphatically echoing Pericles' challenge at 1. 144. 2: 'we are willing to go to arbitration in accordance with the treaty; we shall not begin the war, but we shall resist you if you begin it.' No doubt Thucydides is overemphasizing Athenian innocence (cf. Badian, *From Plataea to Potidaea* 142–4), but the general principle would have been widely endorsed.

[97] For the text (with illuminating discussion of the background) see Greenblatt, *Marvelous Possessions* 52–64.

Abisares comes sharply to mind). Cortés' reaction was exactly that of Alexander: 'I spoke to these messengers and told them that an embassy from so high a prince as Your Sacred Majesty should not be received by persons such as they…therefore the chiefs should appear before me within three days to owe obedience to Your Highness and offer themselves as your vassals. I warned them that if they did not appear within the period I specified, I would march against them and destroy them as rebels who refused to submit themselves to the dominion of Your Highness.'[98] Here the refusal to appear in person is explicitly interpreted as an act of rebellion, and Cortés makes the message even clearer by sending a written command (witnessed by a notary) to declare that those who wished to be vassals would be honoured and aided, while 'those who rebelled would be punished in accordance with the law.'

The trappings of legality are extraordinary. Cortés was in fact issuing the *Requerimiento*, the remarkable document excogitated by Spanish jurists in 1513.[99] This explicitly justified the Spanish claim to the Americas through the territorial donation of Pope Alexander VI, the famous ruling which divided the world between Spain and Portugal. The Indians were therefore called upon to accept the sovereignty of the Catholic church, proclaimed by God's vicegerent, and its secular authorities, the representatives of the Spanish Crown. Thanks to the papal declaration the Spanish king was lord of all the peoples Cortés encountered, and it was their divinely ordained duty to submit themselves as vassals. Alexander's claims to be the successor of the Achaemenids would at least have been understood by the peoples of Gandhara and Sind, but for Cortés' new subjects the claims were starkly incomprehensible. They had no knowledge of the language in which the declaration was made, no concept of the religious and legal structure which underpinned it. The modern reader sympathizes with Las Casas' famous assertion that he did not

[98] Cortés p. 71. Other accounts of the transaction are essentially the same (Gómara pp. 124–5; Díaz pp. 234–7 (Maudslay), pp. 185–8 (Cohen)).

[99] For a translation see Charles Gibson, *The Spanish Tradition in America* (Columbia, SC, 1968) 58–60. If the justification is vague, referring the Indians to 'certain writings which passed on the subject aforesaid, which you can see if you wish', the consequences of resistance are brutally clear: total war, subjection to the Church, dispossession, and enslavement—'and we protest that the deaths and losses which shall accrue from this are your fault, and not of their highnesses, or of ours, or of the soldiers who come with us'. For a brief history of the *Requerimiento* and its genesis see Hugh Thomas, *The Conquest of Mexico* 71–5, and the succinct note of Anthony Pagden in *Hernán Cortés, Letters from Mexico* 453–5 n. 27.

know whether to weep or laugh, or the blunt reaction of the Indian chief who said that the pope must have been drunk. However, for Cortés, as for Alexander, the claims were made in deadly earnest. The people of Cholula were the natural vassals of Charles V. It was obligatory for the chiefs to offer submission, and failure to do so was *ipso facto* rebellion, to be punished as such.

What Cortés meant by due punishment is shown by the sequel. The chiefs of Cholula appeared in person, and swore to be vassals of the Spanish king, an oath which was formally recorded by Cortés' notary.[100] What they conceived themselves to have done can only be guessed, but from Cortés' standpoint it was formal, binding confirmation of their subjection to the Spanish Crown. Thus reassured, Cortés entered Cholula in state, but (so he claims) his worries were soon reactivated. The Cholulans had evacuated their women and children, a step which Cortés, like Alexander, saw as a sign of disaffection.[101] They also supplied insufficient food; and Cortés' interpreter, the formidable Doña Marina, was warned by an Indian native of Cholula that the men of the city were in collusion with an army of Montezuma, in wait to ambush the invaders once they left the city.[102] Cortés' response was to invite the chiefs to a colloquy, where he had them arrested, and simultaneously his men fell upon the population of the city. The result was a bloodbath, in which Cortés' Tlaxcalan allies participated with gusto; and the city itself with its immense pyramid-temple was largely gutted. The surviving chiefs renewed their promises of loyalty, and as the population returned ('all unafraid' is Cortés' disingenuous claim), Cholula was transformed into a peaceful and prosperous vassal state of Spain.

The massacre was one of Cortés' more controversial acts, and his bitter critic, the crusading Dominican, Bartolomé de Las Casas, denounced it as an act of terror, designed to break the spirit of the Mexicans. The allegation was indignantly rebutted by Bernal Díaz, who repeated the story that Cortés and his men were almost the victims of

---

[100] Cortés p. 72; Gómara p. 125 ('they offered to serve and pay tribute...an offer which Cortés had witnessed by notaries and interpreters'). Díaz (p. 244 (Maudslay), p. 191 (Cohen)) agrees on the fact of submission, but denies that a notary was present. If so, it was a serious breach of formalities (see below, n. 106).

[101] Cortés pp. 73–4. According to Francisco de Aguilar 'the city was empty of people. This meant that they were afraid or ready for war' (de Fuentes p. 144).

[102] Cortés p. 73. The revelations of Doña Marina are reported more fully by Díaz pp. 251–2 (Maudslay), pp. 196–7 (Cohen); cf. Gómara p. 127; Andrés de Tapia (de Fuentes pp. 33–4).

a plot, and claimed that the great army sent by Montezuma prudently disappeared as soon as news broke of the repression in Cholula.[103] However that may be, it remains a fact that the main informant was the person closest to Cortés, Doña Marina. She first broke the news of the plot, and was the principal, perhaps the only interpreter when the Cholulan chiefs were interviewed and supposedly confessed their guilt. If they did in fact confess, they were promptly killed,[104] and could not recant later. The 'official' story, which emerges from Cortés and is enlarged by Díaz, is that the peoples of Cholula were slow to confirm their vassalage and mendacious in the vows they took. Their alleged plot was treachery, and the promiscuous, undeclared killing launched by Cortés was justified retribution.

There is a curious complicity here. According to the extant accounts the Indians accepted their new vassal status without complaint or query, and after the salutary lesson of the Cholula massacre they freely confessed their fault and renewed their commitment to the Spanish Crown. Nothing could be better suited to the purposes of Cortés, and we may well doubt that the submission was as categorical as is implied. Cortés' messages were transmitted from Castilian to Mayan by Géronimo de Aguilar, and Doña Marina converted the Mayan into Nahuatl, the language of the Mexicans. The responses of the Cholulans suffered the same process of transformation. They may not have seen themselves as surrendering unconditionally to the Spanish Crown, but, if they made qualifications, they were certainly expunged by the translators. The reply which Aguilar finally delivered to Cortés was precisely the reply Cortés most wished to hear. Something very similar happened when Cortés first met the Mexican emperor, Montezuma. Montezuma's very first address, as Cortés records it, is an explicit acceptance of subjection. His ancestors were brought to the valley of Mexico by a

---

[103] Díaz pp. 202–3 (Cohen), p. 257 (Maudslay). For Díaz the massacre was a wholly prudential measure, and he claims that Las Casas was factually in error: 'He insisted that we punished the Cholulans for no reason at all, or just to amuse ourselves, or because we had a fancy to.' On the accusations of terrorism see Anthony Pagden's note in Cortés, *Letters from Mexico* 465–6 n. 27; Hugh Thomas, *The Conquest of Mexico* 262–3.

[104] Cortés pp. 73–4 implies that all the chiefs he arrested were released, but his chronicler, Gómara (p. 129), concedes that 'several' were put to death, while Díaz (pp. 199–200 (Cohen), pp. 254–5 (Maudslay)) alleges that Cortés actually sentenced his captives to death. According to another eyewitness, Andrés de Tapia, most of the dignitaries arrested, including the five or six who 'confessed', were killed (de Fuentes pp. 35–6).

pioneering chieftain (in Greek terms, an *archegetes*), who subsequently departed to the east.[105] In Montezuma's eyes the Spanish king is the descendant of the Mexican culture hero, the natural lord of Mexico, and the invasion of Cortés is foreshadowed in Aztec folklore. The message is repeated after Montezuma's imprisonment, when the emperor exhorts his chiefs to accept the dominion of the Spanish king, who is the heir of the Aztec empire, 'the same lord for whom we have been waiting'. All the chiefs accordingly accept the story, and declare themselves vassals of the Spanish monarch—and the ubiquitous notary takes it all down in due form.[106]

All this is, of course, too good to be true. Montezuma's foundation legend beautifully vindicates Cortés' behaviour at Cholula, where he treats the chiefs as vassals of Spain even before they make any formal act of submission. The legalism of the *Requerimiento* was underpinned by the Aztecs' own beliefs. Similarly the unconditional acceptance of Charles V as the rightful monarch of Mexico is perfectly tailored to Cortés' self-created persona: not the subordinate of the governor of Cuba with a limited brief of discovery, but the agent of the king himself, endeavouring to secure Mexico as a royal possession.[107] Montezuma therefore acknowledges Charles as his overlord and Cortés as the king's representative: 'from now on you should obey this great king, for he is your rightful lord, and as his representative acknowledge this his captain.' What Montezuma actually said, or thought he was saying, lies beyond conjecture, but the translators clearly represented it as unconditional vassalage. The foundation myth is a clever elaboration, perhaps based on some statement of the admitted truth that the Aztecs were relatively recent

---

[105] Cortés pp. 85–6; cf. Gómara pp. 141–2; Díaz pp. 283–4 (Maudslay), pp. 220–1 (Cohen). On the political implications for the Spaniards see the discussion of V. Frankl, *Saeculum* 13 (1962) 7–12.

[106] Cortés p. 99. See also Andrés de Tapia (de Fuentes p. 39); Francisco de Aguilar (de Fuentes p. 147); Gómara pp. 184–5. This was an episode of capital importance, and it figured prominently in the protracted commission of inquiry (*residencia*) into Cortés' actions, which began in 1529. At least six witnesses confirmed Cortés' account of the Mexicans' act of submission to the Spanish Crown (Hugh Thomas, *The Conquest of Mexico* 324–5), and it was emphasized that the transaction was formally recorded by Cortés' notary (evidence of Francisco de Flores, Thomas 634–5). However, Díaz (p. 336 (Maudslay), p. 264 (Cohen)) alleges that this crucial audience took place 'without Cortés or any of us, excepting Orteguilla the page, being present'. This undermines the whole apologetic story, and Díaz must have been fully aware of the implications of his account.

[107] On Cortés' original brief of discovery see J. H. Elliott, in Cortés, *Letters from Mexico* pp. xii–xvi; Thomas, *Conquest of Mexico* 137–9.

immigrants in the valley of Mexico, but it is warped to legitimize the Spanish claims to empire.

The foundation myth of Montezuma takes us directly back to Alexander. As we have seen, Alexander and his staff created the legend that Heracles and Dionysus had invaded and conquered the Indian lands, and the natives themselves brought corroborative evidence.[108] Alexander came to believe that he was following in the footsteps of his divine forebears. What he took was therefore his own. The Academic pseudo-historian, Antipater of Magnesia, had represented Philip's conquests in Chalcidice as repossession of territory already acquired by Heracles and held in trust for his descendants.[109] In the same way Alexander was repossessing territory which had come into the Hellenic sphere in mythical times. Megasthenes went even further in claiming that the Indian kingship had been established by Dionysus and that the first kings were westerners.[110] In that scheme of things Alexander had a double legitimacy. He was heir to the conquests of the Persian monarchs and heir to Heracles and Dionysus. The gods' conquests were particularly useful because they were indeterminate. Wherever he went, Alexander could always find traces of his predecessors, and there was always a pretext for aggression. The Persian kings may not have penetrated far beyond the Indus, let alone the Hyphasis; but the invincible Dionysus could be portrayed as a universal ruler, subjugating and civilizing the entire world.

Alexander regarded the conquest of India as his right; and our sources show the same apparent complicity on his victims' part that we noted in the Mexican context. After the Malli campaign the Oxydracae sent an embassy of submission, comprising all the dignitaries of the tribe. Their excuse for not having approached Alexander previously was based upon the *fable convenue*. They accepted the tradition of Dionysus' conquest, and claimed that they had been autonomous since the time of the god.[111] Dionysus in effect had authorized their autonomy, and they were entitled to it. However, Alexander resembled the god in boasting divine paternity, and they

---

[108] Above, Ch. 4, pp. 121–4.

[109] *FGrH* 69 F 1 = *Epist. Socr.* 30. 5–7. On the background see M. M. Markle, *JHS* 96 (1976) 93–7; Hammond and Griffith, *History of Macedonia* ii. 514–16.

[110] Above, Ch. 4, n. 126.

[111] Arr. 6. 14. 2. The claims of the Oxydracae were discussed, and dismissed, by Eratosthenes (Strabo 15. 1. 8 (687–8); cf. Arr. *Ind.* 5. 9).

were prepared to surrender to him. The Oxydracae, then, recognize Alexander as the heir of their divine founder, and are willing to compromise their autonomy—but to him alone. Once again we cannot hope to uncover the original substance of the Indians' representations. What we have is the interpretation of the conquerors, and it is an interpretation which confers absolute legitimacy upon the conquest. Alexander is accepted as the heir of Dionysus, the natural ruler of the Indian lands, and the Oxydracae are seen as admitting themselves in the wrong for not having capitulated immediately. Their admission implicitly inculpates the Malli, who shared their guilt. Alexander had a right to their submission, and the horrors of the campaign he unleashed were the direct result of their refusal of his sovereignty. He had every justification to acquire what was his, and acquire it by any means. Even the conquered could be seen to acknowledge his legitimacy. This is the sanitized face of power. An unprovoked and hideously savage campaign of aggression is transformed by propaganda and imaginative translation into a justifiable war against stubborn rebels, defiant of legitimate authority. As so often, the victims have become the culprits.

6

Alexander and the Desert

NOTHING was dearer to Alexander than the belief in his invincibility.[1] By the end of the reign there was a proposal at Athens to erect a statue of 'King Alexander, the invincible god', and the mover was none other than Demosthenes.[2] Whether or not the proposal was carried is irrelevant. What matters is that it was Alexander's invincibility that was identified as his divine attribute. Alexander the invincible is a familiar figure in ancient and modern literature, and an anecdote of Plutarch (*Al.* 14. 6–7) is particularly instructive. The young Alexander supposedly visited Delphi, and wished to consult the oracle. The officiating priestess refused to initiate the procedure, since it was a day of recess. At that he dragged her by force to the temple, and she protested, 'You are invincible (ἀνίκητος), my boy.' Alexander promptly released her, declaring that he had all the prophecy he needed. In all probability the story is apocryphal,[3] but it attests the general belief that Alexander saw conquest as his destiny from the outset of his career.

It is worth diverging for a moment to examine what was made of the story by Tarn. He wished to accept its nucleus, the augury of invincibility, but, as a deeply moral Victorian, he was affronted by

---

[1] That is something Alexander shared with Cortés. A contemporary portrait of the Conquistador (at the age of 63) dubs him *dux invictissimus* (*Hernán Cortés, Letters from Mexico* 7). Cf. Díaz p. 47 (Cohen): 'the plain name Cortés was as highly respected in Spain and throughout the Indies as the name of Alexander in Macedon.'

[2] Hyper. *Dem.* col. 32. On the background see Goukowsky i. 60–6; S. Jaschinski, *Alexander und Griechenland unter dem Eindruck der Flucht von Harpalos* 99–102. The text is fragmentary, but there can be no doubt that Sauppe's reconstruction is correct.

[3] Diod. 17. 93. 4 also refers to the tradition, but it is difficult to insert a visit to Delphi into the chronology of 336 (let alone 335, where Plutarch seems to place it). If the visit is historical, it presumably took place between the recognition of Alexander as head of the Corinthian League and his return to Macedon in winter 336/5. However, the coercion of the Pythia is suspiciously reminiscent of Philomelus' actions in 356, at the beginning of the Sacred War (Diod. 16. 25. 3, 27. 1), and the story may well be a doublet, excogitated to explain the origin of the epithet ἀνίκητος. The scene is transferred to Siwah in a late epitome, the so-called *Fragmentum Sabbaiticum* (*FGrH* 151 F 1. 10).

the imposition of force on any woman, 'let alone a priestess'. Such abuse was unthinkable in his Alexander, and he proceeded to rewrite the text of Plutarch. What the young king did was to take her arm and say 'O, come along,' or something of the sort, and the middle-aged priestess, overcome by the youthful charms of her assailant, replied almost coyly, 'Boy, you are irresistible.'[4] This is pure farce, but it is also an important illustration of bad method. One takes from the ancient evidence only what will support one's preconceived theories, and rejects the rest as biased or distorted. As it happened, Tarn undermined his own case by projecting upon Alexander moral scruples which were anachronistic in 1948, let alone 336 BC. He accepted the apophthegm of the priestess, but rejected the entire literary context in which it was framed. However, such manipulation is not uncharacteristic of Alexander studies. All too often, the concern is to brush aside unpalatable facts, and argue from what the sources should have said.

Fortunately there is no doubt about Alexander's belief in his invincibility. There is an overwhelmingly strong tradition that he presented himself as the successor of Dionysus and Heracles, reconquering the territory they had traversed and equalling or outstripping their greatest feats.[5] The coinage of the reign bears out the story. The famous imperial tetradrachms featured the head of Heracles, the ancestral forebear of the royal house of Macedon, and by the end of the reign the features on the bust had patently become the features of Alexander himself, with the strongly rounded chin and the bulge of the forehead above the nose.[6] The same portraiture occurs in the famous and brilliant tetradrachm of Lysimachus which depicts the king with the horns of Ammon (the ram god of Siwah,

[4] Tarn, *Al.* ii. 346 with n. 1. Plutarch's terminology (βίᾳ εἶλκεν) could not be more explicit on the use of force (see the protest of Hamilton, *Plut. Al.* 35). Nothing incidentally in the anecdote gives any indication of the age of the Pythia.

[5] See above, Ch. 4 *passim*.

[6] Cf. Bellinger, *Essays* 14–21; H. A. Cahn, in *Entretiens Hardt* 22 (1976) 272–3; O. Palagia, *Boreas* 9 (1986) 140–2; Price, *Coinage* i. 33–4. Stewart 158–61 denies that the coin types are in any sense a 'cryptoportrait', but his arguments do not convince me. It is, for instance, true that Alexander might have produced his portrait 'clearly and unambiguously' (Stewart 159), had he wished to do so. However, the identification with Heracles was hardly senseless. Given Alexander's emphasis upon Heracles as his great precursor, the example *par excellence* of the attainment of divinity through achievement and benefaction (see above, Ch. 4 *passim*), it was logical enough to represent himself with the attributes of Heracles (Ath. 12. 537 F = Ephippus, *FGrH* 126 F 4), to the point of fusing his identity with that of the hero god.

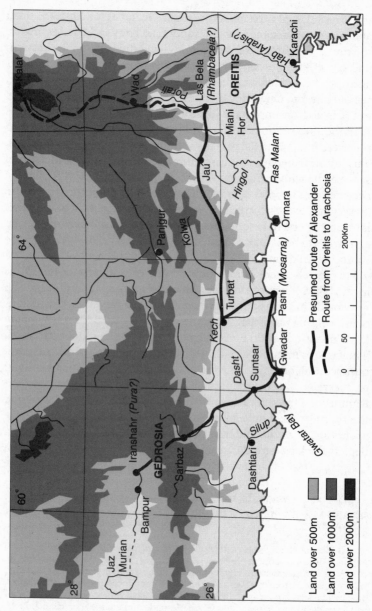

Fig. 10. The Makran

whom he believed to be his spiritual father) and a cloth diadem. The coinage shows Alexander as the superman, the son of Ammon and a second, greater Heracles, sharing Heracles' reputation for invincibility. The same message is proclaimed by the great silver commemorative decadrachms which Alexander issued from Babylon at the end of his reign. One side has a dramatic representation of the king on horseback (with a *sarisa*) attacking two Indians mounted on a elephant—it seems to depict the climactic moment of the Battle of the Hydaspes. The reverse is more interesting. It is inspired by the famous painting of Apelles which depicted Alexander in the guise of Zeus and holding a thunderbolt. Here Alexander in armour brandishes a thunderbolt in his right hand and receives a crown from Victory herself.[7] The royal mint could not have made it clearer that the king was not only son of Zeus Ammon but Zeus incarnate and as such invincible.

In modern writings on Alexander there is one hiccup in the career of conquest. The one serious loss of the reign was not inflicted by any human enemy but by the forces of nature, embodied in the redoubtable Gedrosian desert.[8] In the late summer of 325 BC Alexander had brought an armada of light vessels down the Indus delta. There he set up a naval arsenal and deputed his friend and admiral Nearchus to take a fleet along the coast of the Indian ocean to the Persian Gulf. He himself set off in advance of the fleet with his land army, first via modern Karachi to the plain of Las Bela and then across the Kirthar Range into what was then called Gedrosia, now the Makran. There followed a march of some 460 miles (*c.* 750 km.) direct, ending after 60 days at the Gedrosian capital of Pura (in the vicinity of modern Bampur).[9] The march began early in October and ended in December. The hardships, it is alleged, were enormous. According to the original historians of Alexander they far surpassed all the hardships endured in the previous ten years of campaigning.[10] Modern scholars have envisaged fantastic wastage; even a prudent writer such as Hermann Strasburger could argue that

---

[7] On the portraiture, borrowed from Apelles' canonical painting at Ephesus (Pliny, *NH* 35. 92) see J. B. Kaiser, *JDAI* 72 (1962) 233–5; Goukowsky i. 63–5; Stewart 201–6.

[8] The main discussion of the Gedrosian adventure remains the great article of Hermann Strasburger (*Hermes* 80 (1952) 456–93 = *Studien* i. 449–86), which combines exhaustive discussion of the sources with a very useful commentary on points of detail. See also Bosworth, *Conquest and Empire* 143–6, for a necessarily brief outline.

[9] Arr. 6. 24. 1; Strabo 15. 2. 7 (723). On the location see Stein, *Archaeological Reconnaissances* 113; *GJ* 102 (1943) 222.   [10] Arr. 6. 24. 1; *Ind.* 26. 1.

Alexander lost 45,000–55,000 out of a total strength of 60,000–70,000, and there have been far wilder estimates.[11] It has even been suggested that the losses were so calamitous that Alexander was forced to inaugurate a witch hunt among his senior officers and governors, in an attempt to shift the responsibility on to other shoulders.[12] This is a bleak and depressing picture, a stark counterpoint to the blatant propaganda of the coinage and, if justified, the modern interpretations give us an instance of reckless, ill-calculated bravado to set against the catalogue of uninterrupted victory. We need to examine the record of hardship and the evidence for Alexander's motives, to elucidate just how adventurous and how calamitous that desert march was.

Let us begin with the record of hardship. That is most eloquently provided by one of Alexander's first historians, almost certainly the fleet commander Nearchus. The original is lost but it was used by two later, extant writers, Strabo and Arrian, who provide very similar digests of it.[13] They emphasize the pervasive heat and the long marches between the sources of water; they emphasize the difficulties caused by marching over the deep sands, which drifted into steep ridges of dunes, and record a disaster which occurred when rains in the northern mountains generated a flash flood, causing havoc among the camp followers and destroying all the royal baggage train.[14] Men were lost during the night-long forced marches, as they collapsed from exhaustion and were abandoned;[15] others died from excessive drinking when an abundance of water was encountered.[16]

---

[11] Strasburger, *Studien* i. 479–80: 'wird man die Gedrosien-Armee schwerlich auf weniger als 60–70,000 Soldaten schätzen dürfen, von denen allerhöchstens 15,000 überlebt haben können' (for guarded scepticism see Brunt, *Arrian* ii. 481). Engels 114–15 seems to calculate the total losses at something over 100,000!

[12] Badian, *CQ* 18 (1958) 148; *JHS* 81 (1961) 21; *CHIran* ii. 473–7.

[13] Arr. 6. 24. 2–26. 5; Strabo 15. 2. 5–6 (721–2). On the identification of the source as Nearchus see the detailed discussion of Strasburger (*Studien* i. 451–9, approved by Brunt, *Arrian* ii. 475–6). The alternative attribution to Aristobulus (Schwartz, *RE* ii. 1245; Jacoby, ii. D 420; Pearson, *LHA* 128 n. 151; Hammond, *Sources* 274–7) is to my mind inadmissible. Arrian (6. 24. 4) continues a named citation of Nearchus (λέγει Νέαρχος) in accusative and infinitive (τό τε οὖν καῦμα...διαφθεῖραι), while Strabo similarly refers to Nearchus' famous story of the failures of Cyrus and Semiramis in the general context of the horror narrative. In both cases the exposition is unitary, and is ascribed to Nearchus.   [14] Arr. 6. 25. 4–5; Strabo 15. 2. 6 (722).

[15] Arr. 6. 24. 6, 25. 3; Strabo 15. 2. 6 ('travelling by night for the most part'). Cf. Curt. 9. 10. 14–16.

[16] Arr. 6. 25. 6; on Strabo's version see below, pp. 173–4.

This record is very vivid, and it is easy to parallel all the items of horror in the accounts of modern travellers. Nowadays Baluchistan and the Makran coast can indeed be a fearful place. A Persian proverb, often quoted, has it that when Allah created the world he made Baluchistan out of the pieces of refuse. I myself recall looking out of an aeroplane window as dawn broke on the flight west from Bombay, and seeing an appalling tangle of eviscerated mountains, the Kirthar range, followed by a view of two parallel ridges which went for mile after mile along the coast with what seemed nothing but pure sand between them. It could have been the inspiration for Tolkien's description of the ramparts of Mordor. The Makran is indeed a bleakly inhospitable place. Its coast is sandy and largely waterless, with almost impenetrable tangles of eroded hills, which from time to time block any transit. Inland to the east there is the dull, featureless Dashtiari plain which extends northwards to a maze of hills dividing the coast from the inland valley of Bampur. The rainfall is low, particularly in the Iranian Makran, with an average of no more than 5 inches of rain a year (though two inches and more may fall in a single day).[17] In the west, in Las Bela, the rainfall is slightly higher, about 7 inches per year, almost all of it during the summer months.[18] The difficulties of the sand dunes are notorious, and almost every traveller has stories to tell of being bogged and delayed by flash floods.[19]

If (and I stress the if) conditions were comparable in antiquity and Alexander led a large force into the Makran, then it is inevitable that losses were immense. Not surprisingly, there have been a number of modern attempts at rationalization. It has been argued that Alexander took only a skeleton force with him, to prepare the way for the larger fleet with Nearchus.[20] That runs against the explicit evidence that Alexander's ambition was to cross the desert safely with an

---

[17] For statistics see *CHIran* i. 246, under the entry for Bam.

[18] *Baluchistan District Gazetteer Series* VIII: Las Bela (Allahabad 1907) 18: 'The rainfall is capricious and uncertain. Most of it is received in the summer during June, July and August, but a little rain falls during the winter during January and February.' In 1905/6 the total rainfall was 7.9 inches.

[19] Notably Sir Aurel Stein, whose lorries were bogged in a river bed near Turbat in a flash flood early in January (*An Archaeological Tour in Gedrosia* (Calcutta 1931) 56–7). See also Strasburger, *Studien* i. 478 n. 1, for other reports.

[20] So Tarn, *Al.* i. 106–7. The case was most fully argued by Kraft, *Der 'rationale' Alexander* 106–18.

army[21] (in contrast with the legends of Semiramis and Cyrus the Great, who were said to have lost all but a handful of their troops in transit). What is more the record of hardship refers to the straggle of women and children who followed the army.[22] This was no picked corps of pioneers but a full expeditionary force with all its impedimenta. An alternative explanation has accordingly been devised by some recent scholars.[23] According to this interpretation Nearchus' fleet was intended to provision the land army, and his fleet comprised great flat-bottomed freighters which would take grain from the Indus delta to feed Alexander's men in the desert. The hardships and losses were inevitable when Nearchus was delayed by adverse winds and failed to meet his rendezvous. This is a pleasing enough story, but it is sheer romance, comparable to Tarn's extravaganza with the Delphian priestess. The ancient sources, particularly Arrian, make it clear that one of Alexander's prime objectives was to provision his fleet. He sank wells along the mouth of the delta and near Karachi and arranged for stockpiles of grain to be amassed on the coast south of Las Bela.[24] Even in the desert regions of Gedrosia he contrived to requisition a surplus of grain and transported it south to the coast.[25] The consignment was eaten by its famished escort, but it was at least intended to provision the fleet. There is, moreover, no evidence for grain transports in Nearchus' fleet. The *kerkouroi* mentioned by Arrian are clearly light pursuit vessels,[26] not slow flat-

---

[21] Arr. 6. 24. 2 ('hearing that nobody as yet had come off safely crossing by that route with any army'); Strabo 15. 1. 5 ('what an august thing if he and his army could win through with victory intact'); so 15. 2. 5. See below, p. 182.

[22] Arr. 6. 25. 5, claiming that the majority of the women and children succumbed. Hammond, *Sources* 275 n. 27, curiously attempts to minimize the disaster, alleging that τὰ πολλὰ τῶν ἑπομένων can *only* mean 'the majority (of the women and children) of the camp followers'. Hence the wives and children of the *soldiers* were safe and sound with Craterus. However, this is a gross misinterpretation. The genitive, as invariably with τὰ πολλά, is *partitive* (Arr. 1. 3. 4, 2. 11. 9, 5. 12. 3; cf. 4. 24. 7, 5. 10. 3). Those who perished were 'the majority of women and children who followed the army'; the text does not restrict the casualties to the dependants of the camp followers, the traders and sutlers. Strabo 15. 2. 6 (722) mentions severe losses to life and property, but gives no specific details (πολλὰ δὲ κατέκλυσε καὶ τῶν σωμάτων καὶ τῶν χρηστηρίων).

[23] Green 430–1; Engels 111–17; R. Lane Fox, *The Search for Alexander* 348–50. For detailed criticism see G. Schepens, *AncSoc* 20 (1989) 36–43.

[24] Arr. 6. 21. 3, 22. 3, 23. 7; cf. Strabo 15. 2. 3 fin. (721). See below, pp. 177–9.

[25] Arr. 6. 23. 4–5. Nearchus has no record of provisions left for him west of Oreitis. It was only in the last stage of his voyage, along the coast of Persis, that food depots could be arranged (Arr. *Ind.* 38. 9).

[26] *Kerkouroi* (κέρκουροι) are mentioned at Arr. 6. 2. 4 (= Ptolemy, *FGrH* 138 F 24), 18. 3, 20. 4; *Ind.* 23. 3, 31. 3. These ships were included in the squadron of fast vessels

bottomed lighters, which were fine for the Nile but hardly designed for ocean conditions. It is worth repeating yet again that any historical reconstruction must be based solidly on what ancient evidence there is; otherwise it is intellectual speculation and nothing more.

What then are we to make of the narrative of horror? We have no right to reject the details in it, but, if those details are placed in context, a less horrific picture may emerge. Indeed it must emerge, if we are to make any historical sense of the episode. Our chief source for the desert journey, Arrian, is a highly elaborate and sophisticated author. He draws on contemporary historians but rearranges the material in them for the maximum dramatic impact. The account of the passage of the desert is divided into three parts, neatly separated to illustrate different aspects of the episode. The first is based on Aristobulus (a contemporary who probably took part in the desert march) and deals with the exotic flora of the region: perfume-bearing plants, mangroves, and giant thorns.[27] Here there is no hint of hardship. The second passage focuses on Alexander's efforts to provision the fleet. It is a sober narrative, mentioning the pressures of hunger but not laying any special emphasis on the suffering.[28] That comes in the third section, based on Nearchus, where Arrian concentrates explicitly upon the hardships, carefully contrasting the torments of thirst and heat with the losses from flash flooding and over-supply of water.[29] He has deliberately taken the material out of context and manipulated it to give the most dramatic picture of hardship that he could conceive. When we turn to Strabo, the other source for Nearchus' narrative, we find the same lurid details. But there are also mitigating factors which we do not find in Arrian, who was preoccupied by his record of suffering. In particular Strabo sets on record the precious information that Alexander deliberately chose the most promising season for his crossing, so as to take advantage of the summer rainfall.[30] When he moved into

---

which Alexander took to the Ocean (6. 18. 3, 19. 3). In later war fleets they were used alongside light pirate vessels (*myoparones*), and proved very effective (App. *Lib.* 121, 576; 122, 580; Livy 23. 34. 4 stresses their *celeritas*). For the grain transports of the Nile see L. Casson, *Ships and Seamanship* 164–6.

[27] Arr. 6. 22. 4–8, explicitly ascribed to Aristobulus (*FGrH* 139 F 49).

[28] Arr. 6. 23. 1–24. 1. This chapter probably derives from Ptolemy (so Strasburger *Studien* i. 451–2; Kornemann 86–7; Brunt, *Arrian* i. 474–5).

[29] Arr. 6. 24. 6–25. 3 (heat); 6. 25. 4–6 (water).

[30] Strabo 15. 2. 3 (721): 'they made their return from India in the summer on

Gedrosia the seasonal watercourses were running and what wells and underground cisterns existed were full. That recurs later in his record when he notes that thirst-crazed soldiers would plunge into the wells in full armour, die in the very act of convulsive drinking and float up to the surface to pollute the water.[31] It is a sensational and exaggerated detail, which should put us on our guard; but it does imply that water was often in very abundant supply.

Next there is plenty of indication that the region in antiquity was hardly the wilderness of desolation that it is today. Both Aristobulus and Nearchus noted the profusion of incense-bearing plants resembling myrrh and spikenard.[32] This is presumably the mukul tree which is still harvested for its aromatic resin. In Alexander's day the plant was enormously prolific, so much so that the troops used its branches for bedding, and it was harvested by the Phoenician traders who followed the army. They at least were not deterred by the desert conditions. In the same way the mangroves which still exist in small clumps along the Makran coast flourished in great stands.[33] Sadly these are the plants which have receded. The cactus-like thorns vividly described by Aristobulus have become more prevalent; nearly a century ago a jaundiced observer remarked of the vegetation: 'they look like the skeletons of plants, the grey ghosts of a vegetation which has perished of thirst. The glaucous aspect of all, and the universality of spines, are remarkable.'[34] The country has clearly degenerated. That is nowhere more evident than in the Bampur valley, the centre of Gedrosia, where Alexander ended his march. This was an area of relative plenty, where Alexander rested his troops for a short while before moving west to the more fertile

purpose, for at that time Gedrosia has rains, and the rivers and the wells are filled, though in winter they fail.'

[31] Strabo 15. 2. 6 (722). Arr. 6. 25. 6 describes the same phenomenon, but in rather more restrained terms. Both versions presuppose that the wells and watercourses were full to overflowing.

[32] Arr. 6. 22. 4–5 (Aristobulus); Strabo 15. 2. 3 (Nearchus?) claims that the plants were used for bedding and tent covering. For the identification with the mukul tree (*Balsamodendron mukul* Stocks) see H. Bretzl, *Die botanische Forschungen des Alexander-zuges* 282–4.

[33] Arr. 6. 22. 6–7 (cf. Theophr. *HP* 4. 7. 4). Aristobulus described the mangroves (*Rhizophora mucronata*) with their characteristic flowers, which he observed during the march (the flowering season is October/November). Modest growths of mangrove have been reported in the eastern Makran in recent times (R. E. Snead, *Physical Geography Reconnaissance: Las Bela Coastal Plain* (Baton Rouge 1966) 68).

[34] Major D. Paine, Director of the Botanical Survey of India, quoted in the *Baluchistan Gazetteers Series* VIII Las Bela 16–17.

area of Carmania.[35] Nowadays the Bampur valley is near desolate, its waste of sand dunes hardly less forbidding than the desert country to the south. In December 1935 an eyewitness noted a mere trickle of water in the Bampur river and remarked that 'the country would be taxed to feed a battalion for long, let alone a brigade'.[36] In December 325 BC the region must have been far better watered, verdant, and productive.

I am not for a moment trying to deny the veracity of the details in Nearchus' horror narrative. What I am doing is, as far as possible, to set them in their proper context. Nearchus, we must recall, was not with Alexander on the desert crossing. His account therefore is not a personal record, but his compilation of reports from survivors, presumably made shortly after the event. The stories certainly reflect the experiences of the march, the struggle against drifting sand, thirst, and sheer distance, but equally certainly they are embellished in the desire to make the best of the story—the besetting vice of war memoirs of every age. We may well believe that there were long overnight marches, but hardly of 50 or 70 miles, as Strabo suggests.[37] Otherwise how could a direct journey of 460 miles or so have taken 60 days of hard marching—as both Arrian and Strabo record? The details are clearly coloured, exaggerated by the reporters and by Nearchus himself, who was prone to draw a long bow and could coolly describe one of his vessels disappearing into thin air close to the magic island of Nosala.[38] What is clear is that for part of the march at least there was an abundance of water. There was also at times no shortage of foodstuffs. Arrian notes that there was at least one area of Gedrosia (almost certainly the modern oasis of Turbat)

[35] Arr. 6. 24. 1, 27. 1. Diod. 17. 106. 1 stresses the abundance of the area; so Curt. 9. 10. 18.

[36] J. V. Harrison, *GJ* 101 (1943) 214, adding that the road to Kerman across the north of the Jaz Murian basin (the route taken by Alexander into Carmania) had to be furnished with dumps of fodder and grain to enable horses to make the passage.

[37] Strabo 15. 2. 6 (722) attests marches of 200, 300, or even 600 stades. Arr. 6. 24. 5 also stresses the distance between water sources, but gives no figures. It is sheer desperation to assume (with Strasburger, *Studien* i. 459–62) that Nearchus was operating with a short stade (of 0.11 km.). It is unlikely that the bematists were working with strict accuracy in the Gedrosian wilderness; and most of the participants in the march had no way of measuring the distance they traversed. However, they would have been aware of the numerous digressions from the direct route (Arr. 6. 25. 2), which would have encouraged them to give the most exaggerated estimates. It would have felt like walking in circles—for ever.

[38] Arr. *Ind.* 31. 3; Strabo 15. 2. 13 (726). See above, Ch. 3, p. 72.

where grain was relatively plentiful.[39] The surplus remained after his army was fed and was conveyed in a baggage train to the coast. Other provisions he amassed by sending out foraging parties, and the inhabitants of the northern Panjgur district, who were fortunately untouched by his expedition, were ordered to convey their surplus of grain and dates to the coast.[40] It was not required by Alexander and his troops. Here we have an apparent paradox. Part of the source tradition stresses thirst and famine, another reports at least a modicum of provisions. How can the two be reconciled?

It is time to introduce the chief actor in our drama, not a human protagonist but the south-west monsoon, which dominates the weather of the Indian subcontinent. From late May a prevailing southerly wind-current sets in south of Sri Lanka, and the rain shadow moves steadily north. By mid-July it reaches its furthest northern limit in Pakistan, persists for two months and recedes by mid-September. It deposits 50 per cent and more of the annual rainfall and is the essential prerequisite for the winter harvest. Now Alexander and his men had made the acquaintance of the monsoon in the northern Punjab during the campaign of 326. It lasted for over 70 days, from the summer solstice to the rising of Arcturus, late in September.[41] The deluge was consistent, turning the rivers into dangerous flood spates[42] and gradually rotting the men's equipment and morale. Ultimately they refused to advance further into the rains and forced Alexander to retrace his steps from the River Hyphasis in the most effective display of resistance he ever encountered from his own men. Very much present in 326, the monsoon rains were notable for their absence the following year. As Alexander's fleet came down the Indus in the spring and summer of 325 not a drop of rain was experienced, so the invaluable Aristobulus informs us. They reached their destination, Patala, at the rising of Sirius, in the middle

---

[39] Arr. 6. 23. 4. For the identification of the area see Stein, *An Archaeological Tour in Gedrosia* 53; Engels 115; Brunt, *Arrian* ii. 478.

[40] Arr. 6. 23. 6. Panjgur is the most fertile area of the northern Makran, and in medieval times it boasted the capital of the area, Fannazbûr (G. Le Strange, *Lands of the Eastern Caliphate* (Cambridge 1905) 329).

[41] The details were supplied by Aristobulus, *FGrH* 139 F 35 (= Strabo 15. 1. 17 (691)). The effects of the monsoon are vividly depicted in the Vulgate (Diod. 17. 94. 3; cf. Curt. 9. 3. 10; Strabo 15. 1. 27 (697)), but are ignored by Arrian, except for an incidental reference to storm damage (Arr. 5. 29. 5; cf. Bosworth, *HCA* ii. 323, 359–60).

[42] Note Ptolemy's description of the crossing of the Acesines, resumed by Arr. 5. 20. 8–9 (= *FGrH* 138 F 22); cf. Bosworth, *HCA* ii. 322–4.

of July.[43] By that time the monsoon had not begun. Alexander was able to visit the mouth of the Indus and even venture into the Ocean, before the continuous onset of the adverse southerlies[44] which were later to keep Nearchus confined to his shore base. The season was delayed. The monsoon winds only set in consistently late in August, when Alexander was about to leave S. Pakistan for Las Bela (ancient Oreitis), and he was informed that the winds could persist until the setting of the Pleiades, early in November.[45] Those predictions were fulfilled. Nearchus was storm-bound in Patala until early October, when pressure from the hostile natives forced him to attempt a premature embarcation. The renewed monsoon caught him in the open sea and he was marooned on a small island for a further 24 days.[46] There was a full monsoon, but its onset came late and in consequence the entire growing cycle of the region was retarded. The rainfall, Aristobulus claims, was sparse on the plains, but the rivers flooded, swelled by the precipitation in the mountains, where the monsoon deluge was heaviest. That enabled the sowing to proceed.

The growing season for the autumn harvest normally lasts three months. The crops (sorghum, wheat, and barley) are sown in mid-July ('a local saying runs that if a man's mother dies in that month he has no time to bury her'),[47] and the harvest comes in October or November. In 325 there was at least a month's delay in sowing. Alexander led his forces out of S. Pakistan at the end of August. It was absolutely vital that he took his army away from Patala where food had been stockpiled for the fleet and his forces had been supported for nearly two months.[48] The next area to be visited was

[43] Strabo 15. 1. 17 (691–2): the fleet set out from the Hydaspes a few days before the setting of the Pleiades (early Nov. 326), and spent 10 months on the voyage. There were no rains even at the height of the Etesians, when continuous sea winds prevented navigation.

[44] Arr. 6. 18. 3–20. 5; Curt. 9. 9. 1–10. 3; Diod. 17. 104. 1–3; Plut. *Al.* 66. 1–2. Arr. 6. 18. 4–5 mentions an adverse gale at the start of Alexander's voyage, but it was only a forerunner of the monsoon proper. It did not prevent his venturing into the open sea, which would have been impossible after the advent of the full monsoon.

[45] Arr. 6. 21. 1: navigation possible between the setting of the Pleiades and the winter solstice (just when it would be impossible in the Aegean).

[46] Arr. *Ind.* 21. 1; Strabo 15. 2. 5 (721) = Nearchus, *FGrH* 133 F 1a. Both Arrian and Strabo agree on the date, early in Oct. 325 (20 Boedromion, according to the Attic calendar, or the evening rising of the Pleiades); and, according to Strabo, Alexander was then completing his journey through Gedrosia. For the 24-day delay see Arr. *Ind.* 21. 11–13.

[47] *Baluchistan District Gazetteer* VIII Las Bela 78.

[48] Arr. 6. 20. 1, 5 (4 months' supply of grain at Patala).

Oreitis, the modern region of Las Bela. There Alexander overran the territory, forced the inhabitants into submission and established the capital as a new foundation, one of the many Alexandrias, with a dominant élite of Greek mercenaries. His marshal, Leonnatus, stayed for a few months, until the harvest was ripe. Much of this he commandeered and stored in a great depot near the coast. He also suppressed the rebellion which his activities provoked.[49] At all events when Nearchus and his ocean fleet put in at the coast of Oreitis in mid-November he could take on board full rations for 10 days.

By that time Alexander had forged westwards across the Kirthar range into the Kolwa valley.[50] He avoided the coast which was practically impassable and inhabited by aborigines who lived on fish and cultivated no crops.[51] The interior was watered, by flood waters from the mountains if not by direct rainfall, and when he entered the Makran early in October the crops were close to maturity. By the time he reached the area of Turbat, some 160 miles (260 km.) from the passes into Gedrosia, the harvest, such as it was, was ready and he exploited it ruthlessly, arranging for it to be conveyed to the sea for the fleet. At this point his good intentions foundered. Whatever Alexander's expectations were of the yield in the Makran, he was disappointed. There was a surplus, but that surplus was rapidly devoured by the troops escorting the convoy, who were pressed to

---

[49] Arr. *Ind.* 23. 5–8; Curt. 9. 10. 19. Leonnatus was decorated the following year at Susa in recognition of his achievement (Arr. 7. 5. 5; *Ind.* 42. 9; cf. Heckel 102–3).

[50] The exact route is irrelevant to my argument here. What is evident is that Alexander avoided the coast, as was necessary if provisions were to be left for the fleet. He discovered the poverty of the eastern coastline around Ormara through Thoas' reconnaissance mission (Arr. 6. 23. 1–3), and Arrian is explicit that he kept away from the sea (προσωτέρω ἀπὸ θαλάσσης), except for the 7-day march along the coast south of Turbat (Arr. 6. 26. 5; Strabo 15. 2. 6 (722 fin.)). Similarly Nearchus' report of his voyage excludes Alexander's presence on the eastern coast of the Makran. Strabo 15. 2. 4 (721) claims that the king kept a *maximum* of 500 stades from the sea, and often impinged upon the coastline. That is totally inconsistent with Arrian, and is probably garbled. Strabo could be reporting Alexander's *intention* to keep close to the sea (cf. Arr. 6. 23. 1), so as to prepare for the fleet. That intention, as Arrian demonstrates, was frustrated by Thoas' forbidding reports of the coast. I assume, like Stein (*GJ* 102 (1943) 216; so Engels 137–43; Brunt, *Arrian* ii. 478–9) that Alexander followed the Kolwa valley, where the population was denser and food (such as it was) more abundant. The coastal route (advocated by Strasburger, *Studien* i. 459–62, 487–90; so J. Seibert, *Die Eroberung des Perserreiches* 175) would have been practically impassable, and Strasburger himself concedes that the massif of Ras Malan would have required a substantial detour (*Studien* i. 460/1, n. 2).

[51] Arr. *Ind.* 24. 9, 29. 12–13; Strabo 15. 2. 2 (720–1), all mentioning that they had a small supply of grain. Cf. Arr. *Ind.* 26. 8–9.

extremities by hunger.[52] No supplies remained for the fleet later in
the season, and, when Nearchus passed along the coast towards the
end of November and reached the eastern Makran, all that remained
of the harvest was straw piled in bales near the sea.[53]

Alexander's forces themselves were presently in difficulties. His
army preceded the grain convoy to the coastline south of Turbat.
Even on this relatively well-trodden route there were problems. The
monsoon southerlies drove up such a cloud of sand that the land-
marks were obliterated, and Alexander himself led a small mounted
reconnaissance force to find the sea. He continued west for 7 days
along the shore relying on the fresh water dug up above the tide-
line.[54] Here there were no inhabitants and no food, except for the
wild date palms, which provided sustenance of a kind. Even so the
unripe, green dates played havoc with the digestion.[55] What was
worse, Alexander had passed beyond the rain shadow of the
monsoon. What we now know (and he probably did not) is that the
climate of the eastern, Iranian, side of the Makran is quite different
from that in the west. There the summer rainfall is minimal. The
winter rains, such as they are, begin only in late November after five
months of total aridity.[56] Even when Alexander diverged north
through the Dashtiari plain there was no relief. The harvest there
was a distant memory and there was no prospect of food apart from
the ubiquitous date palms. It was in these latter stages that the
march became a rout, when the watercourses were predominantly
dry. As the food disappeared the baggage animals were slaughtered
by the famished troops. Alexander could not prevent the practice
and so diplomatically pretended ignorance.[57] He was in no position
to enforce discipline, but he could not reveal the fact. Accordingly
the transport wagons were broken up and the horses and pack mules
gradually consumed. The column which finally limped into the

---

[52] Arr. 6. 23. 4–5. For some reason Hammond (*Sources* 275 n. 27) believes that
'those who were starving were camp followers, who accompanied the army at their
own risk'. The text seems to me to imply that the guards of the convoy *and* the
starving recipients of their largesse were both soldiers (στρατιῶται).

[53] Arr. *Ind.* 27. 9, 28. 8, 29. 5.   [54] Arr. 6. 26. 4–5; Strabo 15. 2. 6 (722 fin.).

[55] Strabo 15. 2. 5 (722), 15. 2. 7 (723); cf. Arr. *Ind.* 29. 1–2; Theophr. *HP* 4. 4. 12;
Pliny *NH* 13. 50.

[56] See the rainfall figures adduced by Siddiqi 14–17. During the monsoon period
Las Bela averages 208 mm., Ormara (in the eastern Makran) 68 mm., Pasni (further
west still) 25 mm., and Jask (in the Persian Makran) 0 mm.

[57] Arr. 6. 25. 1–2; Strabo 15. 2. 5 (722) mentions that the pack animals 'gave out'
(ἐπέλιπε), but adds no details.

Bampur valley was a rabble, without equipment, food, or morale and clearly in the last stages of exhaustion.

But how calamitous was the march? Plutarch claims that hardly a quarter of the forces Alexander had in India reached the far side of the Makran.[58] But the figure he gives for the troops in India is vast (120,000 foot and 15,000 horse) and, if there is any substance in it, it must refer to the huge number of auxiliaries who swelled his armies in India and returned home before the desert crossing. Far more significant is the fact that there is no evidence of wastage in Alexander's army. The Macedonian infantry numbers were surprisingly high at the end of Alexander's reign. By 324 there were 18,000 rank-and-file in the phalanx, a greater number than inaugurated the campaign in 334, and there had been no large-scale reinforcement since the winter of 331/30.[59] In other words the crossing of Gedrosia did not perceptibly reduce the infantry numbers, and we cannot speak of a large-scale military calamity. The women and children in the expedition will have been less fortunate. They were the victims in the flash flood; the soldiers were strong enough to force their way out of danger.[60] Similarly one may assume that the fighting men had privileged access to food and water.[61] The non-combatants probably perished in much greater numbers. Even so, what emerges is not a picture of disaster. It is one of appalling hardship, and the loss of life was probably less than the loss of morale. The army which found its way into Pura was a disorganized rabble which needed careful recreation, but there was no military threat to contain. Alexander's military machine soon regained its fearful efficiency.

We can now address the most intriguing question. Why did Alexander lead his army through the desert? We have stressed the factor of provisioning the fleet, which certainly bulked very large in

[58] Plut. *Al.* 66. 4–5. For justified scepticism see Kraft, *Der 'rationale' Alexander* 115–17. The figures given for Alexander's forces in India correlate pretty well with Arrian's statement (from Nearchus) that 120,000 fighting men were in his entourage by the end of 326 (Arr. *Ind.* 19. 5); Curtius 8. 5. 4 gives the same figure. Given that the forces with Alexander at Susa were considerably smaller, it was a facile assumption that the losses had come about in the Gedrosian desert.

[59] For the calculations see Bosworth, *JHS* 106 (1986) 3–4. Whatever the validity of the general argument, there can be no doubt about the number of Macedonians at Opis. It precludes any calamitous losses (among *Macedonians*) during the desert march.

[60] Explicitly stated at 6. 25. 5: the soldiers escaped with difficulty, with the loss of *some* of their weapons. [61] See above, n. 52.

his calculations. But that was not the whole story. The force Alexander took with him was very large indeed. We can only guess at the numbers. Part of the army had already gone. Before he left the Indus valley he had separated something under half of the infantry phalanx and an unspecified number of Macedonian veterans and sent them under the command of Craterus on a northern route into Afghanistan and the Helmand valley.[62] The rest of the army remained with Alexander and crossed the desert with him together with all the impedimenta of camp servants, concubines, and children. The total must have exceeded 30,000. Now the Makran could be readily traversed by a small, properly equipped force. In AD 711, one thousand years after Alexander, the 17 year-old Arab conqueror, Muhammad ibn Qasim, set out from Hormuz to cross the Makran with a land and naval force. His land force, 12,000 strong, mounted on camels and horses, crossed the desert without incident and embarked immediately on the conquest of the Indus valley.[63] But then the Makran was an Arab dependency (since 643) and the transit was well prepared. By contrast Alexander was moving into unknown territory with a much larger force, and there were obvious limits on the amounts of foodstuffs he could have taken into the desert with him. From the outset the army would need to live from the land, and merely to survive it would need to monopolize the majority of the food it found. The very size of the force was an absurdity if the only object was to provision the fleet.

Was there any alternative to the route Alexander chose? We have seen that he needed to keep moving, so as not to exhaust the sources of supply in any given region. He might well have been reluctant to retrace his path up the Indus through lands devastated by his campaigns of the past year, where the means for supporting his forces were dramatically reduced. But the Makran was not the only corridor between the Indian and Iranian lands. Today there is a relatively well-trodden route between Las Bela and Afghanistan, winding north through the Kirthar Range through Kalat and Quetta to Kandahar and the Helmand valley (ancient Arachosia).[64] The

[62] Arr. 6. 17. 3; Strabo 15. 2. 4–5 (721), 15. 2. 11 (725); Justin 12. 10. 1. Cf. Berve ii. 224–5; Heckel 124–5.

[63] On the Arab conquest of Sind see H. T. Lambrick, *Sind* 152–64; F. Gabrieli, *East & West* 15 (1964/5) 291–5. The parallel is mentioned briefly, and with some scepticism, by Strasburger, *Studien* i. 481.

[64] The various components of the route were described by Charles Masson,

route was very much in evidence in Alexander's day. The agricultural population for Alexander's new settlement in Las Bela was conscribed from Arachosia to the north,[65] and there was clearly a considerable migration. In due course the administration of the entire Las Bela area was placed under the control of the Macedonian governor in Arachosia, and the lines of communication were obviously well defined. Alexander could have split up his forces more evenly, sending a larger contingent with Craterus and hiving off another army group to follow the relatively well-watered route through the Kirthar Range. No more than a token force need have crossed the Makran itself, and the fleet would have been far more effectively supplied.

Instead Alexander kept his army together and took it through what he knew to have been the most desolate route. That leaves us with only one explanation, that given by the contemporary Nearchus. The king wished to surmount a challenge. In the Indus valley he had been informed by the local inhabitants that the passage through Gedrosia was difficult and that two armies had foundered there, led by the legendary Babylonian queen, Semiramis, and the Persian conqueror, Cyrus the Great.[66] The stories were apocryphal, and Alexander surely knew it, but there is no doubt that they were recounted to him. In the next generation Megasthenes, the first Western writer to write extensively on India, took pains to refute the allegations, claiming that there had been no invasion of the Indian lands between Alexander and the mythical expedition of Heracles.[67] Alexander, however, accepted the legends as truth and was inspired to meet the challenge of the desert. Unlike his predecessors *he* would take an army safely through. Bizarre though it may seem to us, the

---

Narrative of Various Journeys in Baluchistan, Afghanistan and the Panjab (London 1842) i. 297–330 (Kandahar to Quetta); ii. 29–52 (Las Bela to Kalat via Wad). Masson describes both routes as relatively easy, traversed by caravans; and he writes with evident pleasure of the verdant area of Kalat (ii. 50).

[65] Curt. 9. 10. 7: 'in hac quoque regione' [sc. Oreitis] 'urbem condidit, deductique sunt in eam Arachosii'.

[66] Arr. 6. 24. 2; Strabo 15. 1. 5 (686), 15. 2. 5 (722) = *FGrH* 133 F 3. Both Arrian and Strabo claim that Alexander was fully aware of the difficulties of the route, and Arrian adds that the allegation was unique to Nearchus (τοῦτο μὲν μόνος...λέγει). What Nearchus maintained was that Alexander had prior knowledge of the difficulties (*contra* Pearson, *LHA* 178 n. 151; Hammond, *Sources* 277); τοῦτο μέν must refer to the entire preceding clause. Other sources must have exculpated Alexander by suggesting that he was incompletely briefed about the difficulties of the desert crossing.

[67] Arr. *Ind.* 5. 4–7, 9. 10–12; Strabo 15. 1. 6 (686–7) = *FGrH* 715 F 11. For discussion see Ch. 4 above, p. 125.

motivation is plausible enough for Alexander. For him there was no firm barrier between myth and history. Heracles was no fairy-tale figure, but the actual ancestor of the Macedonian kings, who had achieved divine status through his labours for mankind. Alexander found traces of his invasion everywhere in India and the Indian deity Krishna he regarded as a local manifestation of Heracles. He surpassed Heracles in capturing Mt. Aornus and had already come to view himself as greater than Heracles, more worthy than his ancestor to be acknowledged a god among men.[68] He had proved his superiority over human and even divine rivals and now he was to assert himself over nature itself. Seven years before he had pressed the siege of Gaza to the bitter end in defiance of any strategic logic simply because the city was considered impregnable.[69] Now the desert itself would succumb to him. His self-confidence was limitless.

The march through Gedrosia was ultimately a grandiose demonstration by Alexander, the final proof of his superiority to mortal frailty. Not only would he take his army through the desert; he would take it intact and supply his fleet with provisions at the same time. He had chosen the season well, and expected to be able to strip the land of everything edible as he progressed. To a degree his calculations worked—until he passed the rain shadow of the monsoon. Then thirst and fatigue took their toll and the great baggage train disappeared into the voracious maw of the starving army. The march became a rout, and the desert was partially victorious. But Alexander kept his men together. He ostentatiously shared the hardships of the march and was diplomatic enough to overlook the breakdown of discipline. There were losses but they affected the classes he considered dispensable. The fighting men won through. The rest were sacrificed on the altar of his egotism. It was no triumph but hardly a disaster. The army was refreshed by a week of systematic dissipation and Alexander's colourful reign proceeded without any noticeable disruption.

I should like to end by taking the focus off Alexander and his army. From their perspective the march could be seen as a heroic record of visionary leadership and hardship surmounted. But there

---

[68] This view is explored at length in Ch. 4.
[69] Arr. 2. 26. 3. On the siege of Gaza see Bosworth, *HCA* i. 257–60; Atkinson i. 333–44.

were other perspectives, and when we look at them the picture becomes more sombre and the martial fanfares modulate into a minor key. What happened to the people who suffered the passage of the army? There is little evidence. Our sources concentrate on the coastal aborigines, the so-called Fish-Eaters, who lived on the Makran coast, west of Karachi. They had evolved a simple way of life wholly dependent on the ocean tides. Their food was obtained by netting fish which would be left stranded when the waters receded at low tide; their water was obtained by scratching into the sand above the tide level. Grotesque in appearance, they had abundant body hair, long claw-like nails, and they dressed in skins. Their technology was stone-based, their housing the spines of stranded whales and sea shells.[70] Alexander sent a reconnaissance party south soon after he crossed into the Kolwa valley, which reported that the coast was totally devoid of sustenance, its inhabitants too primitive to be exploited.[71] Consequently the Fish-Eaters were denied the pleasure of entertaining Alexander and his men. They did encounter Nearchus and his fleet, but after one pathetic attempt to contest a landing they prudently took to their heels and disappeared.[72]

These were the lucky ones. Further west there were scattered village communities with a few meagre herds of sheep and goats (which were reared on dry fish meal), and these Nearchus promptly commandeered.[73] Near Cyiza at the extreme west of the land of the Fish-Eaters there was a little town which even boasted mud walls. Its inhabitants offered token presents of roast fish, cakes, and dates. That was not enough for Nearchus, who proudly describes how he accepted their meagre hospitality and entered with a small entourage as their guest. The entourage promptly seized the gates and exposed the town to the body of the fleet. On pain of total destruction the inhabitants were forced to disclose their scanty harvest of wheat and

---

[70] Arr. *Ind.* 24. 9, 29. 9–16; Strabo 15. 2. 2 (720–1); Diod. 17. 105. 3–5; Curt. 9. 10. 8–10. For a description of modern conditions, which seem to have been remarkably similar, see Siddiqi 27–9, 42–50, 72–6.

[71] Arr. 6. 23. 2–3. See above, p. 178. It is clear that Thoas encountered one of the poorest communities of Fish-Eaters, but his report of the dearth of water was depressingly true. Cf. Siddiqi 19–21: 'The quantity of water available for any settlement depends on the number, size and consolidation of the nearby sand-dunes...the water is generally discovered 2 or 3 feet below the surface. The fishermen, soon after the water is found, stop further vertical digging and draw the water already in the hole, which satisfies the requirements of a few families and lasts from five to six hours.'

[72] Arr. *Ind.* 24. 2–8.   [73] Arr. *Ind.* 26. 6–7, 9, 27. 2, 29. 5.

barley and their reserves of fish meal. Nearchus and his men provisioned themselves from what was there and continued the voyage.[74] I find this a singularly revolting story. A simple, trusting population was coldly manipulated and deprived of its food reserves. For them there was no prospect of replenishment (of the grain at least) until the next season, and the spectre of starvation must have loomed threateningly.

The fate of this little community must have been typical. If anything, it was fortunate in that it only suffered the depredations of the fleet, not the demands of Alexander himself. Where the main army passed the havoc must have been frightful. The personnel to be fed may well have been greater than the total population of the area it visited, and the season of the transit was the most sensitive period of the year, with the autumn harvest ripening and maturing. The productive areas of Gedrosia must have been stripped clean— and the wretched inhabitants had neither the numbers nor the military expertise to withstand the most accomplished horde of looters ever to take the field in antiquity. I can only conclude that large tracts of country were denuded of food, and the inhabitants were left to subsist on the edible hearts of the date palms left over by the troops or dried fish brought inland from the coast. Their agony would have lasted far longer than 60 days and it is all too likely that it ended in starvation.

[74] Arr. *Ind.* 27. 7–28. 9. For the localization of the 'city', near modern Gwatar, see H. Schiwek, *BJ* 162 (1962) 55; Brunt, *Arrian* ii. 387 n. 5.

Appendix
Alexander and the Ganges: A Question of Probability

Most contentious issues in the reign of Alexander have a distinctly cyclical aspect. Long ago Ernst Badian criticized Schachermeyr's claim that 'today we know' that the Greeks of Asia were not in the League of Corinth. 'Yesterday, presumably, we "knew" that they were; and who knows what we shall "know" tomorrow?'[1] Eternal verities are beyond our grasp when there is little or no evidence at our disposal, as is the case with the Asiatic Greeks and the Corinthian League.[2] Interpretation and speculation have free rein. However, even where explicit evidence exists, we may find a comparable cycle of acceptance and scepticism. One school accepts the source testimony at face value and builds upon it; another dismisses the evidence as distorted or tainted and excludes it from any historical reconstruction. Such exclusion can be justified if the source material is in conflict with other evidence adjudged more incontrovertible, or transcends the bounds of possibility. However, what transcends the bounds of possibility often coincides with what is uncomfortable to believe. One sets one's own limits upon what Alexander may have thought, planned, and done, and accepts or rejects the source material by that criterion. *Credo, ergo est* becomes the unstated methodological rule.

The issue which best exemplifies this dilemma is the famous Ganges question. Is it credible that Alexander had reasonably accurate information about the Ganges river system and planned to extend his conquests there? On a priori considerations it would seem highly probable. He spent a spring and a summer in the northern Punjab, penetrating as far east as the river Hyphasis (modern Beas).

---

[1] E. Badian, in *Ancient Society and Institutions: Studies Presented to Victor Ehrenberg* 65–6 n. 56.

[2] Schachermeyr at least absorbed the lesson. In the 2nd edn. of his work on Alexander he weakened his confident assertion. 'Heute wir wissen' became 'Heute glauben wir zu wissen' (*Al.*[2] 177), and in a subsequent fn. he added that the data was insufficient for stringent proof and that his views should be regarded as hypothetical and provisional (*Al.*[2] 258 n. 295).

In the course of that campaign he carried out detailed topographical investigations as far as the Indus mouth (which refuted his rashly formed belief that the Indus and Nile were interconnected).[3] He was in close contact with the local native rulers and naturally questioned them about conditions on the march ahead. It is surely to be inferred that he received information about the river system of the Jumna and Ganges, no more than 250 km., as the crow flies, east of the Hyphasis. When three separate source traditions corroborate that probability it would seem perverse to question it, and it is fair to state that most modern authorities have accepted that Alexander had some knowledge of the Ganges.[4]

There is, however, a strong sceptical minority. The most eloquent and authoritative attack upon the ancient tradition came from Sir William Tarn, who in 1923 argued that Alexander 'never knew of the Ganges or of Magadha, any more than he knew of the vast Middle Country between the Sutlej and the Ganges',[5] and in 1948 he was to refine his case, noting but not addressing the criticisms made in the meantime by Ernst Meyer.[6] In 1965 Dietmar Kienast came to the same conclusion by a somewhat different route,[7] and most recently T. R. Robinson has attempted the demolition of a critical (but not decisive) branch of the source tradition.[8] What these approaches have in common is an insistence that the only evidence which can be accepted without reservation is a single passage of Arrian (5. 25. 1), which describes Alexander's ambitions beyond the Hyphasis without

---

[3] Arr. 6. 1. 5; Strabo 15. 1. 25 (696) = Nearchus, *FGrH* 133 F 20. On this strange episode see above, Ch. 3.

[4] That was the consensus of earlier scholars. The doyen of Indianologists, Christian Lassen, stated categorically that Alexander intended to take his conquests to the mouth of the Ganges (*Indische Altertumskunde* ii.[2] 171–3). Droysen i.[2] 2. 165, was more cautious about Alexander's aims, but took it as axiomatic that he knew of the Ganges. So too the infuential monograph by A. E. Anspach, *De Alexandri Magni expeditione Indica* (Leipzig 1903) 77–9. In more recent times the most eloquent and systematic defender of what may be termed the traditional view has been Fritz Schachermeyr, 'Alexander und die Ganges-Länder', *IBK* 3 (1955) 123–35 (= G. T. Griffith (ed.), *Alexander the Great: The Main Problems* (Cambridge, 1966) 137–49). For a sample of *obiter dicta* see U. Wilcken, *Alexander the Great* 185–6; Green 407–8; N. G. L. Hammond, *KCS*[2] 218: Bosworth, *Conquest and Empire* 132–3.

[5] Tarn, *JHS* 43 (1923) 93–101. He had a forerunner in Niese i. 138–9, 509.

[6] Tarn, *Al.* ii. 275–85. Meyer's criticism (*Klio* 21 (1927) 183–91) is noted in a single footnote (279 n. 2) with a contemptuous aside: the proposal to supplement the name Ganges at Diod. 18. 6. 2 'is indefensible and merely darkens counsel: I need not refute Ernst Meyer's attempts to defend it'.

[7] D. Kienast, *Historia* 14 (1965) 180–8.

[8] T. R. Robinson, *AHB* 7 (1993) 84–99.

reference to the Ganges and without apparent knowledge of the centralized Nanda kingdom in the lower Ganges valley.[9] The vulgate tradition, common to Diodorus, Curtius, and the *Metz Epitome*,[10] reports that Alexander did receive information about the Ganges and the eastern kingdom, and is necessarily dismissed as romantic embroidery, dating from the period when Megasthenes' embassy to Chandragupta had brought eyewitness information about the Ganges and the great eastern capital of Pātaliputra.[11] We therefore have only one piece of 'reliable' evidence; the rest of the tradition is argued away. However, even if we accept the argumentation, it does not prove the sceptical case. The minuscule piece of 'reliable' evidence is silent about Alexander's knowledge of the Ganges. Even if we accept every word of Arrian, one could still argue that he had been informed of the existence of the great river.[12] The intrinsic probability remains. No source contains or hints at the negative.

Of the various pieces of source material buttressing the case for Alexander's knowledge of the Ganges by far the most important (and problematic) is a tradition represented in two passages of Diodorus.[13] In Book 2 he grafts on to his digest of Megasthenes' account of India a description of the Ganges which patently comes from another source.[14] The river is described as 30 stades wide, flowing from north to south (as the Ganges does in its western reaches) and dividing off to the east the Gandaridae, who had the largest and most numerous elephants in India. No foreign king had ever conquered them because of the number and ferocity of these

---

[9] Kienast's exposition (above, n. 7, 180–1) is typical: 'Dieser sehr detaillierte Bericht, der offenbar aus guter Quelle (wohl Aristobul) stammt, weiss also nichts vom Ganges, sondern nur von dem Lande unmittelbar jenseits des Hyphasis.'

[10] Diod. 17. 93. 2–4; Curt. 9. 2. 2–9; *Metz Epit.* 68–9; cf. Plut. *Al.* 62. 2–3; Justin 12. 8. 9–10 (heavily abbreviated and garbled).

[11] So Robinson (above, n. 8) 98–9. Tarn *Al.* ii. 282–3 considered that the 'legends' of Alexander and the Ganges dated to the second century BC and reflect the history of the Indo-Bactrian monarchy. Kienast (above, n. 7) 187–8 comes to a minimalist sceptical position: both Hieronymus and Cleitarchus knew of the Ganges, the former through the campaigns of Eumenes, but there is no conclusive evidence that Alexander planned to take his conquests beyond the Punjab.

[12] As is honestly and candidly admitted by Kienast 181: 'Andererseits kann man auch nicht schlüssig beweisen, dass Alexander vom Ganges keine Kenntnis hatte.'

[13] Diod. 2. 37. 2–3; 18. 6. 1–2.

[14] The width of the Ganges is totally at odds with Megasthenes' well-attested statement that its median (or minimum) breadth was 100 stades (Arr. *Ind.* 4. 7; Strabo 15. 1. 35 (702) = Megasthenes *FGrH* 715 F 9).

beasts.[15] Alexander himself came to the Ganges after subjugating the rest of the Indians but gave up the expedition on learning that his adversaries possessed 4,000 elephants. This information is neatly paralleled in the context of the so-called *Gazetteer of Empire* in Book 18.[16] There Diodorus reviews the various components of the eastern Empire of Alexander's successors and begins his enumeration of the southern lands from the far east. First is India, a large and populous kingdom, boasting several nations, the largest of which is the 'Tyndaridae' against whom Alexander did not campaign because of the number of their elephants. That country is divided from the next portion of India by a river which is not named in the text but is described as the greatest in those parts, with a width of 30 stades.

The similarities of these passages is such that one naturally assumes that they are derived from a single source: the 'Tyndaridae' of the second passage are simply a corruption of the Gandaridae of the first,[17] and the unnamed river of the second passage must be the Ganges. If both passages have a common original, the most likely source is Hieronymus of Cardia, who provided the narrative core for Diodorus in Book 18. The material would be anticipated in Book 2, and engrafted on the body of material from Megasthenes. There is a clear parallel in the anticipatory citation of Cleitarchus which Diodorus imposes upon the surrounding context, from Ctesias.[18] As for Hieronymus, he was much in Diodorus' mind in Book 2. The account of the Nabataean Arabs is patently part recapitulation, part

[15] The statement is restricted to the Gandaridae. It is hardly a sentence of Megasthenes grafted into an alien context, as is argued by Robinson (above, n. 8) 93–5. Megasthenes claimed that *all* India had been immune from invasion until the time of Alexander (Arr. *Ind.* 5. 4–7; Strabo 15. 1. 6 (686–7) = *FGrH* 715 F 11; cf. Diod. 2. 39. 4; Arr. *Ind.* 9. 10–11 = *FGrH* 715 F 14). The uniqueness of Megasthenes was to deny the Achaemenid conquest of western India. *Any* source might have claimed that the eastern land had been immune from invasion.

[16] Diod. 18. 6. 1–2. On the *Gazetteer* in general see Hornblower, *Hieronymus* 80–7. 'Geographical review' is a better label than 'Gazetteer', but the term is now sanctioned by use.

[17] This to my knowledge has never been questioned. Gandaridae to Tyndaridae is an easy scribal error, imposing a recognizable Greek name upon an unfamiliar foreign term. The corruption incidentally supports the traditional correction Γανδαριδῶν at 18. 6. 1; in the Budé Goukowsky restored Γαγγαριδῶν, which coheres with the Latin spellings of the name (see below, n. 29) and supports the interpretation that it is a general ethnic derived from the river ('people of the Ganges': cf. Goukowsky *ad* Diod. 17. 93. 2). However, such a spelling would lend itself less to corruption than Γανδαριδῶν, the invariable form given by the manuscripts at Diod. 17. 93. 2–4.

[18] Diod. 2. 7. 3 = *FGrH* 137 F 10; cf. Curt. 5. 1. 26 with Hamilton, in *Greece & the E. Med.* 126–46, esp. 138–40; Bosworth, *From Arrian to Alexander* 10.

repetition of a long excursus in Book 19, which was derived from Hieronymus, an eyewitness of the area.[19] Part of this secondary draft is in turn extracted from its context and added to Ctesias' account of the campaign of Ninus. In exactly the same way a section from the *Gazetteer* in Book 18 is re-used in the context of Megasthenes' geography of India. In that case Alexander's plans for an invasion of the Ganges valley are attested by the near-contemporary Hieronymus, and Hieronymus is a formidable cachet of authenticity.

The strategy of the sceptics has necessarily been to distance the report of the Ganges from Hieronymus. Tarn in his most sophistical vein excised everything he disapproved of in the *Gazetteer* as an interpolation by Diodorus and failed to address the detailed correspondence with the parallel passage of Book 2.[20] The more recent approach of Robinson is more coherent. It accepts that the second passage is unitary, but claims that the river there described is not the Ganges but the Hyphasis (Beas) and that the Gandaridae should be located not on the Ganges but immediately east of the Hyphasis (see Fig. 8 above).[21] This report Diodorus misinterpreted and combined incompetently with other material from Megasthenes (used in Book 2) and Cleitarchus (used in Book 17). Hieronymus, then, did not mention the Ganges, and it is only Diodorus' proverbial stupidity which gives the impression that he did.

Robinson's argument is undoubtedly ingenious, but its premises are flawed, and unfortunately much of the material is taken directly from Tarn without any probing of the supporting evidence. Most illuminating is the key assertion that in Diodorus there is an eastward displacement of the Gandaridae. 'For the Gandaridae are generally associated with the eastern Punjab and the Indus system, not with

---

[19] Diod. 2. 48. 1–5 resumes the more extended description at 19. 94. 2–10, while 2. 48. 6–10 is a virtual copy of 19. 98. In its turn Diod. 2. 1. 5 epitomizes the exposition at 2. 48. 2–5 (cf. P. Krumbholz, *Rh. Mus.* 44 (1889) 286–98, esp. 291–3). On Hieronymus' excursus in general see Hornblower, *Hieronymus* 144–53.

[20] The fullest exposition is Tarn, *Al.* ii. 277–9; the earlier discussion (*JHS* 43 (1923) 93–5) is less convoluted and involves only one interpolation (98: 'the part of the gazetteer given in Diod. 18. 6. 1 seems to be given with substantial accuracy, subject, of course, to this, that the statement that Alexander turned back from fear of the elephants is a late legend inserted by Diodorus himself').

[21] Robinson (above, n. 8), esp. 84–5. Both hypotheses were foreshadowed by Tarn, who considered that the river of the *Gazetteer* could be the Sutlej, immediately east of the Hyphasis (*JHS* 43 (1923) 97–8; 25 years later (at *Al.* ii. 279) the 'unnamed river' becomes an interpolation by Diodorus), and argued repeatedly that the Gandaridae were displaced (see below).

the Gangetic plain.'[22] This categorical assertion is documented by a reference to Kiessling's Pauly articles on 'Gandaris' and 'Gandaridae', which unequivocally locate the Gandaridae in the Ganges plain.[23] As Kiessling makes plain, there is no reference to Gandaridae west of the Ganges. We hear in passing that the princedom of the 'bad' Porus, which lay between the rivers Acesines and Hydraotes, was named Gandaris.[24] That may or may not indicate some association with the people named Gandaridae, and in any case the location does not help Robinson. The 'bad' Porus ruled an area well to the west of the Hyphasis, not to the east of the river, where Robinson would locate the Gandaridae. Now this Porus fled in the face of Alexander's advance across the Punjab, in the early summer of 326, and we are informed that he fled to the land of the Gandaridae.[25] All that proves is that these Gandaridae were located *somewhere* east of the Hydraotes; it provides no information as to how far east they were found. Robinson suggests that they were directly beyond the Hyphasis, but it might also be argued that any Indian rajah who cared to flee rather than submit to Alexander would put the greatest distance possible between himself and the invader and seek sanctuary in the Ganges kingdom,[26] as far away as possible.

Apart from the single reference to the princedom of 'Gandaris' there is only an oblique reference in Dionysius Periegetes to 'Gargaridae' near the 'gold-bearing Hypanis' (another name for the

[22] Robinson (above, n. 8) 89 with n. 13. Tarn in 1923 (above, n. 5, 98) suggested that the Gandaridae of the *Gazetteer* were somehow distinct from the Gandaridae of the vulgate and were located east of the Sutlej. In 1948 he was more radical and claimed that the Gandaridae were in fact the Indians of Gandhāra, the old Achaemenid satrapy of the Kabul valley (*Al.* ii. 277–8).

[23] Kiessling, *RE* vii. 694–5 ('Gandaridai'), 695–6 ('Gandaris'); cf. 703–7 ('Ganges'). Kiessling was categorical that there were three separate areas: Achaemenid Gandhāra, Gandaris in the Punjab, and the land of the Gandaridae in the lower Ganges, and considered the similarity of name an important indicator of the progress of Aryan migration (695, lines 49–58).

[24] Strabo 15. 1. 30 (699). For the general location of the realm of the 'bad' Porus see Arr. 5. 21. 1–4.

[25] Diod. 17. 91. 1 (cf. Arr. 5. 21. 3—destination unnamed).

[26] That was the automatic and plausible assumption of Lassen, *Indische Altertumskunde* ii.[2] 163 n. 3 (so Droysen i.[2] 2. 148 n. 1). Why Anspach (above, n. 4) 64 n. 199 commented 'iam veri dissimile est trans Gangem tum fugisse Porum' I do not understand. There was the instructive object lesson of the regicide Barsaentes, who fled from his satrapy in central Iran to the Indians of Gandhāra (cf. Berve ii. 102, no. 205). If we may believe Curtius (8. 13. 4), both Barsaentes and his Indian collaborator had been delivered to Alexander's justice shortly before the battle of the Hydaspes and the flight of the 'bad' Porus. It gave a defector every encouragement to fly as far as possible and choose the strongest possible protector.

Hyphasis/Beas).[27] Before we are transported by excitement at this, we should look at the context in Dionysius, which is a farrago of nonsense. The 'Hypanis' is associated with another mysterious river, the Magarsus, and both are said to flow down from the northern mountains into the Gangetic plain.[28] If the Gargaridae of Dionysius are in fact the Gandaridae of Diodorus, they are as much associated with the Ganges as they are with the Hyphasis. There is no other trace of the supposed western Gandaridae. Against this dearth of attestation there is solid testimony linking the Gandaridae with the Ganges plain. One important qualification needs to be made. Latin authors almost invariably refer to the people as *Gangaridae*. Why that is the case is obscure, but the fact is certain and proved by Curtius (9. 2. 3) who clearly follows the same source as Diodorus (17. 93. 1) and reads *Gangaridae*[29] whereas Diodorus and Plutarch refer to Gandaridae. What is more, the vulgate tradition associates both Gandaridae and Gangaridae with the Prasii,[30] whom the eyewitness Megasthenes attests in the vicinity of the capital of the Ganges kingdom. Even if one writes off this unanimous testimony as deriving from a single tainted source, there is independent corroboration in Pliny, who locates the Gangaridae explicitly on the Ganges, gives their capital (Pertalis), and adds an estimate of their army size.[31]

[27] Dion. Per. 1143–8. Kiessling also adduced *Peripl. M. Rubr.* 47, in which a people named 'Tanthragoi' are attested inland from Barygaza (by the Rann of Kutch) and associated with Bucephala. But, even if the traditional correction 'Gandaraioi' is accepted, the passage is extraordinarily imprecise (cf. L. Casson, *The Periplus Maris Erythraei* 204–5) and contains the egregious error that Alexander penetrated to the Ganges. It cannot be used as evidence for Gandaridae in the Punjab.

[28] Dion. Per. 1146–7: ἀπὸ δ᾽ οὔρεος | ὀρνύμενοι προρέουσιν ἐπὶ Γαγγήτιδα χώρην. It may be added that Dionysius (1152–60) also places Nysa (see below, p. 199) in the Gangetic plain. His view of Indian geography can only be termed chaotic.

[29] So apparently Justin, 12. 8. 9 (some manuscript variation); *Metz Epit.* 68 reads 'candaras'. I suspect that Vergil (*Georg.* 3. 27) became canonical for the Latin tradition. The form *Gangaridae* may even have been his creation, to suggest the Ganges as a counterpart to the Nile (*Georg.* 3. 29). If so it inevitably influenced Curtius the rhetorician, and Pompeius Trogus, who wrote immediately after Vergil.

[30] The combination occurs in all branches: Diodorus, Curtius, Plutarch, Justin and the *Metz Epitome*. For Megasthenes' location of the Prasii around Pātaliputra see Arr. *Ind.* 10. 5; Strabo 15. 1. 36 (702) = *FGrH* 715 F 18.

[31] Pliny, *NH* 6. 65–6. These 'Gangaridae' are mentioned immediately after the description of the Ganges, which includes Megasthenes' figure of 100 stades for its median breadth. They are termed the *novissima gens* of the Ganges; whether that implies nearest the mouth or nearest the headwaters cannot be determined. Ptolemy (*Geogr.* 7. 1. 81) at least located the Gangaridae around the mouths of the Ganges. All this is desperately obscure but it does establish the key point that the peoples of the Gangetic plain could be termed (in whole or part) Gandaridae or Gangaridae.

The appropriate conclusion is surely the reverse of that drawn by Robinson. There is no evidence that the Gandaridae were located in the Punjab, but there are several independent attestations of them in the Ganges plain. If, then, the *Gazetteer* mentions the Gandaridae in the context of a great river, then that river can only be the Ganges, as Diodorus makes explicit in Book 2.

If there is no eastward displacement of the Gandaridae, the case for identifying the unnamed river of Diodorus 18. 6. 2 with the Hyphasis is fatally weakened. The surrounding description is, as Robinson admits, hard to reconcile with the ancient testimony about the Hyphasis. It was certainly *not* the largest of the rivers in the area. Even if one limits the area in question to the western border of Alexander's conquests in the Punjab,[32] there can be no doubt that the largest river in that district was the Acesines whose breadth was estimated at 15 stades in the flood season (as opposed to 7 stades for the Hyphasis).[33] It was the Acesines which (for Alexander's men) preserved its identity through successive confluences until it reached the Indus,[34] and it was the Acesines whose flood spate impressed the Macedonians. By contrast the Hyphasis was important as the boundary of Alexander's conquests, not for its size.[35] And, *pace* Robinson, it is size that Diodorus emphasizes. The boundary river was the largest in the area, which is most naturally understood as the Indian lands in their entirety, and had a width of 30 stades. Now the Ganges was agreed to be the largest Indian river, and although estimates of its width vary dramatically, there is some agreement on 30 stades. The figure recurs in the vulgate tradition of Alexander's plans against the Gandaridae,[36] and more seriously in Strabo (15. 1. 35 (702)), who mentions 'some authors' who gave 30 stades as the

[32] So Robinson (above, n. 8) 89: 'its description...will have to be taken in a limited sense to mean that it is the greatest river in its own immediate area.' That is perhaps just possible, but it is not likely and is contradicted by Diodorus' own usage (cf. 2. 16. 7, where the Indus is 'the greatest of the rivers in those parts' ($\mu\acute{\epsilon}\gamma\iota\sigma\tau\sigma\varsigma$ $\check{\omega}\nu$ $\tau\tilde{\omega}\nu$ $\pi\epsilon\varrho\grave{\iota}$ $\tau\sigma\grave{\upsilon}\varsigma$ $\tau\acute{\sigma}\pi\sigma\upsilon\varsigma$) and the context is clearly India as a whole: see also 17. 85. 3).

[33] Arr. 5. 20. 8 = Ptolemy, *FGrH* 138 F 22 (the Acesines was the one river whose breadth was mentioned by Ptolemy). See also Strabo 15. 1. 18 (692) = Nearchus, *FGrH* 133 F 18; Aristobulus, *FGrH* 139 F 35. The width of the Hyphasis is given by Diodorus 17. 93. 1.

[34] The most important passage is Arr. 6. 14. 4–5.

[35] Cf. Pliny, *NH* 6. 62 = *FGrH* 119 F 2a: the bematists made the Hyphasis the terminus of their measurements in Asia.

[36] Diod. 17. 93. 2 (32 stades: so Plut. *Al.* 62. 2); *Metz Epit.* 68 gives 30 stades, and Curtius affords no figure.

minimum width of the Ganges (others made it as little as 3)[37] and contrasts the more exaggerated estimate of Megasthenes. The description in Diodorus' *Gazetteer* most naturally applies to the Ganges, and the estimate of its breadth is not too inflated (according to modern measurements the width of its bed varies between $1\frac{1}{4}$ and $2\frac{1}{4}$ miles). The boundary river west of the Gandaridae looks remarkably like the Ganges, where the Gandaridae are elsewhere attested, and the exposition in the *Gazetteer* is practically identical to the earlier description of the Ganges in Diodorus Book 2.

There are awkwardnesses, to be sure, as is almost always the case with Diodorus. The *Gazetteer* purports to be a list of satrapies, but the concept of satrapy is very elastic: Lycaonia, Lycia, and Pisidia are entered as separate entities, whereas they were never more than satrapal subdivisions,[38] and there is some confusion between what is inside and outside the Empire. Armenia is included despite its dubious status and so notably is the eastern Indian kingdom, even though Diodorus makes it abundantly clear that Alexander never annexed it. But the territory *is* described as a populous kingdom, and the description suits the Nanda kingdom of the Ganges, rather than the territory immediately east of the Hyphasis, which *may* not have been a kingdom in any sense. Indeed for Robinson the area was not a kingdom, rather the territory of the autonomous Yaudheyas, who are named by Pāṇini and attested some centuries later between the Beas and Sutlej.[39] He can hardly have all the factors of his equation. If the boundary river of the *Gazetteer* was the Hyphasis, then there was no kingdom to the east, and if there *was* a kingdom to the east of the boundary river, then the river cannot have been the Hyphasis.

Next, Diodorus (18. 6. 2) makes a clean distinction between the

[37] Strabo 15. 1. 35 (702). Tarn (above, n. 5, 96) claims that 'we know of nothing to which this can refer except Diodorus' source (Cleitarchus)?' It would be more helpful to add that there is no source other than Megasthenes whom we can confidently exclude. Our ignorance is profound, and the most economical hypothesis is that *several* traditions gave the width of the Ganges at or around 30 stades. It is ironic that the eyewitness, Megasthenes, gives the most patently inflated figure.

[38] See, most conveniently, the characterization of Antigonus' satrapy at Triparadeisus (and Babylon), including Lycaonia, Lycia, and Pamphylia as subgroups (Arr. *Succ.* F 1. 37 (Roos); cf. Diod. 18. 3. 1, 39. 6). Hornblower's conclusion (84) is characteristically level-headed: 'Though the word "satrapy" is used everywhere, this may be the fault of Diodorus, and the term cannot be pressed too hard.'

[39] Robinson (above, n. 8) 98. The Yaudheyas are described as autonomous by Pāṇini (15. 3. 117; cf. Agrawala 445). Their coins (2nd century BC to 2nd century AD) have been found in the general area between the Beas and Jumna. For a brief statement see *The Oxford History of India*[4] (Oxford 1981) 166.

kingdom of the east with its great boundary river and the land conquered by Alexander, which was intersected by several rivers. Diodorus' wording is obscure, and may require emendation;[40] but on any interpretation, as Robinson concedes, what is at issue is a distinction between the multiple river system of the west and the single boundary river of the east. That boundary river cannot be the Hyphasis/Beas, which was one—and not the most important—of the tributaries of the Indus. It is a counsel of desperation when Robinson (92) asserts without a shred of evidence that Diodorus concluded that the Hyphasis/Beas flowed independently into the Ocean and inferred in Book 2 that his source meant the Ganges when it referred to the boundary river. On the contrary the *Gazetteer* can only mean the Ganges when it defines the Indians to the east of the subcontinent,[41] and it makes a rough distinction between the kingdom of Pātaliputra and the western lands conquered by Alexander and dominated by the river system of the Indus. The west was not all overrun by the Macedonians but most of it definitely was, and there is a valid distinction between the eastern kingdom bounded by the Ganges which Alexander never attacked and the western lands which he largely overran.

This rough distinction explains the one error of fact in the recapitulation of the passage in Book 2. Diodorus carelessly states that Alexander penetrated as far as the Ganges. If the source of the *Gazetteer* made the Ganges the boundary of eastern India and stated loosely that Alexander conquered the lands to the west, it was easy for Diodorus to write that he took his conquests to the Ganges—even though he is later explicit that the turning point was the Beas. The inexactitude is paralleled elsewhere[42] and easily compre-

---

[40] Fischer's Teubner (followed in the Loeb) reads [παρα]ποταμίοις ('irrigated by river waters'), a somewhat vacuous expression, but with some justification in Diodorus (2. 39. 3; 5. 19. 3). Goukowsky's πέντε ποταμῶν ὕδασι ('irrigated by the waters of five rivers') strays too far from the received reading and presupposes that Diodorus' source knew of the Sutlej (cf. Arr. 6. 14. 5, where only *four* Punjab rivers are named).

[41] Tarn made much of the statement in the vulgate (Diod. 17. 93. 2; cf. Curt. 9. 2. 3; Plut. *Al.* 62. 2; *Metz Epit.* 68) that the Gandaridae were situated across the Ganges. In 1923 (above, n. 5, 95) he assumed that this meant that they were *beyond* the Ganges and repeated the point in 1948 (*Alexander the Great* ii. 281). But surely all the vulgate is signifying is the western reaches of the Ganges which extend northwards to the Himalayas. It would need to be crossed (or was conceived as being crossed) by any traveller aiming at Pātaliputra, the capital of the east.

[42] *Peripl. M. Rubr.* 47 (see above, n. 27). Strabo 15. 1. 35 (702) adduces a clearly fictitious letter of Craterus which claimed that Alexander advanced to the Ganges.

hensible. The misunderstanding, moreover, presupposes that Diodorus was working with a single source, not conflating material from the *Gazetteer* and the report of the eastern kingdom which he includes in Book 17. The latter report is embedded in the context of the return from the Hyphasis, and the Hyphasis is explicitly mentioned in the previous sentence (17. 93. 1). If he were working with that source in Book 2, he was unlikely to have concluded that Alexander reached the Ganges. The fact that his figures for the elephant army of the Gandaridae are exactly those he gives in Book 17[43] need only imply that the sources were in relative agreement. The description of the elephants, 'decked out for war', is practically a stock theme in Diodorus, and recurs in the account of Alexander's funeral carriage in Book 18;[44] it certainly does not imply that Diodorus combined two separate narrative strands.

Indeed there is a fatal objection to the hypothesis of conflation. In the vulgate tradition the reports of the eastern kingdom whet Alexander's appetite for conquest and it is the resistance of the troops which forces him to abandon the project.[45] In the other tradition the king considers discretion the better part of valour, and decides against attacking such a formidable army.[46] This is a fundamental contradiction. It should also be noted that in Books 2 and 18 the Gandaridae stand alone, whereas in the vulgate they are associated with the Prasii. Diodorus clearly used two distinct sources. In Book 17 he worked from the vulgate (Cleitarchus?), whereas the two other passages, in Book 2 and Book 18, derive from a single authority, most probably Hieronymus of Cardia. The two

---

However, Strabo claims that the tradition was unique (οὐχ ὁμολογοῦσα οὐδενί) and that the sighting of the Ganges was its strangest point. It can hardly have been a feature of the Alexander literature. When Diodorus (17. 108. 3) mentions the army's refusal to cross the Ganges, it is a general reference to reluctance for the proposed eastern campaign; it does not entail that the army had reached the Ganges. It was a refusal in prospect. So too in Plut. *Al.* 62. 2 where the Macedonians resist Alexander's forcing them to cross the Ganges. It is a flight of rhetoric but not misleading—hardly 'the worst chapter he ever wrote' (Tarn, *Alexander the Great* ii. 281 n. 5).

[43] Diod. 2. 37. 3; 17. 93. 2. No number is given at 18. 6. 2.

[44] Diod. 18. 27. 1. Cf. Diod. 31. 8. 12. One should never underestimate Diodorus' penchant for repetition.

[45] Diod. 17. 93. 4, 94. 5; Curt. 9. 2. 9–10; Plut. *Al.* 62. 2.

[46] Diod. 18. 6. 1; 2. 37. 3. It is likely enough that Hieronymus contracted his reference to the proceedings and obscured the fact that the king's decision was forced upon him by his troops, but it is most improbable that Diodorus twice omitted all reference to the Macedonian resistance, which he described in detail at 17. 94. This distinction is slurred over by Hornblower, Hieronymus 86.

traditions have some measure of agreement, on the width of the Ganges and the number of elephants at the disposal of the Gandaridae. Above all they are categorical that Alexander conceived and abandoned plans of attacking the Gangetic plain.

We can now address the account of Arrian, which prima facie contradicts the rest of the tradition. His narrative of events at the Hyphasis is schematic, dominated by the interplay between Alexander and his troops. The reports of conditions beyond the Hyphasis are brief and vague: the land was rich, its inhabitants good at agriculture and excellently governed, the commons held in check by the enlightened rule of the best men.[47] Their elephants far exceeded in number those possessed by the other Indians, and they excelled in size and courage (Arr. 5. 25. 1). This description contains not a single ethnic name, nor a single geographical pointer except that the territory lay to the east of the Hyphasis. Kienast assumed without question that Arrian was referring *only* to the lands immediately east of the river ('unmittelbar jenseits des Hyphasis').[48] However, he did not add that Arrian's information is largely repeated in an unnamed authority used by Strabo, which reported an aristocratic polity with 5,000 counsellors, each of whom contributed an elephant to the commonwealth.[49] These numbers are even larger than those in the vulgate, and presuppose a catchment area much more extensive than the lands immediately east of the Hyphasis. One may, of course, deny that there is a common source, but one cannot artificially restrict the range of Arrian's description. He is not here interested in the geography but in the valour and virtue of the intended enemy and in the huge number of elephants. That in itself was sufficient to dampen the spirits of the rank-and-file (Arr. 5. 25. 2).

The absence of any geographical limit may mean that Arrian's source was equally unforthcoming, but we cannot assume it. Indeed

[47] The passage is derived from one of Arrian's narrative sources. The most popular candidate is Aristobulus (Strasburger, *Studien* i. 130; Kienast (above, n. 7) 181). Kornemann 79 adjudged the context 'pure Ptolemy'. All that can be said is that it is 'pure Arrian', and, as usual, its provenance is impossible to determine.

[48] Kienast 181, cf. 188. Schachermeyr (above, n. 4) 132 n. 28 had already undermined the assumption in trenchant style: 'Das πέραν τοῦ Ὑφάσιος... muss ebenso wenig "unmittelbar am anderen Ufer" bedeuten, wie wenn man heute von "jenseits des Kanals", "jenseits des Ozean" usw. spricht.'

[49] Strabo 15. 1. 37 (702). Cf. Robinson (above, n. 8) 98, suggesting Aristobulus as a common source. That is certainly a possibility, but Strabo *may* derive from some other authority (Onesicritus?), which gave similar details to those in Arrian but reported the 'facts' independently.

in the speech which is placed in Alexander's mouth Arrian has the king claim that the Ganges and the eastern ocean are relatively close.[50] Not a great deal can hinge upon this. The speeches which Arrian presents here are very elaborate rhetorical constructions, blending diverse and inconsistent material. The sentence after the reference to the Ganges continues with an anachronistic echo of Eratosthenes' doctrine of the gulfs of Ocean,[51] and the reference to the Ganges may be equally misplaced, the product of later rhetorical fantasy. But one could also argue that the Ganges was mentioned in Arrian's narrative sources and held in reserve for the speech.[52] It certainly tells in favour of Arrian's sources having mentioned the Ganges or given an account not inconsistent with its having been Alexander's objective.

The crux is the apparent divergence of fact between Arrian and the vulgate tradition. The vulgate presents us with a kingdom and a somewhat unimpressive king named Xandrames.[53] Arrian has nothing about a king but describes a regime controlled by the best men. Are these accounts mutually exclusive? Perhaps not. A central monarchy may still tolerate aristocratic government within its constituent communities, provided that it can control the *aristoi*. Now there is nothing either in Arrian or in Strabo to suggest that the peoples they describe were autonomous. Elsewhere that is explicitly stated of the numerous Aratta peoples between the Acesines and Hyphasis.[54] The Kśudrakas (Oxydracae) of the Rechna Doab boast

---

[50] Arr. 5. 26. 1: On the nature and derivation of the Hyphasis speeches see most fully Bosworth (above, n. 18) 123–34, esp. 129–30. More recently N. G. L. Hammond, *Sources for Alexander the Great* (Cambridge 1993) 258–9, has argued that they were 'based on speeches incorporated in their histories by Ptolemy and Aristobulus'. If this were accepted (and I find it frankly incredible), it would entail that the first-generation historians did refer explicitly to the Ganges and credited Alexander with knowledge of the river.

[51] In his last year Alexander was agnostic on the Caspian question and commissioned an expedition to determine whether or not it was a gulf of Ocean (7. 16. 1–2). Previously he had accepted the theory that the Iaxartes and Tanais (Syr-Darya and Don) were connected, a theory which entailed that the Caspian was an enclosed sea. This is obscured by Hammond, *Sources* 258: Arr. 3. 29. 2 and 5. 5. 4 represent Arrian's view (from Eratosthenes) not Alexander's.

[52] That again was Schachermeyr's suggestion (above, n. 4, 132): 'da es der Autor wohl zu vermeiden wusste, die Erwähnung des Ganges zweimal zu bringen'. It is not the best argument, for repetition of narrative detail is a feature of Arrian's speeches. Reservation of source material for the speeches is more a trait of Curtius Rufus.

[53] Diod. 17. 93. 2–3; Curtius 9. 2. 3, 6–7; *Metz Epit.* 68; cf. Plut. *Al.* 62. 9.

[54] Arr. 5. 20. 6, 21. 5, 22. 1–2, 24. 6, 8; 6. 6. 1, 11. 3, 15. 1, 21. 3; cf. *Ind.* 11. 9, 12. 5–6.

of their freedom and autonomy and are ruled by an aristocracy.[55]
The same is said of the state of Nysa in the mountains of Bajaur.
The language used of its polity echoes what Arrian says of the
peoples east of the Hyphasis—but Nysa is specifically termed free
and autonomous.[56] It *may* be sheer chance that Arrian does not state
that the eastern Indians were also free, but on the other hand the
omission *could* be significant. Arrian's description is compatible with
a paramount regal authority. That, according to Megasthenes, was
the situation in the Mauryan kingdom in the generation after
Alexander, under the enlightened rule of Chandragupta. The king's
counsellors were noted for their wisdom and justice, and it was from
their number that their local rulers were selected.[57] They were a
small class but the most distinguished in birth and intelligence, and
they acted as judges and administrators of the masses.[58] This might
almost be Arrian's description of the peoples beyond the Hyphasis.
He concentrates on the intermediate level of counsellors and ignores
the monarch. There were good compositional reasons for doing so.
Arrian is concerned to explain the reluctance of the Macedonians
and stresses the formidable nature of the opposition they faced. A
weak, unpopular king, as Xandrames is portrayed in the vulgate, was
not particularly to be feared, but the local governors, men of integrity and intelligence, certainly were. Their local administration
proved their quality and made them worthy opponents of Alexander,
proper objects of fear for his troops. The difference between the
sources, then, is a difference of perspective rather than fact. The vulgate tradition gives a fairly discursive report on the geography,
manpower, and politics of the eastern kingdom, while Arrian singles
out the aspects which made it a formidable adversary: agricultural
wealth, a warlike population well controlled by the government, and
an unparalleled number of war elephants. The two traditions are
complementary, not contradictory.

We may now conclude. There is a strong source tradition attesting
that Alexander was informed about the Gangetic plain, its popula-

---

[55] Arr. 6. 14. 1–2: the Oxydracae are represented by nomarchs and city rulers,
backed by 150 of their notables, and they stress their freedom and autonomy,
continuous since the time of Dionysus.

[56] Arr. 5. 1. 5–6 ; cf. 2. 2.

[57] *Ind.* 12. 6–7; Strabo 15. 1. 49 (707) = Megasthenes, *FGrH* 715 F 19.

[58] Diod. 2. 41. 4 (= *FGrH* 715 F 4). Cf. Pliny *NH* 6. 66: 'res publicas optumi
ditissimique temperant, iudicia reddunt, regibus adsident.'

tion, and its government. The vulgate tradition preserves the substance of detailed reports made by friendly princes in the Punjab, reports which encouraged him to invade.[59] Another tradition, based on Hieronymus of Cardia, also records the size of the Gangetic elephant army and insinuates that Alexander was deterred from invasion. In both cases the reports are connected with the retreat from the Hyphasis. For Hieronymus they were the ultimate cause of the retreat: Alexander made a prudential decision not to invade the eastern lands. For the vulgate it was his troops who were reluctant to advance. The latter theme is expanded by Arrian who gives no names but writes generally of the elephants, warlike population, and good internal government of the territory east of the Hyphasis. He supplies extra detail but does not directly contradict the other sources. What is more, the source tradition blends perfectly with all rational arguments from probability. There *was* a centralized monarchy in the Ganges plain and its king *was* weak and unpopular. Alexander had been in the Punjab for several months by the time he reached the Hyphasis, and he enjoyed the society of the rulers of the area. Is it credible that they knew nothing of the lands to the east or that they kept the knowledge to themselves? What is more, if it is true that the 'bad' Porus took refuge with the Gandaridae of the east, then the name would have come to Alexander's attention before he reached the Hyphasis, and further enquiries were practically inevitable. The sceptical view by contrast involves accepting a chain of remotely possible alternatives. Alexander *may* not have enquired carefully about conditions in the east. He *may* not have been informed about the Ganges kingdom. The tradition that he did *may* be the result of later imaginative embroidery. However, each of these probabilities is small, the cumulative probability infinitesimal. It is surely preferable, for once, to accept what the sources say.

[59] On their substantial accuracy see above, Ch. 3.

Bibliography

1. Ancient Sources

The texts, translations, and commentaries which I consider most helpful are:

Arrian:
P. A. Brunt, *Arrian* (2 vols.: Loeb Classical Library, Cambridge Mass. and London: 1976–83), reprints the standard Teubner text of A. G. Roos, with translation, historical annotation, and general appendices. For full commentary on Books 1–5 see Bosworth, *HCA*, and for general discussion of Arrian's life and œuvre one may consult the works of P. A. Stadter and H. Tonnet listed below.

Curtius Rufus:
Quinte-Curce, *Histoires*, ed. and tr. H. Bardon (2 vols.: Paris (Budé) 1947–8). There is also a useful Penguin translation: Quintus Curtius Rufus, *The History of Alexander*, tr. J. Yardley, introd. and notes W. Heckel (Harmondsworth 1984). For full commentary on Books 3–7. 2 see the works of J. E. Atkinson listed below.

Diodorus Siculus:
Diodore de Sicile, *Bibliothèque Historique* XVII, XVIII, ed. P. Goukowsky (Paris (Budé) 1976, 1978). Diodorus of Sicily vols. 8–10, Books 16. 89–20, ed. C. B. Welles and R. M. Geer (Loeb Classical Library: Cambridge, Mass., and London 1963, 1947, 1954).

Plutarch:
Plutarchus, *Vitae Parallelae* ii. 2., 152–253, ed. K. Ziegler (Leipzig (Teubner) 1968). This is the text cited in the footnotes and in the standard commentary by J. R. Hamilton (see below). The paragraphing in the Loeb edition by B. Perrin (*Plutarch's Lives* vii. 224–439 (Cambridge, Mass., 1919)) is significantly different. There is an accessible translation in the Penguin collection: Plutarch, *The Age of Alexander*, trans. I. Scott-Kilvert (Harmondsworth 1973).

Justin:
M. Iuniani Iustini Epitoma Historiarum Philippicarum Pompei Trogi, ed. O. Seel (Stuttgart (Teubner) 1972). There is a forthcoming translation and commentary by J. Yardley and W. Heckel, *Justin's Epitome of the Philippic*

History of Pompeius Trogus: Books 11–12 (Oxford 1996).

Strabo:
The Geography of Strabo, ed. and tr. H. S. Jones (8 vols.: Loeb Classical Library: Cambridge, Mass., and London 1917–32).

FGrH:
F. Jacoby, *Die Fragmente der griechischen Historiker* ii. B (Leiden 1962) 618–828, prints the surviving citations of the non-extant historians of Alexander, listed by number. There is a German commentary in ii. D 403–542. The text of the fragments is translated by C. A. Robinson, Jr., *The History of Alexander the Great* i (Providence, RI, 1953) 30–276, and there is discussion of the content in the works of L. Pearson and P. Pédech listed below.

2. Spanish Sources

I list only those works which I have used to provide parallels for the Alexander period. The source tradition of the Spanish conquest is vast and complex, far beyond the scope of my necessarily restricted coverage. For a guide to the archives and the literary sources see Hugh Thomas, *The Conquest of Mexico* 774–93.

Cortés:
Hernán Cortés: Letters from Mexico, tr. and ed. A. Pagden, with introd. by J. H. Elliott (New Haven 1986).

Díaz:
Bernal Díaz del Castillo, *The Discovery and Conquest of Mexico*, tr. A. P. Maudslay (London 1928). Bernal Díaz, *The Conquest of New Spain*, tr. J. M. Cohen (Harmondsworth 1963).

de Fuentes:
The Conquistadors: First Person Accounts of the Conquest of Mexico, ed. and tr. P. de Fuentes (Norman, Okla., 1993).

Gómara:
Cortés: The Life of the Conqueror by His Secretary, Francisco López de Gómara (Berkeley and Los Angeles 1965).

3. Modern Authors

The following list gives full details of all works of more than peripheral significance, that I have cited in the footnotes. It does not pretend to be even a representative coverage of the period of Alexander. For that one may consult the bibliographical surveys of J. Seibert, *Alexander der Große* (to 1972) and J. M. O'Brien, *Alexander the Great: The Invisible Enemy* 279–322 (to 1992).

AGRAWALA, V. S., *India as Known to Pāṇini* (Lucknow 1958).

ALTHEIM, F. and STIEHL, R., *Geschichte Mittelasiens im Altertum* (Berlin 1970).

ANDREOTTI, R., 'Per una critica dell'ideologia di Alessandro Magno', *Historia* 5 (1956) 257–302.

ANSPACH, A. E., *De Alexandri Magni expeditione Indica* (Leipzig 1903).

ATKINSON, J. E., *A Commentary on Q. Curtius Rufus' Historiae Alexandri Magni: Books 3–4* (Amsterdam 1980).

—— *A Commentary on Q. Curtius Rufus' Historiae Alexandri Magni: Books 5 to 7, 2* (Amsterdam 1994).

ATKINSON, K. M. T., 'Demosthenes, Alexander and Asebeia', *Athenaeum* 51 (1973) 310–35.

AUSTIN, M. M., 'Hellenistic Kings, War, and the Economy', *CQ* 36 (1986) 450–66.

AVENARIUS, G., *Lukians Schrift zur Geschichtsschreibung* (Meisenheim am Glan 1956).

AYMARD, A, *Études d'histoire ancienne* (Paris 1967).

BADIAN, E., 'The Eunuch Bagoas: A Study in Method', *CQ* 8 (1958) 144–57.

—— 'Alexander the Great and the Unity of Mankind', *Historia* 7 (1958) 425–44.

—— 'Harpalus', *JHS* 81 (1961) 16–43.

—— *Studies in Greek and Roman History* (Oxford 1964).

—— 'The Date of Clitarchus', *PACA* 8 (1965) 5–11.

—— 'Alexander the Great and the Greeks of Asia', *Ancient Society and Institutions: Studies Presented to Victor Ehrenberg*, ed. E. Badian (Oxford 1966) 37–69.

—— 'Nearchus the Cretan', *YCS* 24 (1975) 147–70.

—— 'The Deification of Alexander the Great', *Ancient Macedonian Studies in Honor of Charles F. Edson*, ed. H. J. Dell (Thessaloniki 1981) 27–71.

—— 'Alexander in Iran', *Cambridge History of Iran* ii, ed. I. Gershevitch (Cambridge 1985) 420–501.

—— 'The Ring and the Book', *Zu Alexander dem Großen*, ed. W. Will (Amsterdam 1988) i. 610–25.

—— 'Two Postscripts on the Marriage of Phila and Balacrus', *ZPE* 72 (1988) 116–18.

—— 'Eduard Meyer's American Paralipomena', *Eduard Meyer, Leben und Leistung eines Universalhistorikers*, ed. W. M. Calder and A. Demandt (Mnemosyne Suppl. 112: Leiden 1990) 1–40.

—— *From Plataea to Potidaea* (Baltimore 1993).

BALSDON, J. P. V. D., 'The "Divinity" of Alexander', *Historia* 1 (1950) 363–88.

BAUER, A., 'Der Brief Alexanders des Großen über die Schlacht gegen Porus', *Festgaben zu Ehren Max Büdinger's* (Innsbruck 1898) 71–88.

BELLEN, H., 'Der Rachegedanke in der griechisch-persischen Auseinander-setzung', *Chiron* 4 (1974) 43–67.

BELLINGER, A. R., *Essays on the Coinage of Alexander the Great*, Numismatic Studies 11 (New York 1963).

BERNARD, P., 'Alexandre et Aï Khanoum', *JS* (1982) 125–38.

—— 'Le monnayage d'Eudamos, satrape grec du Pandjab et maître des éléphants', *Orientalia Iosephi Tucci memoriae dicata*, ed. G. Gnoli and L. Lanciotti (2 vols.: Rome 1985).

—— 'Fouilles de la mission franco-soviétique à l'ancien Samarkhand (Afrasiab)', *CRAI* (1990) 356–80.

BERVE, H., *Das Alexanderreich auf prosopographischer Grundlage* (2 vols.: Munich 1926).

—— 'Die Verschmelzungspolitik Alexanders des Großen', *Klio* 31 (1938) 135–68 = G. T. Griffith (ed.), *Alexander the Great: The Main Problems* (Cambridge 1966) 103–36.

BILLOWS, R. A., *Antigonos the One-Eyed and the Creation of the Hellenistic State* (Berkeley 1990).

BONGARD-LEVIN, G. M., *Studies in Ancient India and Central Asia* (Calcutta 1971).

BOSWORTH, A. B., 'The Government of Syria under Alexander the Great', *CQ* 24 (1974) 46–64.

—— 'Arrian and the Alexander Vulgate', *Entretiens Hardt* 22 (1976) 1–46.

—— 'Eumenes, Neoptolemus and *PSI* XII 1284', *GRBS* 19 (1978) 227–37.

—— *A Historical Commentary on Arrian's History of Alexander*, i– (Oxford 1980–).

—— 'Alexander and the Iranians', *JHS* 100 (1980) 1–21.

—— 'The Indian Satrapies under Alexander the Great', *Antichthon* 17 (1983) 37–46.

—— 'Alexander the Great and the Decline of Macedon', *JHS* 106 (1986) 1–12.

—— *Conquest and Empire: The Reign of Alexander the Great* (Cambridge 1988).

—— *From Arrian to Alexander: Studies in Historical Interpretation* (Oxford 1988).

—— 'Plutarch, Callisthenes and the Peace of Callias', *JHS* 110 (1990) 1–13.

—— 'Aristotle, India and Alexander', *Topoi* 3 (1993) 407–24.

—— 'A New Macedonian Prince', *CQ* 44 (1994) 57–65.

BOWERSOCK, G. W., *Roman Arabia* (Cambridge, Mass. 1983).

BRELOER, B., *Alexanders Kampf gegen Poros*, Bonner Orientalische Studien 3 (Stuttgart 1932).

—— 'Megasthenes über die indische Gesellschaft', *ZDMG* 88 (1934) 130–63.

BRIANT, P., *Antigone le Borgne: Les Débuts de sa carrière et les problèmes de l'assemblée macédonienne* (Paris 1973).

BRIANT, P., *État et pasteurs au Moyen-Orient ancien* (Cambridge 1982).

——*Rois, tributs et paysans: Études sur les formations tributaires du Moyen-Orient ancien* (Paris 1982).

——*L'Asie Centrale et les royaumes proches-orientales du premier millénaire* (Paris 1984).

BRETZL, H., *Die botanische Forschungen des Alexanderzuges* (Leipzig 1903).

BRODERSEN, K., 'Appian und Arrian. Zu einer Vorlage für Appians Emphylia II 619–649', *Klio* 70 (1988) 461–7.

BROWN, T. S., *Onesicritus: A Study in Hellenistic Historiography* (Berkeley, Calif. 1949).

——'Alexander and Greek Athletics, in Fact and in Fiction', *Greece and the Eastern Mediterranean in History and Prehistory*, ed. K. Kinzl (Berlin 1977) 70–88.

BURN, A. R., 'Notes on Alexander's Campaigns 332–330 BC', *JHS* 72 (1952) 81–91.

——*Persia and the Greeks* (2nd edn.: Stanford, Calif., 1984).

BURSTEIN, S. M., 'Alexander, Callisthenes and the Sources of the Nile', *GRBS* 17 (1976) 135–46.

——*Agatharchides of Cnidus: On the Erythraean Sea* (London 1989).

CAMMAROTA, M. R., 'Il *De Alexandri Magni fortuna aut virtute* come espressione retorico: il panegyrico', *Ricerche plutarchee*, ed. I. Gallo (Naples 1992) 105–24.

CASSON, L., *Ships and Seamanship in the Ancient World* (Princeton 1971).

——*The Periplus Maris Erythraei* (Princeton 1989).

CAWKWELL, G. L., 'The Deification of Alexander', *Ventures into Greek History*, ed. I. Worthington (Oxford 1994) 293–306.

CHANANA, D. R., *Slavery in Ancient India as Depicted in Pali and Sanskrit Texts* (New Delhi 1960).

CONOMIS, N. C., 'Notes on the Fragments of Lycurgus', *Klio* 39 (1961) 72–152.

CORSTEN, T., 'Zum Angebot einer Schenkung Alexanders an Phokion', *Historia* 43 (1994) 112–18.

DELCOURT, M., *Légendes et cultes de héros en Grèce* (Paris 1942).

DEVINE, A. M., 'The Battle of Hydaspes: A Tactical and Source-Critical Study'. *AncW* 16 (1987) 91–113.

DIHLE, A., *Der Prolog der 'Bacchen'* (Sitzungsberichte der Heidelberger Akademie der Wißenschaften, Phil.-hist. Kl. (1981) 2).

——'Dionysos in Indien', *India and the Ancient World*, ed. G. Pollet (Louvain 1987) 47–57.

DROYSEN, J. G., *Geschichte des Hellenismus* (2nd. edn.: 3 vols.: Gotha 1877–8).

ELLIOTT, J. H., 'The Mental World of Hernán Cortés', *Transactions of the Royal Historical Society*[5] 17 (1967) 41–58.

ENGELS, D. W., *Alexander the Great and the Logistics of the Macedonian Army* (Berkeley 1978).

ERRINGTON, R. M., 'Bias in Ptolemy's History of Alexander', *CQ* 19 (1969) 233–42.

—— 'The Nature of the Macedonian State under the Monarchy', *Chiron* 8 (1978) 77–133.

—— *A History of Macedonia* (Berkeley and Los Angeles 1990).

FARBER, J. J., 'The Cyropaedia and Hellenistic Kingship', *AJP* 100 (1979) 497–514.

FERRINI, M. F., 'Il prologo delle 'Bacchanti': La critica e le interpolazioni', *AFLM* 18 (1985) 117–43.

FLEMING, D., 'Achaemenid Sattagydia and the Geography of Vivana's Campaign (DB III, 54–75)', *JRAS* 1982. 102–12.

Fouilles d'Aï-Khanoum, ed. P. Bernard *et al.* vols. i– (Paris 1985–).

FRANKE, P. R., 'Dolmetschen in hellenistischer Zeit', *Zum Umgang mit fremden Sprachen in der griechisch-römischen Antike*, Palingenesia 36, ed. C. W. Müller, K. Sier, and J. Werner (Stuttgart 1992) 85–96.

FRANKL, V., 'Die Begriffe des mexikanischen Kaisertums und der Welt-monarchie in den "Cartas de Relación" des Hernán Cortés', *Saeculum: Jahrbuch für Universalgeschichte* 13 (1962) 1–34.

FREDRICKSMEYER, E. A., 'Divine Honors for Philip II', *TAPA* 109 (1979) 39–61.

—— 'On the Final Aims of Philip II', *Philip II, Alexander the Great and the Macedonian Heritage*, ed. W. L. Adams and E. N. Borza (Washington 1982) 85–98.

FULLER, J. F. C., *The Generalship of Alexander the Great* (London 1958).

GABRIELI, F., 'Muhammad ibn Qasim ath-Thaqati and the Arab Conquest of Sind', *East & West* 15 (1964/5) 291–5.

GOODENOUGH, E. R., 'The Political Philosophy of Hellenistic Kingship', *YCS* 1 (1928) 55–102.

GOUKOWSKY, P., 'Les Juments du Roi Érythras', *REG* 87 (1974) 111–37.

—— *Essai sur les origines du mythe d'Alexandre* (2 vols.: Nancy 1978–81).

GREEN, P., *Alexander of Macedon* (London 1974).

GREENBLATT, S., *Marvelous Possessions* (Oxford 1991).

GULLATH, B., *Untersuchungen zur Geschichte Boiotiens in der Zeit Alexanders und der Diadochen* (Frankfurt 1982).

HABICHT, C., *Gottmenschentum und griechische Städte*, Hypomnemata 14 (2nd edn.: Munich 1970).

HAMILTON, J. R., 'The Cavalry Battle at the Hydaspes', *JHS* 76 (1956) 26–31.

—— *Plutarch Alexander: A Commentary* (Oxford 1969).

—— 'Clitarchus and Diodorus 17', *Greece and the Eastern Mediterranean in History and Prehistory*, ed. K. Kinzl (Berlin 1977) 126–46.

HAMMOND, N. G. L., *Three Historians of Alexander the Great: The So-called Vulgate Authors, Diodorus, Justin and Curtius* (Cambridge 1983).

—— 'Papyrus British Library 3085 verso', *GRBS* 28 (1987) 331–47.

—— 'The Royal Journals of Alexander', *Historia* 37 (1988) 129–50.

—— *Alexander the Great: King, Commander and Statesman* (2nd edn.: Bristol 1989).

—— 'Royal Pages, Personal Pages and Boys Trained in the Macedonian Manner during the Period of the Temenid Monarchy', *Historia* 39 (1990) 261–90.

—— *The Macedonian State* (Oxford 1990).

—— *Sources for Alexander the Great: An Analysis of Plutarch's Life and Arrian's Anabasis Alexandrou* (Cambridge 1993).

HAMMOND, N. G. L., and GRIFFITH, G. T., *A History of Macedonia* ii (Oxford 1979).

HANSEN, G. C., 'Alexander und die Brahmanen', *Klio* 43–5 (1965) 351–80.

HANSON, V. D. (ed.), *Hoplites. The Classical Greek Battle Experience* (London 1991).

HARRISON, J. V., 'The Jaz Murian Depression, Persian Baluchistan', *GJ* 101 (1943) 207–25.

HECKEL, W., 'A grandson of Antipatros at Delos', *ZPE* 70 (1987) 161–2.

—— *The Marshals of Alexander's Empire* (London 1992).

HEIMPEL, W., 'Das Untere Meer', *ZA* 77 (1987) 22–91.

HERZFELD, E., *The Persian Empire* (Wiesbaden 1968).

HEUSS, A., 'Alexander der Große und die politische Ideologie des Altertums', *Antike und Abendland* 4 (1954) 65–104.

HÖGEMANN, P., *Alexander der Große und Arabien*, Zetemata 82 (Munich 1985).

HOLLSTEIN. W., 'Taxiles' Prägung für Alexander den Großen', *SNR* 68 (1989) 5–17.

HORNBLOWER, J., *Hieronymus of Cardia* (Oxford 1981).

HORNBLOWER, S. (ed.), *Greek Historiography* (Oxford 1994).

HORST, J., *Proskynein* (Gütersloh 1932).

HUXLEY, G., 'The Sogdian Tanais and Aristobulus', *BASP* 22 (1985) 117–21.

INSTINSKY, H. U., 'Alexander, Pindar, Euripides', *Historia* 10 (1961) 250–5.

JASCHINSKI, S., *Alexander und Griechenland unter dem Eindruck der Flucht von Harpalos* (Bonn 1981).

KAISER, W. B., 'Ein Meister der Glyptik aus dem Umkreis Alexanders', *JDAI* 77 (1962) 227–39.

KARTTUNEN, K., *India in Early Greek Literature* (Helsinki 1989).

KIENAST, D., 'Alexander und der Ganges', *Historia* 14 (1965) 180–8.

KORNEMANN, E., *Die Alexandergeschichte des Königs Ptolemaios I von Aegypten* (Leipzig 1935).

KRAFT, K., *Der 'rationale' Alexander* (Kallmünz 1971).

KRUGLIKOVA, I., 'Les fouilles de la mission archéologique soviéto-afghane sur le site gréco-kushan de Dilberdjin en Bactriane (Afghanistan)', *CRAI* (1977) 407–27.

KRUMBHOLZ, P., 'Wiederholungen bei Diodor', *Rh. Mus.* 44 (1889) 286–98.

LAMBRICK, H. T., *Sind. A General Introduction* (Hyderabad 1964).

LAMMERT, F., 'Alexanders Verwundung in der Stadt der Maller und die damalige Heilkunde', *Gymnasium* 60 (1953) 1–7.

LANE FOX, R., *Alexander the Great* (London 1973).

—— *The Search for Alexander* (London 1980)

LASSEN, C., *Indische Altertumskunde* (2nd edn.: 4 vols.: Leipzig, Bonn, and London 1861–74).

LATEINER, D. and STEPHENS, S. (eds.), *Selected Papers of Lionel Pearson* (Chico, Calif., 1983).

MARKLE, M. M., 'Support of Athenian Intellectuals for Philip: A Study of Isocrates' *Philippus* and Speusippus' *Letter to Philip*', *JHS* 96 (1976) 80–99.

MARTIN, V., 'Un recueil de diatribes cyniques: Pap. Genev. inv. 271', *MH* 16 (1959) 77–115.

MEDERER, E., *Die Alexanderlegenden bei den ältesten Historiker* (Stuttgart 1936).

MEYER, EDUARD, 'Alexander der Große und die absolute Monarchie', *Kleine Schriften* (2nd edn.: Halle 1924) i. 267–314.

MEYER, ERNST, 'Alexander und der Ganges', *Klio* 21 (1927) 183–91.

MOOKERJI, R. M., *Chandragupta Maurya and his Times* (3rd edn.: Delhi 1960).

NARAIN, A. K., 'Alexander and India', *G&R* 12 (1965) 155–65.

NIESE, B., *Geschichte der griechischen und makedonischen Staaten seit der Schlacht bei Chaeronea* (3 vols.: Gotha 1893–1903).

NEWMAN, W. L., *The Politics of Aristotle* (4 vols.: Oxford 1887–1902).

NOCK, A. D., *Essays on Religion and the Ancient World* (Oxford 1970).

O' BRIEN, J. M., *Alexander the Great: The Invisible Enemy* (London 1992).

PALAGIA, O., 'Imitation of Herakles in Ruler Portraiture. A Survey, from Alexander to Maximinus Daza', *Boreas: Münstersche Beiträge zur Archäologie* 9 (1986) 137–51.

PARKE, H. W., 'The Massacre of the Branchidae', *JHS* 105 (1985) 59–68.

PEARSON, L., *The Lost Histories of Alexander the Great* (Philological Monographs 20: Am. Phil. Ass. 1960).

PÉDECH, P., *Historiens compagnons d'Alexandre* (Paris 1984).

POTTS, D. T., *The Arabian Gulf in Antiquity* (Oxford 1990).

PRANDI, L., *Callistene. Uno storico tra Aristotele e i re macedoni* (Milan 1985).

PRICE, M. J., 'The "Porus" Coinage of Alexander the Great: A Symbol of Concord and community', *Studia Paulo Naster oblata*, ed. S. Scheers and J. Quaegebeur (2 vols.: Louvain 1982) i. 75–85.

—— The Coinage in the Name of Alexander the Great and Philip Arrhidaeus (2 vols.: Zurich 1991).

RAU, W., Staat und Gesellschaft im Alten Indien nach den Brāhmana Texten (Wiesbaden 1957).

REA, J., SENIOR, R. C., and HOLLIS, A. S., 'A Tax Receipt from Hellenistic Bactria', ZPE 104 (1994) 261–8.

ROBERT, L., 'De Delphes à l'Oxus: Inscriptions grecques nouvelles de la Bactriane', CRAI (1968) 416–57 (= OMS v. 510–51).

ROBINSON, T. R., 'Alexander and the Ganges: The Text of Diodorus XVIII. 6. 2', AHB 7 (1993) 84–99.

ROISMAN, J., 'Ptolemy and his rivals in his history of Alexander the Great', CQ 34 (1984) 373–85.

SALLES, J.-F., 'Les Achéménides dans le golfe arabo-persique', Achaemenid History 4 (Leiden 1990) 111–30.

SCHACHERMEYR, F., 'Alexander und die Ganges-Länder', IBK 3 (1955) 123–35 = Griffith, G. T. (ed.), Alexander the Great: The Main Problems (Cambridge 1966) 137–49.

—— Alexander der Große: das Problem seiner Persönlichkeit und seines Wirkens (Sitzungsberichte der österreich. Akad. der Wißenschaften, phil.-hist. Kl., 285 (1973)).

—— 'Alexander und die unterworfenen Nationen', Entretiens Hardt 22 (1976) 46–79.

SCHEPENS, G., 'Zum Problem der "Unbesiegbarkeit" Alexanders des Grossen', AncSoc 20 (1989) 15–53.

SCHIWEK, H., 'Der Persische Golf als Schiffahrts- und Seehandelsroute in Achämenidischer Zeit und in der Zeit Alexanders des Großen', BJ 162 (1962) 4–97.

SCHOBER, L., Untersuchungen zur Geschichte Babyloniens und der Oberen Satrapien von 323–303 v. Chr. (Frankfurt 1981).

SCHRÖDER, S., 'Zu Plutarchs Alexanderreden', MH 48 (1991) 151–7.

SCHWARTZ, E., Griechische Geschichtschreiber (Leipzig 1959).

SEIBERT, J., Alexander der Große, Erträge der Forschung 10 (Darmstadt 1972).

—— Untersuchungen zur Geschichte Ptolemaios' I (Munich 1969).

—— Das Zeitalter der Diadochen, Erträge der Forschung 185 (Darmstadt 1983).

—— Die Eroberung des Perserreiches durch Alexander den Großen auf kartographischer Grundlage (Beih. zum Tübinger Atlas des Vorderen Orients B68: Wiesbaden 1985).

SHARMA, R. S., Śudras in Ancient India (Delhi 1958).

SIDDIQI, M. I., The Fishermen's Settlements on the Coast of West Pakistan, Schriften des geographischen Instituts der Universität Kiel XVI 2 (Kiel 1956).

SIMPSON, R. H., 'A Possible Case of Misrepresentation in Diodorus XIX', *Historia* 6 (1957) 504–5.

STADTER, P. A., *Arrian of Nicomedia* (Chapel Hill, NC, 1980).

STEIN, A., *On Alexander's Track to the Indus* (London 1929).

—— *An Archaeological Tour in Gedrosia* (Calcutta 1931).

—— 'The Site of Alexander's Passage of the Hydaspes and the Battle with Porus', *GJ* 80 (1932) 31–46.

—— *Archaeological Reconnaissances in North-West India and South-East Iran* (London 1937).

—— 'On Alexander's Route into Gedrosia. An Archaeological Tour of Las Bela', *GJ* 102 (1943) 193–227.

STEIN, O., *Megasthenes und Kautilya* (Sitzungsberichte der österreich. Akad. der Wißenschaften, phil.-hist. Kl., 191. 5 (1921)).

STEWART, A., *Faces of Power: Alexander's Image and Hellenistic Politics* (Berkeley and Los Angeles 1993).

STONEMAN, R., 'Who Are the Brahmans? Indian Lore and Cynic Doctrine in Palladius' *De Bragmanibus* and its Models', *CQ* 44 (1994) 500–10.

—— 'Naked Philosophers: The Brahmans in the Alexander Historians and the Alexander Romance', *JHS* 115 (1995) 99–114.

STRATEN, P. VON, 'Did the Greeks Kneel Before Their Gods?', *BABesch* 49 (1974) 159–89.

STRASBURGER, H., *Studien zur Alten Geschichte*, ed. W. Schmitthenner and R. Zoepffel (3 vols.: Hildesheim 1982–90).

TARN, W. W., 'Alexander and the Ganges', *JHS* 43 (1923) 93–101.

—— 'Two Notes on Seleucid History', *JHS* 60 (1940) 84–94.

—— *Alexander the Great* (2 vols.: Cambridge 1948)

THAPAR, R., *Aśoka and the Decline of the Mauryas* (2nd edn.: Delhi 1961).

—— *The Mauryas Revisited* (Calcutta 1987).

THOMAS, H., *The Conquest of Mexico* (London 1993).

TONNET, H., *Recherches sur Arrien: Sa personnalité et ses écrits* (2 vols.: Amsterdam 1988).

TAPLIN, O., 'The Shield of Achilles within the *Iliad*', *G&R* 27 (1980) 1–21.

VEITH, G., 'Der Kavalleriekampf in der Schlacht am Hydaspes', *Klio* 8 (1908) 131–53.

VOGELSANG, W. J., *The Rise and Organisation of the Achaemenid Empire* (London 1992).

WILCKEN, U., *Alexander the Great*, with preface, notes and bibliography by E. N. Borza (New York 1967).

ZAMBRINI, A., 'Gli Indika di Megastene', *ASNP*[3] 12 (1982) 71–149; 15 (1985) 781–853.

General Index

Abii, Saca people 3 n. 7, 151–2
Abisares, Indian dynast:
  ally of Porus 9–11, 79 n. 50
  delayed submission to Al. 152,
    159–60
Abulites, Persian, satrap of
  Susiana 23–4 n. 64
Acesines, R. (Chenab) 9, 54, 127, 191,
  198
  confluence with Hydaspes 73, 133
  flooding of 193
  lotus growths on 70
Achilles:
  model for Al. 47, 59
Agalasseis, Indian people 142–3
Agatharchides, of Cnidus:
  on legend of Erythras 68–9
Agesilaus II, Spartan king 109
Agis, of Argos, poet 110
Agrianians 14 n. 35, 43 n. 39, 49, 51–2,
  135
Aguilar, Géronimo de, interpreter 124–5, 162
Alexander III, of Macedon, the Great:
  as *exemplum* 1–3
  attitude to divinity ch. 4 *passim*,
    164–5
  attitude to glory 57–61, 119, 149–50,
    182–3
  attitude to resistance:
    Brahmans 94–6; *see also* Malli,
      Musicanus, Sambus
    Sogdians 28, 99, 108, 144–5
  campaigns:
    Aornus 49–53, 118, 183
    Bajaur (Aspasii) 41–9, 143–4
    Battle of Hydaspes 5–21
    Cossaeans 146–7
    Malli 53–4, 57, 73–4, 133–41
    passage of Gedrosia 64, ch. 6
      passim
    Rock of Ariamazes 37–8, 99
  city foundations 2–3

claims to Achaemenid empire 152–6
coinage of 6–7, 47 n. 52, 116 n. 89,
  167–9
Exiles' Decree 29, 130–2
flattery of 64, 100–3
geographical investigations:
  Chorasmia 80–3
  Ganges plain 74–9, 186–200
  Indus voyage 73–9
  Nile/Indus link 70–2, 187
  Ocean 79
'policy of fusion' 4
propaganda of invincibility 166–9
propaganda of revenge 145–6, 148–9
suppression of dissent:
  Cleitus 102–4, 113
  Pages 22–3, 114
  'Reign of Terror' 23–4
wounds of 22–3, 53–64, 114–15, 143–4
Alexander, Macedonian
  hypaspist 52–3
Alexander, son of Aeropus ('the
  Lyncestian') 108
Alexander VI, Pope 160
Amazons 81–3
Amisus, democracy at 156 n. 83
Amminapes, Persian satrap of
  Parthyaea 20 n. 54
Ammon, *see* Zeus
Anaxarchus, of Abdera, philoso-
  pher 100
  on monarchy 29, 104–5
  at *proskynesis* banquet 110
Antigone, of Pydna, courtesan 92
Antigonus (Monophthalmus), son of
  Philippus:
  at Gabiene 27
  Nabataean campaign 147–8
  victories after Issus 157, 158
Antipater, son of Iolaus, regent:
  family of 107 n. 42, 158
Antipater, son of Asclepiodorus,
  page 113 n. 71

Antipater, of Magnesia, historian 164
Aornus (Pir-sar):
  Al.'s capture of 12, 29, 49–53, 118,
    119, 183
Apelles, painter 169
Aphamiotae, Cretan serfs 85–6
Aphrodite, wounded by Diomedes 64
    n. 105, 114–15
Apollodorus, general in Babylo-
    nia 22–3
Apollonides, Pseudo-Boeotian 61
Appian:
  on conquest of Cappadocia 156, 157
  use of Arrian 59 n. 87
Arabia, Arabs:
  Al.'s proposed invasion of 132, 150,
    152–3
Arabitae, Indian people 152
Arachosia 181–2
Aratus, Achaean general 127
Araxes, R.:
  in Armenia 119
  name of Syr-Darya 151
Archidamus II, Spartan king 46
Areilycus, killed by Patroclus 46–7
Ariamazes, Sogdian dynast 37–8
Ariarathes I, of Cappadocia 156–9
Ariaspae (Euergetae), Iranian people 3
    n. 7, 151
Aristobulus, of Cassandreia, historian:
  on Al.'s wound at Massaga 115
  analogous to Díaz 35
  on Arabian campaign 150, 152–3
  on Brahmans 93
  on Callisthenes' death 112 n. 66, 114
  date of 32
  on Gedrosian flora 173–4
  on Hydaspes crossing 15 n. 37
  on monsoon rains 11 n. 28, 176 n. 41
Aristotle:
  on absolute monarchy 105–7
  on Cretan serfs 86
  on echoes 55
  on flooding of Nile 69, 71 n. 19
  on geography of India 79
  on political divisions 92
  see also Nearchus
Armenia, Armenians:
  satrapal status 194
  Thessalian origins of 119
Arrian (L. Flavius Arrianus), historian:
  on elephants at Hydaspes 18–19
  on India east of Hyphasis 197–200
  literary echoes:

Herodotus 90 n. 92
Thucydides 18 n. 46, 64
Xenophon 46, 50 n. 55, 55–6, 58
  on Malli invasion 136–7
  on Massaga 29 n. 85
  metrical passages in 46
  on Porus and Al. 8–9
  Renaissance translations of 38
  use of sources 15 n. 37, 32–3, 42,
    53–6, 66 n. 1, 103, 113 n. 70,
    149–50, 153, 156, 173–4, 182 n. 66
  see also Nearchus, Ptolemy
Artaxerxes II 106
Artaxerxes III 71, 154
Aspasians, Aspasii, Indian people of
    Bajaur 41–9, 143–4, 155
Assaceni, Indian people of Swat 49–53
Astis, Indian prince 20 n. 54
Athenaeus, Antigonid general 147
Athens:
  absence of slavery in 86
  divine honours for Al. 132, 166

Bacchiads, Corinthian clan 91
Bactra (Balkh) 99, 109
Balacrus, son of Nicanor, body-
    guard 158
Bampur, *see* Pura
Barba, Pedro, Spanish captain 39
Barsaentes, Persian regicide 191 n. 26
Bindusāra, Mauryan king 91
Bithynians 26
Black Sea 81–2, 126
Boxus, Iranian in Athens 68–9
Brahmans:
  caste 93–4, 97
  city of 94, 96, 138, 143
  privileged status of 95
  resistance to Al. 94–6
  royal advisers 87, 93–4, 157
  see also Calanus, Musicanus
Bucephalas 29

Calanus, Brahman sage 93 n. 100, 94,
    96
Callisthenes, of Olynthus, historian 32,
    100
  death of 33 n. 8, 112, 114, 117
  opposition to *proskynesis* 111–12
candalas, untouchables 88, 92
Cappadocia 156–9
Carduchi, Armenian people 26
Cathaei, autonomous Indian people 11
    n. 25, 135 n. 5, 155

Chaeronea, Battle of 100
Chalco, Mexican town 35
Chandragupta (Sandracottus),
    Mauryan king 76, 77, 199
Chares, of Mytilene, historian 112
    n. 66
Charles V, Spanish emperor 161, 163
Charus, Macedonian hypaspist 51–3
Chimualcan, Mexican village 35
Cholula, Mexican city 144 n. 33,
    159–62
Chorasmia (*Uvārazmish*),
    Chorasmians 80–3
Cilician Gates 156
Cimmerian Bosporus 82
Cineas, founder of Aï Khanum 127
Cleander, son of Polemocrates, Mace-
    donian general 23–4 n. 64
Cleitarchus, of Alexandria, historian:
    on Amazon Queen 81 n. 56
    analogous to Gómara 35
    date of 32
    on Indian geography 78
    on Nanda dynasty 77
    on 'Red Sea' 66 n. 1
    on repression of Brahmans 94–5
Cleitus, son of Dropides, 'The
    Black' 59, 100–4, 113, 121, 140
Cleon, of Syracuse, courtier 110
Coenus, son of Polemocrates, Macedo-
    nian marshal:
    in Bajaur 43
    death of 117
    at the Hydaspes 16
    at the Hyphasis 55 n. 75
    with transport in Punjab 13
    victory in Sogdiana 108
Columbus 159
Corinthian League 29, 129–30, 166
    n. 3, 186
Corral, Cristóbal del, Spanish standard
    bearer 39
Corrhagus, Macedonian 116
Cortés, Hernán, conquistador:
    capture of Mexican rock fortresses
        34–41, 45, 53
    comparison with Al. 166 n. 1
    expedition to Honduras 39
    political motivation of vii, 36–7,
        163–4
    sack of Cholula 159–62
    transport of brigantines 12 n. 31
    use of interpreters 124–5, 161–2
    use of quotations 60–1

Corupedium, Battle of 47 n. 51
Cossaeans, mountain people of
    Zagros 146–7
Craterus, son of Alexander, Macedo-
    nian marshal:
    in Bactria (328) 99
    fictitious letter of 195 n. 42
    at the Hydaspes 14 n. 36
    operations against Aspasians 144
    opposition figure 111, 117
    reproves Al. after Malli cam-
        paign 57–8
    in Sogdiana (327) 111
Critobulus, of Cos, physician 63 n. 102
Ctesias, of Cnidus, historian:
    Diodorus' use of 189–90
    on 'Red Sea' 67–8
Cunaxa, Battle of 26
Curtius Rufus, Q., historian:
    on Al.'s recovery 56–9
    on Aornus 50–2
    on barbarian wisdom 150
    echoes of Vergil 52
    use of by Gómara 38
Cyiza, Gedrosian town 72 n. 23, 184–5
Cyrsilus, of Pharsalus 119
Cyrtaea, city on Persian Gulf 66 n. 3
Cyrus I, the Great 106, 157 n. 86
    alleged passage of Gedrosia 126, 170
        n. 13, 172, 182–3
    Massagetic campaign 149, 151
Cyrus, son of Darius II, the
    Younger 26, 145–6, 158

Dandamis, Indian sage 2, 8, 93 n. 100
Danube, R. 12
Darius I:
    commissions Scylax 71
    conquests in India 154–5
    Scythian invasion 148
Darius III 20 n. 54, 47 n. 52, 66, 102
    n. 19, 139, 148, 154
Dascylium, capital of Hell. Phrygia 68
Dataphernes, Sogdian rebel 108
Deinias, of Argos, historian 68–9
Delphi 166
Demetrius, son of Althaemenes, cavalry
    commander 139
Demetrius (Poliorcetes), son of
    Antigonus:
    Nabataean campaign 147–8
    susceptibility to flattery 100, 115,
        129
Demosthenes, Athenian orator 166

Díaz del Castillo, Bernal, historian:
  on capture of rock fortresses 38–40,
    42, 49
  criticism of Cortés 39
  date of 35
  on Doña Marina 124–5
  'doublethink' in 121
  quotations in 60
  on sack of Cholula 161–2
  on Spanish expertise 142
  sympathy for Mexicans 87
Diodorus Siculus, historian:
  on Aornus 50–1
  on cult of Dion 127–8
  on Ganges 188–97
  Gazetteer of Empire 189, 194–6
Dion, of Syracuse 127–8
Dionysus:
  Arabian deity 132
  in Argead lineage 125–6
  as precedent for Al. 98, 110, 119–23,
    164–5, 167
Dioscuri:
  cult in Bactria 102 n. 17
  precedents for deification 101–3
Dioxippus, of Athens, pancratiast 100
    n. 9, 114–17
Doña Marina, Mexican inter-
    preter 124–5, 161–2

Egypt:
  introduction of lotus 70–1
elephants 6, 15–16, 18–19, 189, 197
  in Chandragupta's army 74, 76
  in Gandhara 144, 154–5
Ephippus, of Olynthus, pamphle-
    teer 24, 117
Eratosthenes, of Cyrene:
  on Al.'s attitude to race 3
  on gulfs of Ocean 198
  scepticism regarding myth 82 n. 60,
    118–19, 122, 123, 164 n. 111
Erythras, mythical king in Persis 66–70
Ethiopians, in Herodotus 148
Eumenes, of Cardia:
  in Cappadocia 157
  cavalry commands of 51
  in coalition war (321) 47 n. 51, 58
    n. 85
  compiles 'Court Journal' 33
  organises *proskynesis* for deceased
    Al. 112
  use of *Syria grammata* 4–5 n. 11

Euripides:
  on lineage of Dionysus 125–6 n. 128
  quotations of 4, 60–1, 101, 116 n. 83
  on wanderings of Dionysus 120
'European Scyths' 82, 120, 148

Gabiene, Battle of 27
Gandaridae, Indian people 74, 189–94,
    200
'Gandaris', territory of 'bad Po-
    rus' 191–2
Gandhara, Achaemenid satrapy 122,
    154–5
Ganges, R. 74–5, 186–200
Gaugamela, Battle of 8, 16, 139, 154,
    157
Gaza, siege of 22–3, 27, 119 n. 99, 183
Gazetteer of Empire, see Diodorus
    Siculus
Gedrosia, Gedrosians:
  Al.'s passage of 63, ch. 6 *passim*
  under Arab rule 181
  flora 174–5
  harvest 177–9
  rainfall 171, 179
  terrain 171–2
Gómara, Francisco López de, chroni-
    cler of Cortés 34–5, 37–8
Granicus, Battle of 19, 27, 66, 101, 104

Halicarnassus, siege of 27, 32–3 n. 7
Harmatelia, Indian city 94
Harmozeia (Minab, Old
    Hormuz) 66–7
Hephaestion, son of Amyntor:
  death of 24, 146
  favourite of Al. 24, 47
  hero cult of 128–9
  in Malli campaign 136
Heracles:
  precedent for Al. 98, 101–2, 110,
    116, 118–19, 164–5, 167–9,
    182–3
  supposed cult in India 75 n. 35, 119,
    125
Heracon, general in Media 23–4 n. 64
Hermolaus, son of Sopolis, conspira-
    tor 22, 112–13
hero cult 127–30
Herodotus:
  on Arabia 154
  consults Zopyrus 69 n. 9
  on Egyptian society 90, 92

on Indian 'ants' 83–4
on just wars 148–9
on slavery in Athens 86
suppression of names 61
Hesiod 104
Hieronymus, of Cardia, historian:
  on Al. and the Ganges 189–90,
    196–7, 200
  on Battle of Gabiene 27
  on Cappadocia 156
  on Nabataeans 147–8, 189–90
Hippodamus, of Miletus 92
Homer:
  on Abii 151
  influence on Nearchus 73 n. 28
  influence on Ptolemy 45–6
  on wounding of gods 64, 114–15
Hydaspes, R. (Jhelum):
  Al.'s voyage on 54–5, 142
  ancient course of 13 n. 34
  Battle of 5–21
  confluence with Acesines 73, 133
  dimensions of 11
Hydraces, Gedrosian interpreter 72
Hydraotes, R. (Ravi) 54, 73, 137–8, 191
hyparchs, significance of 155–6
Hypereides, Athenian orator 105, 115
    n. 79, 129
Hyphasis (Hypanis), R. (Beas) 186–7,
    190–2, 195, 197, 198
  'mutiny' at 13, 55 n. 75, 74, 117, 176
Hyrcania 81

Iaxartes, R. (Syr-Darya):
  identified with Tanais 81–2, 120,
    151, 198 n. 51
India, Indians:
  fauna of 83–4
  fire sacrifice 128
  identify Al. with Dionysus 122–3,
    127–8
  resistance to Al. 28, 149
  slavery in 84–9
  social system of 91–2
  weaponry of 6–7, 15, 141
  see also Agalasseis, Brahmans,
    Cathaei, Gandaridae, Malli,
    Musicanus, Sambastae, Taxiles
Indus, R.:
  campaign on (325) 28, 64, 73, 142–3
  hypothetical linkage with Nile 71–2,
    187
interpreters 72, 98, 124–5, 161–3

Ipsus, Battle of 32 n. 3, 76 n. 39
Isaura, city of Lycaonia 158
Issus, Battle of 19–20, 27, 157
ivy, provenance in East 82, 120, 122

kerkouroi, light vessels 172–3

Laomedon, of Mytilene 5 n. 11
Laranda, city of Lycaonia 158
Las Bela, *see* Oreitis
Las Casas, Bartolemé de 160, 161–2
Leonnatus, bodyguard 42–3, 178
lotus ('Egyptian bean') 70–1
Lysimachus, son of Agathocles, body-
    guard 47 n. 51

Macedonia, Macedonians:
  customs:
    army assembly 104, 107
    king's illness 57
    treason 22
  army:
    cavalry 14 n. 35, 17–18
    disaffection in 13, 25, 117, 176
    expertise of 27, 138–9, 141–2
    infantry 14 n. 35, 27, 44 n. 39,
      51–3, 113 n. 72
Maka, *see* Oman
Makran, *see* Gedrosia
Malli (Malavas), Indian people 23, 28,
    53–4, 57, 73–4, 94, 116, 133–41,
    152
Maracanda (Samarkand) 80, 99–100
Mardi, mountain people of Zagros 29
Massaga, Indian city 29, 114
Massagetae, Sacan tribe 149
Mazenes, Persian governor 66, 70
Medeius, of Larisa 119
Megabyzus, Persian dignitary 66 n. 3
Megasthenes, historian:
  on absence of Indian slavery 88–9
  on Brahmans 93
  at court of Chandragupta 76, 78, 80,
    188
  development of Dionysus
    myth 125–6
  on Ganges 75
  on Indian 'ants' 84
  on Indian immunity from inva-
    sion 182–3, 189 n. 15
  on Indian society 89–93, 199
Meyer, Eduard:
  on Al.'s divinity 131–2

Miletus, siege of 27
Mithropastes, son of Arsites, Persian
    exile 66–70
monsoon 11–12, 69, 176–8
Montezuma, Mexican emperor 124–5,
    159, 162–4
Mosarna, Gedrosian roadstead 72
Muhammad ibn Qasim, Arab con-
    queror 181
Musicanus, Indian ruler:
    delayed submission of 152
    kingdom of 85–9
    revolt against Al. 87, 95–6, 114, 145,
        157, 159
Myllenas ('Mullinus'), son of
    Asander 51, 52

Nabataeans 147–8
Nearchus, son of Androtimus, admiral
    and historian:
    on Al.'s recovery in India 53–7, 60–2
    Arrian's use of 32, 170
    on Brahmans 93
    on Cyrus and Semiramis 182–3
    on hardships in Gedrosia 170, 173–6
    imitation of Herodotus 61–2
    imitation of Homer 73 n. 28
    influenced by Aristotle 54–5, 69
    on monsoon rains 11 n. 28
    on Nile/Indus linkage 70–2
    on nomenclature of 'Red Sea' 66–70
    on Nosala 72, 175
    ocean voyage of 25, 96, 169, 171–3,
        177–8, 184–5
    on tigers and ants 82–3
Nebuchadnezzar 126
Neoptolemus, hypaspist com-
    mander 47 n. 51, 119 n. 99
Nicesias, Macedonian courtier 100
    n. 9, 115
Nile, R. 69, 71–2, 187
Nosala, magic island 72, 175
Nysa, Indian city 28, 30, 121–3, 192
    n. 28, 199

Oaracte (Qeshm) 66, 69
ocean:
    boundary of empire 79–80
    recipient of Indus system 71, 195
Ogyris, island 66, 70
Oman (Maka) 70 n. 14, 154
Onesicritus, of Astypalaea, historian:
    on Al. and the Brahmans 2–3, 8
    on realm of Musicanus 85–8

Opis 25, 117
Oreitis (Las Bela), Indian prov-
    ince 152, 169, 172, 178, 181–2
Oxathres, Persian satrap 23–4 n. 64,
    107–8
Oxus, R. 99
Oxydates, Persian satrap 20 n. 54
Oxydracae ('Kśudrakas'), Indian
    people:
    allied with Malli 134–5
    polity of 198–9
    surrender to Al. 115–16, 123, 141,
        152, 164–5
Oxythemis, of Larisa, courtier of
    Demetrius 115

Pages, conspiracy of 21–4, 112–14
Parapamisus (Hindu Kush), identified
    with Caucasus 118
Parysatis, Persian queen 106
Patala, Indian city 28, 96, 144, 176–7
Pātaliputra (Palimbothra), Indian capi-
    tal 76–7, 78, 188, 195 n. 41
Patroclus, *aristeia* of 46–9
Peithagoras, seer 23–4
Peithon, son of Agenor:
    in Malli campaign 137, 139
    satrap of Sind 96–7
Peleus, ancestor of Al. 101
Peneius, R. 119
Perdiccas, son of Orontes, bodyguard:
    in coalition war (321) 47
    conquest of Cappadocia (322) 156–9
    in Malli campaign 73, 137, 140
    in march on India 44 n. 39
Persepolis, destruction of 145
Pertalis, Indian city 192
Pharasmanes, ruler of Chorasmia 80–3
Pharnabazus, Persian satrap 109
Pharnuches, Persian interpreter 98 n. 1
Phegeus, Indian ruler 74, 77–9, 80
Phila, daughter of Antipater 158
Philip II, of Macedon:
    denigration by Al. 100–1
    divine pretensions 130
    legitimation of conquests 164
    war of revenge 148
Philomelus, Phocian general 166 n. 3
Philotas, son of Parmenion 92, 113
Phocion, Athenian general 130–1
Pindar:
    on divinity and mortality 111 n. 61
    on 'Red Sea' 67
Pisidia, Pisidians 146, 194

Plato, political theory of 86, 89–90, 104–5
Plutarch:
　on Al.'s visit to Delphi 166–7
　on Cossaean campaign 146

　on Hydaspes crossing 15 n. 37
　on losses in Gedrosia 180
　the treatise *de Al. fortuna* 2–5
Polyperchon, son of Simmias 44 n. 39, 107 n. 42, 112 n. 64
Porus, Indian ruler:
　army strength 16, 76
　enmity with neighbours 10–11, 79 n. 50, 135 n. 5
　fights at the Hydaspes 6–21, 58–9
　honoured by Al. 8–9, 155 n. 78
　informant of Al. 74–7
　size of domains 8–9
Porus, 'the bad', Indian ruler 11, 95 n. 111, 191, 200
'Porus coinage' 6–8, 47 n. 52, 169
Prasii, Indian people 75–6, 192, 196
Prometheus 118
proskynesis, prostration 109–12
Ptolemy, son of Lagus (Ptolemy I Soter):
　on Acesines 176 n. 42, 193 n. 33
　on Al.'s wound in India 62–4, 140, 142
　analogous to Cortés 35, 45
　career:
　　at Aornus 49–53
　　in Bajaur 41–9
　　in coalition war (321) 47
　　in Malli campaign 57, 136
　　on fall of Callisthenes 114
　　on Hydaspes crossing 15 n. 37
　　references to *hyparchs* 156
　　self-portraiture 45–9
　　use of, by Arrian 8, 31–3, 41, 49–50
Puertocarrero, Alonso Hernandez, lieutenant of Cortés 60
Pura, Gedrosian capital 169, 174–5

'Red Sea', nomenclature of 67–8
Requerimiento, Spanish proclamation of possession 160–1

Sacae:
　female warriors among 81
　relations with Al. 120, 150–1
Sambastae (Sabarcae), Indian people 127, 129

Sambus, Indian ruler 94–5
Schachermeyr, Fritz, Austrian scholar:
　on Al. and the Ganges 187, 197, 198
　on Al.'s cosmopolitanism 4 n. 9
　on Corinthian League 186
　on value of official records 33–4
Scylax, of Caryanda 71, 106 n. 35
Seleucus, son of Antiochus (Seleucus I Nicator):
　at Corupedium 47 n. 51
　treaty with Chandragupta 76, 80 n. 52
Semiramis, Assyrian queen 126, 170 n. 13, 172, 182–3
Seneca, attitude to Al. 2 n. 1
Sibi, Indian people 119, 142, 143
Sibyrtius, satrap of Arachosia 80
Sisicottus, Indian notable 20 n. 54, 122 n. 114
Sismithres, Sogdian dynast, fortress of 108
Sitalces, general in Media 23–4 n. 64
Sogdiana, Sogdians:
　in Al.'s army 14 n. 35
　ivy in 120
　language of 98 n. 1
　revolt of 27, 81, 82, 99–100, 108, 144–5
Sophocles 4, 60
Sostratus, son of Amyntas, conspirator 22, 113
Sparta, Spartiates:
　attitude to *proskynesis* 109
　divine honours for Al. 132
　parallel to Indian serfdom 85–6
　in Peloponnesian War 25 n. 70, 159
Spitamenes, Sogdian rebel 100 n. 11, 108, 145
Strabo:
　digest of Aristobulus on Arabs 153
　digest of Onesicritus on Musicanus 85–6
　use of Nearchus 67, 170, 173–4
śūdras, Indian caste 77, 87, 92, 95
Sutlej, R. 190 n. 21, 195 n. 40
Syr–Darya, *see* Iaxartes

Taharka, Ethiopian dynast 126
Tanais (Don), R. 82, 120, 198 n. 51
Tapia, Cristóbal de, royal envoy 36
Tarn, Sir William Woodthorpe:
　on Al. at Delphi 166–7
　on Al.'s divinity 131
　on Al.'s knowledge of Ganges 187, 190

Tarn, Sir William Woodthorpe (*cont.*):
  on brotherhood of man 4
  on Malli campaign 133, 136
Tauron, son of Machatas, commander
    of archers 51
Taxila, Indian city 6 n. 16, 13, 93, 122,
    155
Taxiles, Indian ruler:
  enmity with Porus 11, 79–80
  invites Al. to India 11, 83, 122, 155
  recommends Calanus 94 n. 103
Tenochtitlan, Mexican capital 12 n. 31,
    34, 87 n. 80
Thar desert 77–8
Thebes, destruction of 129–30
Thoas, son of Mandrodorus, Macedo-
    nian 178 n. 50, 184 n. 71
Timaeus, of Tauromenium, histo-
    rian 86
Tissaphernes, Persian satrap 57–8
    nn. 84–5
Tlaxcala, Tlaxcalans, Mexican state
    and people 12 n. 31, 141–2,
    159–61
Tomyris, Massagetic queen 149
Torone 71
Tyre 115
  Al.'s siege of 12, 23 n. 59, 27

Uxii, mountain people of Zagros 146

Valerius Maximus, treatment of Al. 2
    n. 2
Verethragna, Iranian counterpart of
    Heracles 102 n. 17, 118
Vergil:
  on 'Gangaridae' 75 n. 34, 192 n. 29
  literary echoes 52, 54 n. 70

Xandrames, Nanda king 75, 76–7,
    198–9
Xenophon:
  on battle experience of Ten Thou-
    sand 26
  compared with Díaz 39
  imitation by Arrian 46, 50 n. 55,
    55–6, 58
  on monarchy 106

Yaudheyas, autonomous Indian peo-
    ple 194

Zeno, of Citium, Stoic 3
Zeus:
  as Ammon, purported father of
    Al. 103, 130, 167, 169
  analogue of monarchy 29, 104–7
  imitated by Al. 6